China Airborne

China Airborne

★

James Fallows

Pantheon Books, New York

All rights reserved. Published in the United States by Pantheon Books,
a division of Random House, Inc., New York, and in Canada by
Random House of Canada Limited, Toronto.

Pantheon Books and colophon are registered trademarks of
Random House, Inc.

Library of Congress Cataloging-in-Publication Data
Fallows, James M.
China airborne / James Fallows.
p. cm.
Includes bibliographical references and index.
ISBN 978-0-375-42211-9
1. Aeronautics—China 2. Aeronautics, Commercial—China. 3. Aerospace
industries—China. 4. China—Economic conditions—2000– I. Title.
TL527.C5F35 2012 387.70951—dc23 2011046805

www.pantheonbooks.com

Jacket image from a painting by Yu Zhenli, May 1976. (altered detail).
Print: International Institute for Social History, Amsterdam
Jacket design by Peter Mendelsund

Printed in the United States of America

First Edition

2 4 6 8 9 7 5 3 1

For Lincoln Caplan and Eric Redman

Contents

Acknowledgments

This book is dedicated with gratitude to Lincoln Caplan and Eric Redman, friends and advisers through most of my life, who during the evolution of this book have once again been generous and perceptive sources of the right mixture of criticism, support, humor, and inspiration. I am fortunate to have them as friends and to know I can rely on them, as I have done very often over the years.

The Atlantic has been my professional home since the late 1970s; through that time I have grown only more appreciative of its journalistic values and its internal culture. David Bradley and Justin Smith have made one of America's oldest literary institutions into a viable modern business. James Bennet and Scott Stossel have guided it (and me) editorially, and were generous in letting me take time to work on this book during an already short-staffed period for the magazine. Before them I worked closely with a sequence of wonderful *Atlantic* editors: Robert Manning, William Whitworth, Michael Kelly, and Cullen Murphy. In recent years I have worked directly with Corby Kummer, Sue Parilla, Marge duMond, and Janice Cane on most of my articles for the magazine, including during my years in China, and with Bob Cohn and John Gould for items on the *Atlantic*'s web site. As with previous books, I really should list every name on the magazine's masthead, but I will mention those I worked with most often during the time I was in China:

Nicole Allan, Marc Ambinder, Lindsey Bahr, Jennifer Barnett, Ashley Bolding, Ben Bradley, Lucy Byrd, Ben Carlson, Steve Clemons, Cotton Codinha, Abby Cutler, Stacey Pavesi-Debre, Betsy Ebersole, Geoffrey Gagnon, James Gibney, Jeffrey Goldberg, Chris Good, Bruce Gottlieb, John Gould, Joshua Green, Jennie Rothenberg Gritz, Alisha Hathawa, Carl Holscher, Shana Keefe, Elizabeth Keffer, Aaron Kenner, Jay Lauf, Clair Lorell, Alexis Madrigal, Megan McGuinn, Justin Miller, Chris Orr, Don Peck, Lyndsay Polloway, Michael Proffitt, Natalie Raabe, Yvonne Rolzhausen, Emmy Scandling, Suzanne Smalley, Ellie Smith, Maria Streshinksy, John Fox Sullivan, Derek Thompson, Jason Treat, and Robert Vare.

Since its founding in 2008, the United States Studies Centre at the University of Sydney has been an additional, welcome professional home. I thank Geoffrey Garrett for building and leading the Centre and making me a part of it; his colleagues Sean Gallagher, Nina Fudala, Craig Purcell, Will Turner, Amber D'Souza, and others; and Joe Skrzynski for his hospitality in Sydney. My other long-term unofficial journalistic home has been National Public Radio, and in particular I thank Guy Raz, Phil Harrell, Matthew Martinez, Rick Holter, Daniel Shukhin, and others with whom I have enjoyed working on the *Weekend All Things Considered* program.

Wendy Weil, my literary agent for more than thirty years, represented me with skill, toughness, understanding, and tact on this project as she has on seven previous ones. At Pantheon, my publisher for most of the past twenty years, I am grateful for the insight and guidance of my editor, Dan Frank, who originally had the idea for this book and saw it through several stages of evolution, and for the patience, flexibility, and help of Jill Verrillo, Altie Karper, and Josie Kals.

I have been fascinated by and involved with Cirrus aircraft

since the late 1990s, when I first wrote about the start-up Cirrus Design company for *The New York Times Magazine*. Soon thereafter I bought a Cirrus SR20 and flew it frequently around America and Canada, before selling it when I moved to China in 2006. This book describes the important roles played in China by first Peter Claeys and then Paul Fiduccia of Cirrus. I am grateful to both of them for their time and trust. Also I thank Ian Bentley, Gary Black, Scott Jiang, and Gary Poelma, now of Cirrus. Plus, in other roles in aviation, Alan Klapmeier, Kate Dougherty, Bruce Holmes, and Lane Wallace; and Michael Klein, Boni Caldeira, and Steve Musgrove of Open Air, with whose guidance I have bought and happily flown a used Cirrus SR22. For this book I should also acknowledge my original flight instructors, Ken Michaelson and Chris Baker. Everyone who follows aviation has learned from the insights of Richard Aboulafia, of the Teal Group. I am grateful for all the time he spent helping me clarify the arguments in this book.

In and around China, for friendship, advice, and help of different sorts between 2006 and 2012, I would like to thank: Andy Andreasen, Fr. Ron Anton, Phil Baker, Andrew Batson, Bing and Daniel Bell, Dominic Barton, Richard Burger, Liam Casey, Liz Rawlings and Steve Chalupsky, Francis Chao, Dovar Chen, Patrick Chovanec, Ella Chou, Chen Xin, Duncan Clark, Melanie and Eliot Cutler, Simon Elegant, Pamela Leonard and John Flower, Rebecca Frankel and Mike, Julio Friedmann, Gao Yuanyang, Jeremy Goldkorn, Jim Gradoville, Paola Sada and Jorge Guajardo, York-chi and Stephen Harder, Guo Liang, Hu Shuli, Andrew Houghton, Andrew Hutson, Ann and Ken Jarrett, Jeremiah Jenne, Isaac Kardon, Kent Kedl, Elizabeth Knup, Kaiser Kuo, Showkee Lee and her family, Kai-fu Lee, Yumin Liang, Mei Fong and Andrew Lih, Rebecca and Kenny Lin,

Jeanee and Brian Linden, Barbara and Robert Liotta, River Lu, Damien Ma, Jim McGregor, Kirk McDonald, Adam Minter, Russell Leigh Moses, John Northen, Evan Osnos, Herve Pauze and Lisa Robins, Minxin Pei, Michael Pettis, Fr. Roberto Ribeiro, Sidney Rittenberg, Robin Bordie and Andy Rothman, Bob Schapiro, Rita O'Connor and Ted Schell, Baifang and Orville Schell, Shi Hongshen, Sam Popkin and Susan Shirk, Anne-Marie Slaughter and Andrew Moravcsik, Sherry Smith and Marcus Corley, Nina Ni and Sun Tze, Andy Switky, Shane Tedjarati, Joe Tymczyszyn, Michele Travierso, Ping Wang, Sean Wang, Louis Woo, Candice and Jarrett Wrisley, Jenny and Bill Wright, Kevin Wu, Michael Zakkour, and Dan Guttman and ZeeZee Zhong.

During a ten-week period early in 2010, I turned my part of the *Atlantic*'s Web site over to teams of guest bloggers while I was finishing a draft of this book. For their excellent work I am grateful to them all. For the record, the full list, including a number of people already mentioned, is: David Allen, Phil Baker, Mark Bernstein, Eric Bonabeau, Keith Blount, Don Brown, Liam Casey, Ella Chou, Parker Donham, Kate Dougherty, Xujun Eberlein, Lizzy Bennett Fallows, Deborah Fallows, Eamonn Fingleton, Julian Fisher, Julio Friedmann, Piero Garau, Brian Glucroft, Edward Goldstick, Sriram Gollapalli, Paola and Jorge Guajardo, Glenna Hall, Shelley Hayduk, Bruce Holmes, Jeremiah Jenne, Alan Klapmeier, Christina Larson, Damien Ma, Adam Minter, Grace Peng, Lucia Pierce, Guy Raz, Sam Roggeveen, David Ryan, Sanjay Saigal, Kate Sedgwick, Chuck Spinney, Andrew Sprung, John Tierney, Kentaro Toyama, Michele Travierso, and Lane Wallace.

As for technology: This book was written using Literature & Latte's wonderful Scrivener writing software. I relied on the different and complementary strengths of the programs DEVON-think Pro, Zoot, PersonalBrain, and TinderBox for storing, organizing, and retrieving research data.

Our extended family—our son Tom and his wife, Lizzy, our son Tad and his, wife, Annie, and their new son, Jack—was of course a source of joy and support to my wife and me during the years in which I reported and then wrote this book. My wife, Deborah Fallows, is the key to everything I have done.

Washington, D.C.
January 2012

China Airborne

Introduction

The flight to Zhuhai

In the fall of 2006, not long after I arrived in China, I was the copilot on a small-airplane journey from Changsha, the capital of Hunan province near the center of the country, to Zhuhai, a tropical settlement on the far southern coast just west of Hong Kong.

The plane was a sleek-looking, four-seat, propeller-driven model called the Cirrus SR22, manufactured by a then wildly successful start-up company in Duluth, Minnesota, called Cirrus Design. Through the previous five years, the SR22 had been a worldwide commercial and technological phenomenon, displacing familiar names like Cessna and Piper to become the best-selling small airplane of its type anywhere. Part of its appeal was its built-in "ballistic parachute," a unique safety device capable of lowering the entire airplane safely to the ground in case of disaster. The first successful "save" by this system in a Cirrus occurred in the fall of 2002, when a pilot took off from a small airport near Dallas in a Cirrus that had just been in for maintenance. A few minutes after takeoff, an aileron flopped loosely from one of the wings; investigators later determined that it had not been correctly reattached after maintenance. This made the plane impossible to control and in other circumstances would probably have led to a fatal crash. Instead the pilot pulled the handle to deploy the parachute, came down near a golf-course fairway, and walked away unharmed. The plane itself was repaired and later flown around the country by Cirrus as a promotional device for its safety systems.

On the tarmac in Changsha, on a Sunday evening as darkness fell, I sat in the Cirrus's right-hand front seat, traditionally the place for the copilot—or the flight instructor, during training flights. In the left-hand seat, usually the place for the pilot-in-command, sat Peter Claeys, a Belgian citizen and linguistic whiz whose job, from his sales base in Shanghai, was to persuade newly flush Chinese business tycoons that they should spend half a million U.S. dollars or more to buy a Cirrus plane of their own—even though there was as yet virtually no place in China where they would be allowed to fly it. I was there as a friend of Claeys's and because I was practically the only other person within a thousand miles who had experience as a pilot of the Cirrus. In one of the backseats was Walter Wang, a Chinese business journalist who, even more than Claeys and me, was happily innocent of the risks we were about to take.

We were headed to Zhuhai because every two years, in November, the vast military-scale runway and ramp areas of Zhuhai's Sanzao Airport become crammed with aircraft large and small that have flown in from around the world for the Zhuhai International Air Show, an Asian equivalent of the Paris Air Show. Zhuhai's main runway, commissioned by grand-thinking local officials without the blessing of the central government in Beijing, is more than 13,000 feet long—longer than any at Heathrow or LAX. The rest of the facilities are on a similar scale, and during most of the year sit practically vacant. As long-term punishment by the Beijing authorities for the local government's ambitious overreach, the airport has been (as a local manager told me ruefully on a visit in 2011) "kept out of the aviation economy" that has brought booms to the surrounding airports in Hong Kong, Macau, Shenzhen, and Guangzhou.

But briefly every two years, every bit of its space is called into play. So many planes are present there's barely room to maneuver. Because nearly all of the twenty-first century's growth in the world's aviation market has been and is expected to be in Asia, with most of that in China, Zhuhai has become more and more important as the place for aerospace merchants and customers to meet. Boeing has booths there, and so does Airbus, and so do Russian and Brazilian and Israeli suppliers—the Russians and Brazilians and others with squads of "booth babes"—plus American and European architecture firms hoping to design the environmentally friendly new Chinese airports of the future, plus every military contractor from every part of the globe trying to sell fighters or attack helicopters to governments with extra cash. The plane we sat in was the only demonstration model of the Cirrus then available in China, and Claeys was the company's only salesman and company pilot anywhere nearby. If he and the plane didn't get there by that Sunday evening, he would be embarrassingly absent for the next day's demo flights, sales talks, and other events he had been lining up for months.

So Claeys was making the trip because he had to, and Walter Wang because he wanted a ride to Zhuhai to cover the show. I was there to help as Claeys's copilot. At the time I imagined that this would be the first of many small-plane trips I would be making in China.

After all, China would seem to be a country made for travel by air. Like Australia, like Brazil, like Russia or Canada or most of the United States away from the urban Northeast, it is characterized by vast distances; widely separated population centers; mountains and gorges and other barriers separating the cities and making land travel slow and difficult—plus dramatic, interesting scenery to view from above. China's commercial-airline business, starting from a very limited base, was already booming, with nearly twice as many people flying on airlines in 2006 as five years earlier, and twice as many again by 2011.

With the surge of private wealth and the rise of industrial centers at far-flung points across the country, "general aviation" would seem a natural candidate for development. This category includes every sort of non-airline activity, from corporate jets for China's scores of new billionaires and thousands of rising millionaires to crop-dusting activities in its farmlands to search-and-rescue operations after disasters or last-minute organ-transplant flights to purely recreational flight. You could take China's relatively limited numbers of airplanes, airports, and overall aviation activities as a sign of backwardness—or, as was the case in so many other aspects of modern China, as an indication of a gap that could be quickly closed with a huge spurt of construction, investment, and capital outlay.

The many countries of China

Now a word about the territory we would see from above. The main surprise of living in China, as opposed to reading or hearing about it, is how much it is a loose assemblage of organizations and aspects and subcultures, an infinity of self-enclosed activities, rather than a "country" in the normal sense. The plainest fact about modern China for most people on the scene often seems the hardest to grasp from afar. That is simply how varied, diverse, contradictory, and quickly changing conditions within the country are. Any large country is diverse and contradictory, but China's variations are of a scale demanding special note.

What is true in one province is false in the next. What was the exception last week is the rule today. A policy that is applied strictly in Beijing may be ignored or completely unknown in Kunming or Changsha. Millions of Chinese people are now very rich, and hundreds of millions are still very poor. Their country is a success and a failure, an opportunity and a threat, an inspiring model to the world and a nightmarish cautionary example. It is tightly controlled and it is out of control; it is futuristic and it is backward; its system is both robust and shaky. Its leaders are skillful and clumsy, supple and stubborn, visionary and foolishly shortsighted.

Of course there are exceptional moments when the disparate elements of China seem to function as a coherent whole. Over a six-month period in 2008, the entire country seemed to be absorbed by a succession of dramatic political and natural events. First, the pre-Olympic torch relay began its ceremonial progression from Mount Olympus in Greece to Beijing and was the cause of nationwide celebration. ("Happiness Abounds as Country Cheers," read a banner headline in the *China Daily*.) The mood shifted abruptly when the relay was disrupted by Tibetan-rights protestors across Europe, to the widespread astonishment, horror, and, soon, fury of people in mainland China—where the accepted version of Tibetan history is that the territory has always been part of the Chinese nation, and that the people of Tibet should be grateful for Mao's having rescued them from the feudal tyranny of the lamas. Then, on May 12, 2008, everything else vanished from the Chinese media when a devastating earthquake struck Sichuan province and at least eighty thousand mostly poor people were killed. Three months after that, the opening ceremony of the Olympic Games seemed to command attention in every part of the country and again marked a shift of national mood.

During periods like these, it can seem sensible to talk about a single cohesive-minded "China." And when acting on the international stage, or when imposing some internal political rules, the central government can operate as a coordinated entity. But most of the time, visitors—and Chinese people too—see vividly and exclusively the little patch of "China" that is in front of them, with only a guess as to how representative it might be of happenings anywhere else. You can develop a feel for a city, a company, a party boss, an opportunity, a problem—and then see its opposite as soon as you go to another town.

Such observations may sound banal—China, land of contrasts!—but I have come to think that really absorbing them is one of the greatest challenges for the outside world in reckoning with China and its rise. A constant awareness of the variety and contradictions within China does not mean suspending critical judgments or failing to observe trends that prevail in most of the country most of the time.. For instance, it really is true that for most Chinese families, life is both richer and freer than it was in the 1980s, and is immeasurably better on both counts than it was in the 1960s. It is also true that in most of the country, air and water pollution are so dire as to constitute not simply a major threat to public health but also a serious impediment to China's continued prospects for economic growth. So some overall statements about "China" and "the Chinese" are fair. But because of the country's scale, because of the linguistic and cultural barriers that can make it seem inaccessible, and because of the Chinese government's efforts to project the image of a seamlessly unified nation, outsiders are tempted to overlook the rifts, variation, and chaos, and talk about Chinese activities as if they were one coordinated whole. Therefore it is worth building in reminders of how many varied and often conflicting Chinas there really are.

Outsiders have learned to stretch their mental boundaries when it comes to considering China's "scale" in one sense of that term: its billion-plus population, its numerous cities the size of Paris, its collective appetite for commodities and products of all sorts, its influence on the world's markets and environment. The military analyst Thomas P. M. Barnett has come up with a vivid thought experiment to help outsiders envision the advantages and challenges that come from China's huge human scope: The United States and China have about the same geographic area, although China's mountainous and desert expanses mean that it has significantly less arable land. But China's population is about four times larger than America's. To match the challenge of human scale that confronts China, the United States would have to bring in every person from Mexico, more than 110 million in all, plus the 200 million people in Brazil. Then it would also need the entire population of Cuba and the rest of the Caribbean nations, plus Canada, Colombia, and every other country in North and South America. After doing all that, it would be up to around one billion people. If it then also added the entire population of Nigeria, some 155 million, and every person from the hyper-crowded islands of Japan, 125 million more, it would have as many people as China—almost.

Feeding, governing, housing, and employing these vast numbers within the borders of the existing fifty U.S. states would be an almost unimaginable challenge, especially while preserving anything resembling open space or wilderness. At the same time, all this humanity would mean that the resulting superstate could draw on much greater reserves of talent in every field—scientific, athletic, artistic and musical, entrepreneurial, civic. Think of running for President in these circumstances. Think of getting into Harvard (as many Chinese students now aspire to do). Those near-unimaginable strengths and the impossibilities of the situation are China's reality now. They explain the aphorism that has stuck with me since I heard it from a government official in Shanghai in 2006. "Outsiders think of everything about China as multiplied by 1.3 billion," he told me. "We have to think of everything as divided by 1.3 billion." Scale in this sense, as an indicator of variety and contradiction, of occasional chaos and frequent difficulty of control, is at least as important as the sheer weight of China's influence on the world.

I have met people for whom "China" is the export factories surrounding Hong Kong and Shenzhen; others for whom it is the Communist Party Schools and centers of related doctrine in Beijing. For many tens of millions in the countryside, "China" is nothing more than the area they can reach by foot from their farmhouses each day. When I spent several days at the Shanghai World Expo in 2010 with an Italian friend, we were often the only non-Chinese people within sight among the thousands in a given pavilion, public square, or multi-hour line for admission. The vast majority of other attendees were families from China's second- and third-tier cities for whom a trip through the Saudi Arabian or German pavilion was as close as they were ever likely to come to a view of the outside world. Exhibits that seemed cheesy to sophisticates from Europe, Japan, or North America were much more popular with their target audiences of untraveled Chinese. In this way the Expo served the same function for early twenty-first century China as the St. Louis and Chicago world's fairs had done for wide-eyed inland Americans a hundred years before.

On one of my first reporting trips to Guangdong province in southern China, a foreigner who had lived there for more than a decade and worked daily with Chinese factory owners and laborers said, "Each month I'm here, I know half as much as I did the month before." I thought he was being arch, but a few years later I began to grasp what he was saying. It's not that your store of knowledge keeps going down; it's that your awareness of what you don't know—and won't ever know—keeps going up, and at a faster rate. It's like driving away from the city lights at night and, when lifting your gaze, realizing with shock how many more stars are in the sky than you had previously seen, or imagined. It increases the importance of trying to recognize trends while allowing the possibility of change.

On the ground at Changsha

The trip began poorly. I had met Claeys in Changsha on a Friday evening, in plenty of time to make the three-hour flight to Zhuhai by Sunday night before the opening of the show on Monday. This is the way small-plane aviation is, anywhere in the world: "efficient" during the moments the plane is actually in the air and flying point to point, burdened with waits both planned and unplanned much of the rest of the time. Claeys had recently based the airplane in Changsha as part of a long-game strategy for attracting the interest of one of the likeliest-seeming purchasers in China. This was Zhang Yue, or "Chairman Zhang," a stylish industrial entrepreneur then in his mid forties who had trained as a landscape painter in vocational school and then come up with a way to make energy-saving air conditioners for places with unreliable electric-power supplies—like rural China, India, and Pakistan. He succeeded so spectacularly that he had built a surreal company town-utopia on the outskirts of the big industrial city of Changsha, which had been Chairman Mao's home in his student days and now has the biggest statue of Mao in the world (a hundred-foot-high granite bust).

Mr. Zhang's Broad Town factory compound, named for the
Broad Air Conditioning company he and his brother founded
and that he still ran, is on a similarly grand scale. It features a
building modeled on the main palace at Versailles, a heliport,
a gold-colored steel-and-glass replica of the Great Pyramid of
Egypt, and similar other touches around the factory and dormitories themselves. Mr. Zhang is an avid environmentalist—he
said that Al Gore was his hero—and an aviation buff as well,
and Claeys thought he would be a good candidate for one of
China's first Cirruses. He already had a small Broad Corporation air fleet consisting of a helicopter, a small jet, and several
Cessna single-engine propeller planes, and he was always on
the lookout for newer and, he hoped, more environmentally
friendly forms of air travel.

Starting on Saturday morning, Claeys kept asking the Aviation Department at Broad if and when they might be able
to find some fuel for the Cirrus, so it could fly on to Zhuhai. Piston-powered airplanes—most of the small ones with
propellers—use a different sort of fuel from either jets or cars.
They need a form of gasoline, rather than the kerosene used by
jets (or by turbine-powered turboprops); and the gas must be a
higher octane than automobile gas, with the lead additives that
were banned in normal gasoline many years ago. Given China's
tiny fleet of piston planes, this aviation gasoline, or avgas, was
not easy to come by. Hour after hour we heard that the fuel was
"on its way" or "almost here." For a while, it was supposed to be
on a convoy from another province. Then we didn't hear about
a convoy anymore. But perhaps there was gas at a different part
of the airport! Then again, apparently not. Saturday afternoon,
when we had planned to leave, turned into Saturday evening,
and then into pitch dark. It's always easier and safer to fly during daylight, and since we had all of Sunday still ahead of us,

we gave up and went to town, checked into the hotel we had previously checked out of, and decided to try again the next morning.

We got back to the airfield early. Against my own late-rising nature, I have come to respect the flying world's emphasis on getting started as close as possible to first light. There are that many more hours of daylight to work with, and that much more leeway to wait out or plan around bad weather. If you're worried about turbulence, wind, or thunderstorms, those problems are usually mildest early in the day. But Sunday morning passed, with no fuel. We were taken to the Broad Company's huge employee cafeteria for lunch, where we sat among the hundreds of blue-uniformed workers and ate our rice and stir-fried pork with peppers off aluminum trays, with metal chopsticks. Back out to the airfield, where still no one knew about any gas. Claeys kept looking down at his watch and up at the sky. You never want to "have to" make a trip in a small plane, but he felt he *had to* get to Zhuhai by dawn. Two p.m. came and went. Three o'clock. Four. The November sun was getting low in the sky—though not as low as you would expect, given the season. Since the whole continental mass of China runs on Beijing Time, sunrise and sunset both come "late" in cities away from the east coast; it is as if everywhere from Boston to Seattle ran on East Coast time.

Five o'clock, still some remaining light—and the first sign of hope! A delivery truck rolled up toward our airplane, with a large metal barrel in the rear. "Avgas!" the head of the Aviation Department said, in Chinese. (*"Hang kong qi you!"*) Claeys asked him where it had come from. The story involved derelict ex-Soviet training planes that had been parked in a remote section of the airport. There was enough old gas left in their tanks to drain into the barrel. Claeys, who understood the description in Chinese (as I did not), blanched. A little later he let me know what they had said.

At most airports, fuel comes out by way of a motor-driven pump, like at a gas station. At a few of the most remote, you might use a hand-cranked system to drive fuel through the hose and into the airplane's gas tank. In this case, we had the barrel on the truck bed, a gas tank opening on top of each wing of the plane, and a ten-foot-long, inch-wide plastic hose with which to connect them. A luckless member of the Broad Corporation's Aviation Department team began sucking fuel through the hose to siphon it from the barrel into the wing tanks.

At first he dreamed that he could start a flow going without getting gasoline all over his tongue and teeth. But each time he tried, yanking the hose from his mouth just before the gasoline reached his lips and jerking the hose toward the plane, the gas retreated back down the hose as soon as he stopped sucking. Not liking it a bit, and to the laughter of his fellow team members, he faced the fact that he would have to suck the gas along until it was spewing into his mouth—and then hand the hose to one of us to stick in the tank, while he began spitting and wiping off his tongue with a cloth. The Chinese term *chi ku,* "eat bitterness," is shorthand for being tough, doing what it takes, bearing hardship. I imagined that in Changsha they might someday say *he you,* "drink gas," for the same concept.

An hour of this—the flow got slower and slower as the level in the barrel went down—with ever-darkening skies, and we were ready to go. In pilot school, you're taught to be hyperconscious of the quality of the fuel going into the gas tank. After all, it is what will keep you in the air and alive. Claeys and I rationalized that if the fuel was bad enough—who knows how long it had been in those Soviet-airplane tanks, or where else it might have been—the engine wouldn't start at all. And if it was good enough to get the plane through the engine start and the test runup, or trial revving of the propellers before takeoff, it would probably at least get us up to an altitude from which we could deploy the parachute if need be. This is not the way I had been taught to operate an airplane, and not what Claeys would have liked to do, but, I told myself, This is China. Meanwhile, Walter Wang was reading peacefully.

Into the plane; onto the runway; preparing for takeoff. Before the flight, Claeys had spent weeks getting the clearances he needed to operate a foreign-registered airplane, as a foreign citizen, through Chinese military airspace—which virtually all the airspace in China is. As we prepared for a southbound departure on the very long, military-scale runway, Claeys revved the engine repeatedly, to make sure that the gas was actually supporting combustion, and as a proxy for seeing that it would keep doing so once we took off.

The most dangerous time in a small-plane flight is the first thirty or forty seconds after the wheels leave the runway. If the engine fails then, because the fuel flow is obstructed or the engine hesitates when suddenly pushed to full power, you are in danger precisely because you're so close to the ground. If the engine fails when an airplane is 10,000 feet up, that's not good. But because airplanes are designed to glide down relatively slowly even without engine power, rather than plummeting like a rock, the higher an airplane is when the trouble starts, the more time the pilot has to decide what to do, and the wider the range of territory and possible landing sites the plane could reach in a glide. Even with its parachute, the Cirrus is in trouble if an engine fails before it gets at least 400 feet above the ground—there is just not enough time for the parachute to deploy fully and slow the descent. So Claeys tested and retested the engine; I kept my eye on the parachute handle, to use if we got far enough into the air; Walter Wang settled into the back-seat, and we went to the end of the runway to take off.

The engine came up smoothly; the plane reached an air speed of 70 knots, at which point Claeys began easing its nose upward; at about the same time as we got a safe distance off the runway, we disappeared into the brown blear of the standard big-city Chinese pollution shroud. And we were off.

Into the clouds

In flying, the big distinction is in the clouds versus out of the clouds. When out of the clouds, you can see where you're going and steer the plane as if it were a car—with the added ability to go up and down. When you're in the clouds, everything about controlling the plane is different. It's like driving a car while blindfolded, but worse. Assuming he's not near a cliff, even a blindfolded driver can keep a car securely on the ground. In a plane it's simply impossible to tell up from down by your own bodily senses, if you can't *see* the ground or the horizon to assess whether the plane is turning, climbing, or holding a straight-and-level course. This is the hardest aspect of aeronautics to believe unless you have tried it.[1] You control the plane by obsessively "scanning" the dashboard gauges, constantly comparing readings from one with the others, and taking advantage of their gyroscopes, which give an idea of where the horizon would be if you were able to see it.

Because of the clouds, and because it was night, and because it's not possible in China just to fly around without the government's approval as it is in much of the United States, from take-off onward we were already operating under instrument flight rules, following controllers' instructions about when to climb, which direction to turn, and what waypoints to cross on our way south. This should have been fine, but it soon became more complicated than we had foreseen. Around the world, air-traffic controllers are supposed to be able to talk with pilots in English, in addition to their local language. If you listen to controllers' discussions on the radio, you will hear a mixture of Spanish and English in Mexico, Korean and English in Korea, French and English in France, and an improbable English-only discourse most of the time in Japan, even though most of those speaking are clearly Japanese. (I ascribe this to a greater emphasis on doing things the "right" way in Japan than in many other places.) When traveling on an airline that lets passengers listen to air-traffic control, I would hear, at China's main international airports—Beijing, Shanghai, Guangzhou—controllers talking rapid Mandarin to Chinese pilots and careful, accented, but clear English to Germans, Japanese, Americans, Turks, and other outsiders. But here in the interior of China, there would be no reason for controllers to keep up that competency. Claeys, skilled in Chinese, felt for procedure's sake that as a foreign pilot he should speak English over the airwaves. But every exchange was halting—and I began to think that the controllers just wanted to forget that we were there.

Between Changsha and Zhuhai stood the mountains of southern Hunan. They are not tremendously high by world standards, but they were higher than our airplane was at its initial assigned altitude. And unless the controller gave us instructions to climb—as we would routinely expect a few minutes into the flight—we would be headed for trouble soon. Even for airliners, instrument flights usually take place in stages: first up to 3,000 feet, then 5,000 feet, then for the airliners well up into the "flight levels," usually above 30,000 feet. Airliners fly that high precisely because the air is so thin. Within limits, the higher it goes, the less wind resistance, or drag, an airplane has to force itself through, so the better fuel mileage it gets. It looked as if we needed to get to about 10,000 feet to go safely over the mountains—that was our guess from the charts, which themselves were in principle a military secret in China—but the controllers hadn't told us to climb, and we couldn't get their attention to pass along our increasingly urgent request.

On the GPS-based moving map in the cockpit, we saw the ridge draw closer. We couldn't legally turn around, since that would be deviating from our clearance. Nor—again without breaking rules—could we decide to climb on our own. If we kept on straight and level, within ten minutes we'd crash. Then within eight minutes. Then six. Of course, we wouldn't just keep on flying straight into the mountains. Around the world, pilots always have the option to "declare an emergency" and deviate from their assigned course and do whatever else they must to avoid disaster. But that is asking for trouble, even in places where flight is less carefully restricted than it is in China. I learned later that a military jet was trailing us through the flight. What might it have done if we suddenly made an unauthorized move? I was preparing a pitch to Claeys on the lines of: I know that as foreigners we are "supposed" to be speaking English to the controller, but you can speak perfectly good Chinese! Time to switch? Please?

All the chatter between pilots and controllers, anywhere in the world, is over open radio channels, as with truckers' old CBs. The other pilots on the frequency, apparently all of them from airlines, could hear our increasingly tense-sounding attempts to get the controllers' attention. Finally a Japan Airlines pilot who was capable in both English and Chinese (apart, I assume, from Japanese) broke in to ask us, in English, if we would like some help. He then relayed the request, in Chinese, to the controller.

Immediately the controller responded to him—partly because of the language but much more, I suspect, because talking with airline pilots seemed "normal"; we could well have been the first private pilots ever to come through his sector. The JAL pilot passed the word back to us, though we had heard it over the airwaves too. Permission to climb. One hurdle cleared.

On through the dark and clouds toward Zhuhai. Its airport is one of a large number studding the bay around Hong Kong harbor. Geographically, the closest U.S. equivalent would be the coast of Maine or Alaska, with rocky cliffs rising sharply from the bay. Economically and commercially, the equivalent would be the greater Los Angeles basin, with roads, lights, and buildings sprawling as far in all directions as one could see. As we descended (with controllers' permission—they were more comfortable in English here so much closer to Hong Kong) in preparation for landing, we were mainly out of the clouds while still 2,000 feet above the ground. We marveled at the lights of the industrial urban expanse while noting the large, unlit masses that signified mountains and rocky islands. Zhuhai's airport is on the far southern extension of a peninsula, the southernmost point in the Hong Kong area. The instrument approach required circling the hills and island peaks, which is safe enough as long as you can follow the radio-guidance beam all the way down to the airport.

As we came to the coast, the clouds thickened again, and we found ourselves in the middle of them when only 1,000 feet above the ground. Claeys had his eyes glued to the dials that showed how closely we were following the beam. If we drifted "one dot left" relative to the beam, he would nudge the plane toward the right; if we fell "one dot low" beneath the desired glide path, he would edge the plane up. I looked back and forth from those gauges to the window, waiting for the glimpse of the ground or the airport approach lights that we needed before we reached our "decision height" a few hundred feet above the runway.

Suddenly the beam we were following, for an Instrument Landing System approach (or ILS, the most accurate system then in common use) seemed to behave strangely, and even flicker off. Momentarily there was no path to follow. This required immediate attention. We were close to the ground; we were headed down; we were among rocky peaks higher than our airplane was; and because of clouds and the dark we couldn't see what was ahead.

With the rational parts of our brains, we knew—and had discussed during the preceding few minutes, in the "brief the approach" discussion that is supposed to be part of the preparation for every landing—how we should respond. Airplane life is based on backups and contingencies, and every pilot who has trained for an instrument rating has practiced the "missed approach" routine that is called for if you don't see the ground or runway lights when you descend as low as the approach-chart says you safely and legally can. But it is one thing to know that in theory, and to have done it in practice time and again. It is something else to have to decide in real time while knowing that we were lower than the surrounding hills and only a few seconds' flight time away from the hyper-busy airspace for Hong Kong.

The main backup plan in any situation like this is to climb immediately, since you cannot keep heading down when you don't know what you might hit. If we climbed too much too suddenly, that could mean violating our clearance, and would bring us up into airspace where five large commercial airports had airline and air-cargo traffic merging—Hong Kong, Macau,

Guangzhou, Shenzhen, and Zhuhai—with God knows what consequences. Of course we'd climb nonetheless; as the aviation saying went, it's better to be around to argue about possible violations than to miss that disciplinary hearing because you have crashed. We could worry later on, too, about what had gone wrong. Had the landing signal failed or been switched off for some reason? Was it our instruments or their settings?

Claeys and I had begun talking, tersely, about what to do next when, with the relief of a drowning person who breaks the surface to gasp air, I saw out the window that we had left the ragged bottom layer of the clouds and could see all the way to the vast, open, clearly lit main runway at Zhuhai.

We landed. The humid 90-degree air fogged over glasses, camera lenses, and dial faces the second we opened the cockpit door. We had friends take a picture, with smiles that barely masked the tenseness we had felt.

We got out, both sobered and giddy; we went to a nightclub in downtown Zhuhai that was called the Blue Angel and was owned by China's most famous female pilot, Chen Yan, a glamorous bombshell who was frequently on the cover of fashion magazines and who asked me, when I first met her in the presence of her teenaged son, "Do you think I am his mother? Most people think I am his sister!" Over the next few days Peter Claeys was busy at the air show; I stayed the next day and then took a commercial flight back to Shanghai, and we never fully determined what had happened in those seconds that seemed like centuries inside the cockpit. Had there been a power failure, or a disruption in the navigation signal, as sometimes happens? Had we gotten a setting wrong? Had someone at the airport inexplicably decided it was time to shut down? At the time I had been too busy staring for breaks in the clouds to notice all the variables, and afterward there was no way to be sure. We saw the runway in time and got down—and if we hadn't seen it, we had been prepared to divert somewhere else.

I did not fly as a pilot or copilot again in mainland Chinese airspace. But starting that day, parallel to my day job of reporting on financiers and politicians, I followed the people in China who were trying to remake its history through taking to the air.

1 ★ This Is Going to Be Big

The trip to the Four Seasons Club

On a freezing February evening in 2011, a little more than four years since my flight to Zhuhai, my wife and I tried to figure out how to get from our apartment in downtown Beijing to a recently opened restaurant on the far east side of town. Basic navigation in big Chinese cities can be more challenging than it sounds, and not simply for foreigners like us with incomplete language skills. I had been studying Chinese characters for many years, starting when we lived in Japan in the 1980s, and thus am comfortable enough reading Chinese maps and street signs; my wife, trained in linguistics and with a good ear in many languages, is much better at hearing and speaking. Together we are stronger than either of us separately; still the language can be a challenge.

And far from the main challenge in finding our way to an unfamiliar site in a big, fast-growing Chinese city. So many roads are constantly being repaved, redirected, renamed, or torn up. So many subway lines, bridges, tunnels, and flyovers are continually being opened, closed, or redone. Neighborhoods are razed in the course of a weekend—in Beijing both the traditional *hutong* courtyard houses from before the modern era and the squat, badly insulated, brutally ugly walk-up apartments built under Mao from the fifties through the seventies.

In their place, seemingly overnight and literally a few weeks or months later, appear a forty-story condo complex, a mall with car dealerships and Armani or Hermès outlets plus KFC and McDonald's, a government research center, a Carrefour or Walmart. Maps are often of little use. While living in Shanghai, I occasionally saw a taxi driver with a city map in his car, but never once in a cab in Beijing.

The Chinese man who would be our host that night had sent a link to the Web site for the venue he had chosen, the Four Seasons Club restaurant. This club has no connection to the familiar high-end Four Seasons international hotel chain, which has several locations in Beijing. Moreover, its name in Chinese—that is, its "real" name—was entirely different, its characters meaning Star River Club.

From the club's Web site, we found that it is located near the Qingnian Road Station on Line 6 of the Beijing Metro. Good news! We had each taken well over a thousand subway trips through our years of living in Shanghai and Beijing—several trips most days, nearly each day we were in town—and always preferred them as a way of avoiding chronically clogged roads. But how would we get onto Line 6, which we had never used before, from our apartment near the intersection of Lines 1 and 10? Unfortunately, it turned out that the only way there would be via a time machine, since Line 6 would still be under construction for the next year or two. No wonder we hadn't seen it on the subway-system maps inside the stations.

Buses were a possibility, and one we'd used for other sites off the subway grid. But at rush hour along Jianguo Road, one of Beijing's broadest and most heavily trafficked thoroughfares, the windows of each passing bus were dark with the overcoats of people jammed into every available cubic inch of its volume, with further huge crowds waiting expectantly on the sidewalk.

And anyway we would have had to change buses several times to get where we were headed. That left taxis. When we finally saw one with the bright red "empty car" (空车) sign illuminated, meaning that it would take passengers, I raced past a group of young Chinese women also looking for a taxi—forget chivalry, it was either that or stand around waiting all night—and got in, moving over to make room for my wife and an American friend visiting from California.

Over the next half hour, we inched and jolted the five-plus miles to the club, through the east-side congestion of Beijing's Fourth Ring Road and Chaoyang Road as the driver weaved in and out of construction zones. When we got within what we all reckoned to be a few blocks of the destination, he called the restaurant's number on a mobile phone for final turn-by-turn guidance through a particularly chewed-up, trench-ridden, girder-strewn building area.

The satellite map of the neighborhood, which we'd checked before leaving the apartment, was as out of date as any printed map. At the alleged site of the Star River hotel-restaurant-golf-course complex, it had shown only a low warren of Mao-era apartment buildings amid vegetable fields. I knew that at best the satellite view would be approximate. Chinese law requires that images of Chinese cities from Google Maps, Google Earth, and the like must be offset[1] from online street maps, so you can never exactly line up a street address with a satellite image. It's a feint at security, from a government that long viewed maps as highly sensitive information. This mentality reaches a delightful extreme in maps of the west side of Beijing: Satellite views and Google Earth show a huge airport sitting between the Fourth and Fifth Ring Roads, with a runway like the ones at O'Hare or JFK, alongside major malls and business centers. But that airport is used mainly for military and government purposes, and its existence is acknowledged neither by highway exit signs nor on city maps, which show only a big blank spot in that area.

For our trip that evening, the mismatch was an offset in time more than in space, since there was nothing in either the satellite or the map images to suggest a business of any sort anywhere close to the destination. Yet as we neared the assigned address in the cab we saw something that in its neon lighting and its showy architecture would have fit in easily in Las Vegas.

The club's entrance had parapets modeled on a villa in Tuscany, or a castle from a fairy tale. A black Mercedes that appeared to have been washed and polished mere instants before sat gleaming in the driveway. Teams of attractive and spiffily uniformed young male and female attendants saluted us on entry with Chinese and English greetings. *Huanying guanglin!* Welcome, sir and madam! The building's back windows looked onto the recently opened fairways of the club's golf course.

For the next few hours inside, we enjoyed an unusually luxurious version of that staple of Chinese business interactions, the celebratory dinner. Many courses; many welcoming toasts; much gracious plucking with long serving chopsticks of the choicest morsel of fish or meat, for ceremonial placement by the host on the dish of the honored guest. The actual head of the roasted chicken, complete with beak and comb? For me? Why, thank you so much for this gesture of respect! Because the Chinese businesspeople at the dinner had all worked and studied outside China, we were spared the rounds of competitive bottoms-up toasting, toward the intended aim of all-hands drunkenness, that typifies many gatherings in the provinces. We were spared as well a TV set turned on and blaring soap operas, game shows, or karaoke songs inside the private dining room, a standard touch of provincial banquets. Instead we had sips of wine, cups of tea, mobile phones frequently ringing and being answered, and animated discussion of Chinese-American business possibilities.

The main business to be done that night was between representatives of U.S. and Chinese coal and power companies, pooling their efforts for research in "cleaner" coal. American, European, and Japanese companies were all coming to China to see new carbon-control, coal-gasification, and other clean-up techniques tried and improved upon, since China is where so many of the world's plants were being built.

But, as often happens at such gatherings, other side deals were being discussed and dreamed about at the same time, and several Chinese guests went in and out of the room to take phone calls or drop in on other business dinners they had double-booked for that same night. For instance, late in the evening, an unassuming and modestly dressed man arrived from his previous dinner. He was less urbane-seeming than the others and unlike them spoke only Chinese, rather than being able to go back and forth between languages. Despite appearances, he turned out to be the wealthiest person present; as the CEO of one of the largest battery-making companies in the world, he was there to talk not about coal but about electric cars. A few weeks earlier he had been to Washington, where he met congressmen and told them about his dream of opening factories in the United States to produce batteries for a new electric car he was helping design. "This can change the future! If I can reassure those congressmen," he said, according to an interpreter at the table.

Confident, can't-wait talking and planning of this sort is familiar as both an exhausting and an exhilarating trait of modern China. I would hear the phrase "my dream is . . ." more often in the course of a typical month in China than in a typical decade in the United States. The person who appeared to be most excited by his dream that evening was the dinner's host, a stocky man in his late fifties named Xu Changdong. Mr. Xu had a stake in the coal and energy discussion, to put it mildly; he personally controlled development rights to vast coal reserves in the Chinese autonomous region of Inner Mongolia, which the regional government had awarded him in exchange for his plans to open an advanced manufacturing plant there. But what really excited his passion was his newest venture, which he was sure was going to transform the country: a boom in aviation.

The morning after this dinner, one of his companies would announce a plan to sell helicopters inside China and start building them there—including at the plant in Inner Mongolia. Also that next day, the main Chinese newspapers would splash on their front pages the story of China's across-the-board push to become a major aerospace and air-travel power as part of the upcoming Twelfth Five-Year Plan.[2] In American and European discussion, the very term "Five-Year Plan" smacks of the Soviet era, suggesting clumsy central-government efforts that are out of touch with market realities and are therefore doomed before they start. Within China, businesspeople, government officials, and members of the public take very seriously the goals and spending targets laid out in the successive Five-Year Plans. They know that this is where a lot of public money and attention will be directed. The Twelfth Plan, counting from the First in the early 1950s under Chairman Mao, would run from mid-2011 through 2016 and include a big boost for aviation, which it listed as one of the "seven major strategic industries" for the next phase of the country's growth. Public investment in all phases of China's aerospace future over those years would come to 1.5 trillion Chinese yuan renminbi (RMB), or about

$230 billion. That was a 50 percent increase over comparable investment in the previous Five-Year Plan—and, depending on how you count, somewhere between five and ten times as much as the Federal Aviation Administration's budget for capital improvements and airport construction in the same period in the United States. Dozens of brand-new airports were coming, and thousands of new airliners for China's fleets, and many thousands of helicopters, business jets, and small aircraft of all varieties.

"You can't imagine how big this is going to be," Xu Changdong said in English to the guests at the dinner. "People have the money. They have the technology. The airspace is opening."

You can't imagine. By this time in China, I was beginning to.

Xu had grown up in Shanghai, gone to New York as a penniless thirty-year-old graduate student in 1983, and stayed there for nearly twenty years as he built an import-export empire. During the 1990s, after he had established himself, he went out one summer day on an open-ocean fishing expedition off Long Island. Anglers had ringed the boat's railings, with their backs to one another as they cast lines into the sea. Suddenly a hook that one person had flipped over his shoulder, on the backswing of a cast, caught the eyeball of someone on the other side of the boat. Xu, like the other passengers, was horrified and could hardly bear to look. But—as he remembered clearly, when retelling the story to me many years later—he was struck by the firm but low-key manner in which the boat's captain told him and everyone else to remain calm. The captain had radioed the Coast Guard and been assured that within eight minutes a rescue helicopter would arrive to take the victim in for emergency care.

"I looked at my watch, and even before eight minutes, the helicopter was coming," Xu said, when he told me the story in Beijing. The rescue crew lifted the victim from the boat's deck into the helicopter, and thence off to an emergency room.

"I heard later that the man's sight had been saved," Xu told me when reflecting on the role played by the rescue helicopter. "I realized that if he had been in China, absolutely there is no chance to save his eye. I said to myself, Someday I will bring this technology to China." At the current stage of China's growth it is common to hear that kind of "I will change the world / I will transform my country" declaration. Xu was certainly right about the unmet need in his homeland. A dramatic instance occurred after the Sichuan earthquake of 2008, when many thousands of Chinese people survived the initial landslides and building collapses, only to die of exposure or dehydration in the subsequent days. Chinese rescue forces had to trudge in by foot, since roads through the mountainous territory had been buried and the country had far too few helicopters with which to reach those who were still alive.

In the early 2000s, Xu came back to China, to expand his business and reenter the Chinese linguistic and cultural environment. He became a leader of the charmingly named Western Returned Scholars Association, composed of people who, like him, had graduated from American or other foreign universities and come back to China after successful business careers abroad. Xu had had $40 in cash in his pocket when he arrived at Kennedy Airport the first time, in 1983, and had been panicked at the discovery that the taxi to his student dormitory cost $30. Thus he had to find a part-time job immediately, which he did the very next day. By the time he returned to China two decades later, he had become rich by any country's standards. Hearing stories like Xu's, I often felt in China as if I were living through a Horatio Alger novel, or a collection of them simultaneously. The rags-to-riches tales with their emphasis on early hardship, subsequent business success, and gratifying return to a prospering homeland, were so common that I had to remind myself to keep paying attention to them.

As he went on about his dream of what aviation would mean for China, Xu seemed tongue-tied for a moment. He turned to the translator and said, "I am forgetting my English! Let me speak in Chinese." One of the Americans at the dinner, who was making his first trip to China and spoke no Chinese, said with unthinking Blimpish patronization, "Oh, your English is not that bad!" Xu was in fact fully fluent in English, albeit with an accent, having done business in America for decades. He couldn't help himself: "Well, it *is* better than your Chinese." He softened that, somewhat, with a smile, and then switched to Chinese and relied on the interpreter: "It is as if we were talking twenty years ago, and I told you this was going to be the biggest market for cars in the world. You would look around and see the bicycles and the oxcarts, and you would think I was crazy. I would have been evicted from America if I had made that kind of claim!" Of course, by 2010, Chinese companies produced more cars, and Chinese customers bought more—including luxury models—than their counterparts in the United States. At that point General Motors was surviving not simply because of government help in the United States but also because of its strong position in China, where Buick remains a prestigious and best-selling brand.[3] "Or when those first very large Motorola 'mobile' phones came into China twenty years ago. And *The Wall Street Journal* said it would be ten years before China had regular desk phones and another ten before cell phones became popular." Of course, China was the world's largest mobile-phone market by the early 2000s.

"That is how it is going to be with flying. The next step will be the helicopter. Everything is about to take off."

Planning for "takeoff"

The Twelfth Five-Year Plan, the one that included aerospace as a strategic industry, wouldn't officially begin until later in the year, but at the start of 2011 the steps toward China's ambitious future in the skies kept coming. As Xu had said, they paralleled the leaps the country had previously made in electronics, automobiles, and many other fields, and the operative principle did seem to be "everything is about to take off," all at once.

A week after that dinner, the Beijing police force would announce its plans to buy a new fleet of helicopters for traffic and safety patrols over the town. Chinese cities have plenty of street-level noise, to put it mildly, but as soon as you think to notice it, you're struck by the lack of the overhead roar from airliners and helicopters that is the background soundscape in most of the world's other big cities. Later that same month, the head of China's central aviation agency—Li Jiaxiang, a former People's Liberation Army Air Force general who had then become head of China's national airline and who now ran CAAC, the Civil Aviation Administration of China—previewed some of the spending details that would accompany the next Five-Year Plan, including the 1.5 trillion RMB (at the time about $200 billion) for new airports, navigation systems, and airplanes. The story was run across the top of the front page of *China Daily*, the state-controlled English-language paper that is China's face to the outside world. "Aviation Sector Has High Hopes for Next 5 Years" was the headline.[4] In aerospace as in so many areas, China was starting out far behind the United States and many other developed powers—but planned to catch up fast. The country's commercial airline fleet numbered only about 2,600 airplanes as of 2010, roughly half as many as America's for a population four times as large. The target in the next five years was 4,500 airplanes, a rate of purchase that would represent about half of the new aircraft sold anywhere in the world. Back in 2009, when airlines everywhere else in the world were canceling jet orders and stretching out delivery schedules as long as possible, a Boeing executive had pointed out that China was the only "dynamic aviation market" in the world and said that its "strong domestic air-travel growth" was the main indication "that the world aviation industry is beginning to recover."[5]

Total airline passenger volume had increased only modestly in the United States and Europe throughout the whole first decade of the twenty-first century—because of the 9/11 attacks, world financial crises, increased security hassles, and the overall neuralgia of flying. But in China passenger traffic had never stopped growing, and it was predicted to keep doubling every five years. It is tricky to compare market capitalizations of Chinese firms, especially large state-owned enterprises that can draw on government support, with those of outside corporations that usually must rely on normal equity markets. Still, the scale of Chinese carriers is impressive. The flagship carrier, Air China, is in capitalization terms the largest airline in the world, by far. As of 2011 its market capitalization was about $19 billion, or much more than that of the carriers United-Continental, American, US Airways, jetBlue, SkyWest, Hawaiian, and Republic, which, combined, were worth only about $15 billion.[6] The three largest Chinese carriers—Air China, followed by China Southern and China Eastern—are respectively numbers one, three, and four in valuation among all airlines in the world. The three largest U.S. carriers are numbers nine, ten, and eleven, and the top three European lines are five, twelve, and thirteen.

Among passenger airports, Atlanta's is still the world's busiest, with about eighty-nine million passengers in 2010. But Beijing's Capital Airport is already second and gaining, with about seventy-four million passengers and traffic growing by well over 10 percent a year. In 2000, the three largest cargo airports, by tonnage carried, were Memphis (as the hub for FedEx), Hong Kong (for southern China's exports to the world), and Los Angeles (where many Asian imports arrive). In 2010, the three largest were Hong Kong, Memphis, and Shanghai. Traffic at both Hong Kong and Shanghai was up more than 20 percent from the preceding year, versus 6 percent for Memphis.[7] And none of this even counted the ambitions to open China's airspace for the kind of business-aviation boom that has been routine in the United States, Europe, Australia, and Latin America for decades. As of 2011, China still had relatively few airports compared with more developed countries—175 total, compared with nearly 1,000 in the United States capable of receiving commercial flights plus another 4,000 or so where propeller planes and small business jets could land. But the Chinese government was already at work on 150 new airports, mainly in parts of the country that had never previously had air service.

The Chinese ambitions extended to manufacturing too. Apart from the helicopters—and a planned jetliner that might someday take customers from Airbus and Boeing, and the regional jets—during the spring of 2011 a subsidiary of AVIC, China's main state-run aviation corporation, bought Cirrus Aviation, the pioneering company in Duluth, Minnesota, that made the world's most popular small propeller aircraft, including the one in which Peter Claeys and I had gone to Zhuhai.

Around the same time another AVIC subsidiary bought Teledyne Continental, the United States–based company that made
the engines for Cirrus and a number of other small planes.

About ten days after that dinner with Mr. Xu, I was in Hong
Kong, at the Asian Aerospace Expo, where organizations as
large as Boeing and Airbus and as small as tour operators or
three-pilot flight schools looked for customers. A Chinese
man who had for some reason chosen the improbable English
name Vicky—he and his business partner were known as Ricky
and Vicky—had begun operations for an "FBO," or fixed-base
operator, the aviation world's term for the kind of small-airport
facility that would serve non-airline aviation.

"Now that they"—the government—"have got Cirrus, I
think you will see very good support for general aviation in
China," Vicky said. "Today we have only a few airplanes in all
of China. In the United States, there are more than two hundred twenty thousand small airplanes![8] I can say, the market
here will be enormous." Next to Vicky in the booth, I met a
man named Chen, from the northeast zone of China still called
Manchuria in the Western world and Dongbei, "East-North,"
in China. "I had always had a dream to fly, but when I tried
to the military I did not pass the body exam," he told me, in
English, referring to the military's physical screening tests. He
looked perfectly hale, and I assumed that he had run afoul of
the People's Liberation Army Air Force's notoriously strict eyesight standards for pilots.

Mr. Chen was a child during the Cultural Revolution and
ended up in the metal-parts business. Thanks to China's infrastructure boom, he became very rich. His company had the
contract to build metal structures at towers at the 2006 Interna-

tional Horticultural Exhibition in Shenyang, the northeastern city known as Mukden in the colonial days. The soaring symbols of the towers reawakened his interest in flight. He bought a small glider, went to the gigantic international AirVenture gathering in Oshkosh, Wisconsin, and decided he would make aviation part of his business. By the time I met him, he had also decided to buy several "wind-tunnel machines"—huge turbines that supported paying guests on cushions of air and gave them the feeling of skydiving—that he was going to install at the former site of the Shanghai World Exposition, and other places. "The aviation market in China is going to become very big!" he told me, reinforcing what Vicky had said. "Everyone knows this, all around the world!"

On the same day I spoke with him, I interviewed a salesman for a private jet company, who said that he had sold three new jets to Chinese customers within the past twenty-four hours. Each of the planes cost around $20 million; one of the sales was in cash, delivered in suitcases. In some parts of the world, bulk cash payments might come only from drug dealers or arms traffickers. In this instance the purchaser was a regional industrialist and real estate magnate, and the cash was a sign of the fast growth and rough-and-ready nature of Chinese capitalism at the moment.

A few days after that, a company in Shanghai announced the debut of *Wings and Water* magazine, a Robb Report–style publication about yachts and private jets for China's new wealthy class.[9] As a gauge of the potential, an official from Dassault, the French jet firm, pointed out that the United States already had more than eleven thousand business jets, versus two hundred to three hundred in China (only thirty of which were registered—the rest flying illegally). An aviation blogger outside China calculated that China had only 22 private jets per trillion dollars of gross domestic product (GDP), versus 535 for the United States and 138 for Europe.[10] If it were to match the European level—on an income basis, not even adjusting for population—that meant its fleet could expand sixfold. To match the American level, a better comparison given its geography, it could expand by a factor of twenty-five. At the first-ever China Business and Private Jet Expo, held in Shanghai in 2010, the proudly nationalist paper *Global Times*—which chronicled the country's rise with such features as "Chinese vs. Foreign Stars: Who Has the Most Beautiful Legs?"—said China's leading role as an aircraft market, and eventually as a producer, would be another sign of its emergence as a modern power. "We are going to buy *two* business jets this time," the story quoted Li Nonghe, secretary general of the World Chinese Business Advancement Association, as saying. It added, "He showed his feelings of pride as Chinese are becoming richer to the point of owning jets."[11]

The next frontier in Chinese achievement

These plans were grand; some were grandiose. Some of them would succeed; some would become huge money losers and at best would be forgotten, with deluded investors or indifferent state agencies left to cover the eventual loss. Some would represent significant challenges to established businesses and whole industries in the rest of the world. Some would open opportunities for foreign participants. In these aspects and many others, the impending drive to make China a major player in the world's aerospace business resembles many other aspects of the country's rush to modernization since the beginning of its market reforms and opening to the world starting in 1979. The more time I spent in China, the more I thought that this aspect of its industrial ambition, which has received far less attention than comparable pushes for clean-energy, info-tech, biotech, and other fields, was the next great arena and test case for Chinese modernization.

I am a lifelong aviation enthusiast, and for about fifteen years have been an active small-plane pilot. I had flown across the United States several times before arriving in China in 2006, and I imagined, or hoped, that I might be able to explore parts of the country in a small plane. Soon enough, I learned better. A few weeks after arriving in China, I had an unexpected interview with a senior official from the foreign ministry. I innocently explained my hope to see parts of China's western frontier from the air. He managed to keep a straight face while my comments were being translated. "That is interesting," he said in reply.

Ultimately I did manage to fly in a small plane more than once in and around mainland China, apart from the many dozens of trips I made on Chinese airlines. One year after my memorable trip from Changsha to Zhuhai with Peter Claeys in a Cirrus, I was copilot on another Cirrus flight with him. We started at a small airport outside Tokyo, down through Okinawa for a refueling stop on the eve of a typhoon, and after the storm passed to Taipei. From there Claeys took it on to Macau with an Italian pilot friend, Michele Travierso. Even though I had to give up—or, more optimistically, "postpone"—my own ambitions to fly throughout China, I sought out and met a large cast of Chinese and foreign figures who were preparing for the time when China's aviation dreams fully took off. These were the visionaries, hucksters, engineers, business promoters, regional power brokers, environmentalists, military pilots, airline entrepreneurs, and miscellaneous aviation enthusiasts who believe that China is about to enter its own aviation age.

I first looked into their world largely out of personal fascination, but over the years I became convinced that this was another crucially revealing subelement of Chinese life and prospects, with potentially important implications for the rest of the world. Life around the coal mines, life at the universities, life among the veterans of the Cultural Revolution who are trying to cope with (or suppress) memories of their individual and collective past—each of these says something about the country's overall possibilities. So it is with the people who are now negotiating with the military to open up China's skies, imagining a Chinese counterpart to Boeing, Airbus, and NASA, and reflecting on what the aviation boom in China, the world's biggest, will mean for the country's natural environment and that of the entire planet.

The people in this world include: The engineers hoping to build a Chinese counterpart to and competitor for Boeing and Airbus. The Boeing and Airbus officials—and smaller counterparts from Embraer and Dassault and Cessna and Diamond—trying to stay in the Chinese market and remain ahead of the competition. The provincial boosters and dreamers from the wilds of China who imagined that building a vast new airfield would be the secret to their area's prosperity. The foreign pilots who had been furloughed by airlines in the developed world and hired on for service as "freight dogs" (air-freight pilots) or instructors in China's burgeoning flight-academy business. The Chinese officials planning where to build the next dozen new airports, and the foreign architects and engineers and environmental consultants desperately competing to be cut in on those deals. The Chinese and international researchers working to produce jet fuel from algae in hopes of offsetting the environmental effects of the aviation boom, on China and the world. The sales reps for American, European, and Brazilian airplanes and helicopters trying to sell their aircraft—who in some cases ended up selling their companies as a whole to Chinese bidders. And the people across China who, much as happened to Americans with the coming first of the "jet age" in the late 1950s and then of cheap deregulated air travel in the late 1970s, were changing their sense of the country and themselves through the idea of quick travel by air.

Almost any activity in China involves a lot of people, and so it is with Chinese aviation. The city of Xi'an alone has more than 250,000 aerospace engineers and assembly workers, about eight times as many as in the comparable U.S. aviation center, Seattle. That difference in volume says something about the gap in output and productivity levels too—with their much smaller workforce, the U.S. factories still produce most of the world's airplanes, from Boeings down to Cirruses and Cessnas. Still, the scale of the coming Chinese effort can seem fearsome and unstoppable. Late in 2011 a new company called the China Business Aviation Group played on that impression by announcing that "the giant had awakened" and predicting China's inevitable domination of the business-jet market worldwide.[12]

But the realities behind the scale and numbers, in aviation as in so many other aspects of China's development, are more complicated, sometimes less impressive, and always more interesting than they seem from afar. The comedy and infighting that coexist with grandiose national planning; the corruption and small-town parochialism that give policies such a different effect in the hinterland than was intended in the capital—these apply in aviation as they do in the "green tech" boom, the boom in higher education, and many other areas. The biggest difference between being a foreigner inside China and watching it as a foreigner from outside is how much more precarious and uneven the state of China's "success" seems from within, and the different view one gets as to how China's growth will affect the rest of the world.

The many stories that make "the China story"

There is no one China story or "complete" picture of China. That is the theme I stressed repeatedly in the *Atlantic* articles I wrote while I was living in China and that also guides this narrative. The first step toward reckoning with what is knowable about China's rise is remembering how diverse and contradictory conditions within the country can seem to be. Trends both good and bad in China's development can be identified, but every one of them has its exceptions and uncertainties.

Perhaps the strongest and most important of these general trends in China is the sense that *things are possible*. Many Americans and Europeans have that in their personal lives; it's very strong for those in the scientific, technological, and pop-culture businesses, but it has all but vanished from public life in many developed countries. The electorates in most of North America, Europe, and Japan know very well what their countries' main problems are. They just lack any belief that their governments will grapple with those problems or even that governments should try. China's problems are far worse and more obvious, starting with the rampant pollution and thoroughgoing environmental destruction that have become the nation's major public-health threat and challenge to its long-term development. But three decades into the modernization kicked off by Deng Xiaoping, most people seem to imagine that problems will be solved, or at least that life will be better five years from now than it was five years ago.

The part of Chinese ambition that is channeled into aerospace parallels this larger trend, and its progress in this field is a close marker of its overall modernization. In the 1980s, China's airlines were antiquated and genuinely dangerous. Through most of the past ten years, they have been statistically among the safest in the world, and more comfortable than most in North America or Europe. Who remembers the last Economy Class seat on a U.S. airline that came with a meal as part of the price? I cannot remember being on a Chinese airline flight of any duration that did not include a hot meal—usually fish, chicken, or pork with either rice or noodles. The old airline system was a proxy for China's general backwardness, and the current one is an indicator of its progress and ambition, in surprisingly revealing ways.

Designing and building modern airplanes is even more complex than it seems, incorporating simultaneous advances on many separate technological fronts. Materials science (so the planes can be lighter and stronger), engine design (so they can fly more reliably on less fuel), electronics and avionics (as the plane's control systems and sensors become one enormous interconnected computer), large-scale coordination of supply chains and performance schedules, and more. Running a successful airline requires a combination of retail-level customer-handling skills, to keep the level of hatred and frustration felt by the flying public from driving them away from air travel altogether, and complex integration of route structure, fare changes, crew scheduling, the passenger-versus-cargo mix, and many other variables.

At the national level, keeping air travel safe enough to seem First World rather than Third World is the most complex undertaking of all. It requires uniform maintenance and safety standards for airports in every remote corner of the country; a network of air-traffic controllers who know how to work within their own system and with the airlines' pilots and dispatchers; the ability to collect accurate weather reports from around the country, and get them to pilots and controllers in real time, while feeding the data into supercomputers to forecast hazardous patterns; a system for training pilots, mechanics, and inspectors and indoctrinating them into a safety-first culture; check-and-balance procedures that detect and correct those not fully indoctrinated and that keep any individual or organization from taking too many risks; and more. A modern air-travel system also requires a degree of integration across national borders—U.S. planes flying across the Caribbean routinely talk with controllers in Havana—and across organizational boundaries within each country, since military, commercial, and civilian authorities must coordinate their use of airspace. Therefore it is not just techno-chauvinism that leads rising nations to think that a functioning aerospace and air-travel system is a meaningful indication of full-fledged development.

Modern China is the world's great success story at the "hard" elements of this achievement: creating infrastructure, lowering production costs, doing any- and everything at a great scale. But it has yet to show comparable sophistication with the "soft" ingredients necessary for a fully functioning, world-leading aerospace establishment. These include standards that apply consistently across the country, rather than depending on the whim and favor of local potentates. Or smooth, quick coordination among civil, military, and commercial organizations. Or sustaining the conditions—intellectual-property protection, reliable contract enforcement and rule of law, freedom of inquiry and expression—that allow first-rate research-and-developments institutions to thrive and to attract talent from around the world.

If China can succeed fully in aerospace, then in principle there is very little it cannot do. The combination of economic power and autocratic political control that has made the Chinese story so successful thus far seems, from a Western perspective, to be self-limiting, because it is a contradiction. The Chinese model has worked to bring a mainly peasant economy into the low-wage manufacturing era. But—the reasoning goes—it will be hard to sustain the controls as more Chinese people become rich, urbane, independent-minded. Or, if the government insists on maintaining the controls, it will be hard to move the economy beyond the stage of reliance on low-wage industries and copycat goods.

Aviation in all its aspects will be a test of these theories. For success, China will need the strengths it has already demonstrated, and ones it has yet to master.

2 ★ Getting Off the Ground

Starting out far behind

A man who had served in the People's Liberation Army Air Force before immigrating to the United States in the 1980s told me the following story of China's introduction to the world of international aviation.

As Henry Kissinger planned his secret trip to China in 1971, airport officials in Beijing were concerned. Kissinger would be arriving on a Boeing 707 operated by Pakistan International Airlines. To conceal the fact that he was going to China, Kissinger had feigned illness while on a trip to Pakistan, which explained his absence from official functions there. For extra security he traveled from Islamabad to Beijing not in an American-government aircraft but one from PIA, which had operated scheduled service to China since the mid-1960s.

At the time, the 707 was one of the most recognizable aircraft in the world. It was the airplane that more than any other had made jet age intercontinental travel feasible in the 1960s. An Air Force version of the 707 also served in those days as *Air Force One,* as it had during one mission that commanded attention around the world: bringing John F. Kennedy's body back from Dallas in 1963.[1]

But 707s did not normally fly into the People's Republic of China. Its airports were closed to most Western airlines, and its own commercial and military fleets used mainly Soviet-model airplanes. Would it have the right equipment to handle and service the plane? At an even more basic and potentially embarrassing level, how was Kissinger supposed to get from the airplane onto the ground? When the 707's doors opened, they would be some twenty feet above the runway, and at a different height from the Soviet-made planes. Would the VIP passengers have to jump, or climb, to reach the movable stairways the Beijing authorities already had on hand?

According to my friend from the PLA Air Force, the Chinese officials did not want to buy or borrow a standard airport staircase from a Western supplier—such was their sensitivity about revelations of their technological isolation. Instead they built their own in a rush, using pictures and published specs of the 707. When Kissinger's plane arrived they rolled out the staircase as if it were the most natural thing for them to be prepared for any sort of international aircraft.

Forty years later, China's President Hu Jintao took a non-stop flight from Beijing's lavishly modernized Capital Airport to Andrews Air Force Base, outside Washington, for his series of meetings with President Obama. He also traveled in a very familiar Boeing plane, the latest extended-range version of the 747, painted with the livery of Air China. There was an image of a big red Chinese flag near the nose of the plane, and, next to it, the logo of Star Alliance, which linked Air China with United, Lufthansa, ANA (All Nippon Airways), Air New Zealand, and many other international airlines.

Kissinger's trip underscored China's apartness from the world; Hu Jintao's its thorough connectedness. And one of the few elements that remained constant through this forty-year span—that officials of each government traveled to the other's capital on U.S.-made Boeing planes—illustrated another aspect of China's evolution and of the United States–Chinese interaction: the symbolic and also practical significance of American dominance in aerospace and aviation, a field in which China had ambitions but few achievements.

With the unveiling of its Twelfth Five-Year Plan, and presumably with the plans that would come after it, the Chinese government announced its intention to close that gap, much as it had previously done in automobile production, electronics, clean-energy technology, and so many other areas. At the Asian Aerospace Expo in Hong Kong in 2011, COMAC—the Commercial Aircraft Group of China, the country's intended long-term rival to Boeing and Airbus—presented a huge mockup of the C919 commercial airliner whose development was then under way, as a prelude to a similar presentation a few months later at the Paris Air Show.

When visitors walked into a full-scale model of a section of the cabin's interior in Hong Kong, they could watch video renderings of a future in which Chinese-made airliners were taking passengers and potentates all around the world. They reminded me powerfully of the videos I had seen the previous year at the Shanghai World Expo, or that Americans who attended the New York World's Fair of 1964 would have seen there. By the comparison I mean not that the Chinese presentations were out of date but that they were optimistic. The theme of their "let's imagine!" videos was how much brighter, cleaner, and in all ways better a futuristic existence will be. I hope that someday the video that GM China produced for its Shanghai Expo pavilion will be taken on a world tour. It conveyed the same sense of futuristic marvel that I recall from visiting Disney's Tomorrowland as a schoolchild in the early 1960s. A similar spirit guides the future-of-Chinese-aviation videos, with their depictions of suave Chinese businesspeople and happy Chinese families relaxing, enjoying the flight, and looking confidently toward what awaits them at their destination.

That's the goal—with airplanes, and with so many other aspects of life in China now. It is hard for rich-country residents—Europeans, North Americans, Japanese, Australians, New Zealanders, and others—to contemplate such simple joy in material progress without a slight mocking smile. For them, prosperity, in an overall sense, has been thoroughly taken for granted, for a long time, and the uneven and imperfect blessings of progress are well understood. But at least for people over the age of thirty in China, the excitement about modernization is still (largely) genuine and sincere.

Elements of the plan

China's progress from the earliest days of aviation to its current aspirations to create the next Boeing resemble patterns in other areas where it has rushed to modernize. The main themes of that progress are:

- The growth of this industry has been both guided and uncontrolled, at times chaotic and even outside the law.
- It has depended upon efforts by both the country's military and its civilian organizations, both government and business, both enormous state-owned entities and tiny private firms, both central-government guidance and entrepreneurial efforts from provinces and towns.
- It has relied on and been shaped by foreigners, especially Americans, to a degree that few people inside or outside China recognize. Indeed, the transformation of China's airline systems from one of the most dangerous in the world to one of the safest is largely a testament to underpublicized but

highly important efforts by Chinese and American companies and governments.

- Its successes and its impending limitations reflect the same schisms within China's political leadership and tensions between central guidance and regional guidance that appear in many other areas.
- Its efforts to build a modern air-travel system, in parallel with the road-building and track-laying whose effects are so obvious across China, reflect the central government's sharp awareness of a challenge very similar to the one that propelled American development through the United States's first century or so as a nation: the need to create physical connections across a continental nation of great geographic, cultural, and economic extremes.[2]

Here is how they started and how they plan to bring it about.

The Chinese pioneers

In the headquarters of Boeing China's offices, in the Pacific Plaza complex off the Third Ring Road on the east side of Beijing, there is a special small shrine to a Chinese technologist named Wong Tsu. Wong was born in Beijing in 1893. He was ten years old when the Wright brothers made their first flight at Kitty Hawk, and not yet twenty when the Qing Dynasty, which had ruled China since the 1640s, collapsed under its last sovereign, the "boy emperor" Puyi. When Wong Tsu was sixteen, during the turbulent final stages of the Qing decline, he was sent as a naval cadet to England for training—and then, as the regime fully collapsed, he went on to MIT, where he became a student in the very first aeronautical engineering program in the United States.[3]

In 1916, as the Great War raged in Europe and as the forces of Sun Yat-sen were taking over China, Wong received his degree from MIT and also learned to fly, in a seaplane school in Buffalo. In that same year, Bill Boeing, a thirty-five-year-old Yale man who had worked in the timber industry, started an airplane company in Seattle. Wong moved out to Seattle and joined him as the new Boeing company's first chief engineer.

In the shrine at the Beijing office, along with portraits of Wong and testimonials about his work, there is a dramatic black-and-white photo taken in 1919 of Bill Boeing and Eddie Hubbard, one of the company's first pilots. They are wearing the jackets and leather flying helmets we associate with photos of Lindbergh or Earhart; they are standing on a Puget Sound dock, with water lapping up just behind them. In one hand, Boeing is holding a canvas sack of mail. This was, in fact, the first international airmail shipment ever carried to the United States, which Boeing and Hubbard had brought from Vancouver, British Columbia, to Seattle. Behind them in the picture, on pontoons, is Boeing's hugely important Model C seaplane, which was designed by Wong Tsu.

For Beijing, the Model C was a commercial breakthrough. It was the first plane that Boeing had sold to the U.S. military, and also the first to be used in America for postal delivery.

Military purchases and airmail contracts were how early airlines—and aircraft companies—paid for their development. From Bill Boeing onward, the company's chief executives through the decades were careful to note that without Wong Tsu's efforts, especially with the Model C, the company might not have survived the early years to become the dominant world aircraft manufacturer.[4]

In 1918, Wong Tsu returned to China, and over the next two decades he started to build an aviation industry there, in close cooperation with his former colleagues in England and the United States. As World War I was nearing its end, he founded the Mah-Wei aircraft company in southern coastal China, not far from the site where the computer-maker Dell now has its Chinese manufacturing center. There he oversaw production of the first genuinely Chinese airplane, the Sea Eagle, soon followed by the River Bird.

In the late 1920s, Wong worked with a former partner from Boeing to found the Chinese National Aviation Corporation, in Shanghai. He became a colonel in the Chinese Army; he oversaw the construction of China's first military-aircraft fleet. When the Japanese invaded, he went inland, first to Wuhan, along the Yangtze, and then to Kunming, in far southwestern Yunnan province, bordering Burma. During World War II, when Chinese factories were essentially cut off from international supplies, he designed all-bamboo gliders for carrying troops.

But as civil war spread across the country after Japan's surrender, Wong Tsu fled to Taiwan rather than to stay for life under Mao and the communists. He spent the next twenty years, until his death in 1965, teaching aeronautical engineering at a Taiwanese university rather than building airplanes.

Overall he fared much better than the other most famous father of Chinese aviation. This was Feng Ru,[5] an immigrant from Guangzhou in southern China who was known as Joe Fung, or Joe Fong in the Chinatowns of Oakland and San Francisco at the beginning of the twentieth century.

On arrival in the United States, Feng had been dazzled by its technological modernity. He traveled around the country, working in machine shops and shipyards to learn skills he could eventually take back to China.[6] As an article in *Air & Space* magazine put it, "Feng became well known for developing alternate versions of the water pump, the generator, the telephone, and the wireless telegraph, some of which were used by San Francisco's Chinese businessmen." After the Wright brothers' flight, as part of the general romance of flight that swept the world, Feng Ru became obsessed with aviation, produced Chinese translations of reports on the Wright brothers and their competitors, and decided to create an airplane of his own.

He worked in secret, in a tiny room that he grandly called the Guangdong Aircraft Factory; he ordered parts from a variety of manufacturers so that no one supplier would be wise to his plans. By 1909, he had designed and built a biplane that, on September 21, he successfully kept aloft for more than twenty minutes in the hills outside Oakland. For a while his work caused an international sensation, which included coverage in *The New York Times* and a congratulatory message from Sun Yat-sen. He returned to China but was killed, at age twenty-nine, in a crash in 1912 while performing before a crowd of a thousand in Guangzhou. Sun Yat-sen decreed that Feng's grave should carry the words "Chinese Aviation Pioneer."

During the "anti-Japanese war," which is the way Chinese histories refer to the entire period from 1937 to 1945, Chinese forces had essentially no air power of their own. Japanese bombers struck Chinese cities at will during a series of invasions into Manchuria in the north and then Shanghai and eventually Hong Kong in the south. Once the United States entered the war, its main aerial involvement within China was via convoys that went over the hump of the Himalayas, from India and Burma, to deliver armaments and supplies to Chinese forces in Kunming and Chongqing (then referred to as Chungking) and to fight Japanese forces there. More than sixty years after the war's end, in the far southern reaches of Yunnan province that border Burma and India, my wife and I saw the remnants of the radio stations that had guided U.S. aviators over the Hump. This was in a small town near Dali named Xizhou, which happened also to be where the teachers of Yale's China program had fled when Japanese troops overran Chongqing.

Mao's China takes to the skies, barely

When the civil war was over and the communists were in charge, China had only the most rudimentary aviation industry or establishment. Some two hundred airplanes total were left after more than a decade of war—fewer than one day's production for the United States during its World War II peak. This fleet was replenished briefly, with Soviet help, to challenge the American forces during the Korean War. But the industry that emerged from the era of Soviet cooperation, through the 1950s until the split between Mao and Khrushchev in the early 1960s, was autarkic and out of date.

For the country as a whole, the most destructive phase of Mao's economic mismanagement was of course the Great Leap Forward of the mid- and late 1950s. Tens of millions of people starved to death in the countryside—more than the number of Soviet soldiers and civilians who perished during the Great Patriotic War against the Nazis, more than the number of European Jews slaughtered during the Holocaust—as mass levees of manpower took workers from tending the farms to working in fanciful village-level steel mills. When it came to genuine factories, those still producing the nation's trucks and tractors and locomotives and few airplanes, Mao developed a strategy known as *sanxian* (三线), or "third line," as in "third line of defense." Factories were moved away from the coastline and distributed through interior provinces, often nestled into remote valleys in the middle of mountain ranges. Thus an attacking enemy—presumably the United States, but after the Sino-Soviet breakup the Soviet Union became another perceived threat—would face the daunting prospect of fighting a land war through the center of China if it contemplated destroying these facilities. Even if attacking by air, it would have to send its bombers on long, difficult missions to reach the factories, rather than attacking them where they had been, in obvious concentrations near the coast at Guangzhou in the south, Tianjin in the north, or Shanghai in between. One of the predictable surprises of traveling though today's Chinese countryside is coming across steel mills, engine works, and other derelict-looking heavy industrial sites far from major cities—not that the major cities are short on them. The nationwide dispersal of industries, while intended as a national security measure and as a way of bringing opportunity to the hinterland, also meant that areas of rural China you might expect to be "pristine" now can have as heavy a pall of industrial smoke as the biggest cities do.

As applied to aviation, the dispersal plan led to small factories all over the country, plus a major concentration of airplane factories and related plants outside the famous central city of Xi'an. In Chinese history, the city was known as Chang'an—长安, "long peace"—and was a capital through ten dynasties in Chinese antiquity. Its modern name, Xi'an, or 西安, means "western peace." In modern history, Xi'an is known for the thousands of terra-cotta warriors on its outskirts. But among its distinctions, from the *sanxian* perspective, is that among China's major cities it was the one farthest from any land border, the counterpart to a site in Kansas or Nebraska in the United States, and thus theoretically safest from aerial attack. (And of course during the Cold War the United States based much of its nuclear missile and bomber fleets in the Great Plains, for similar reasons.) Today, some quarter million people, more than the total worldwide payroll of Boeing and Airbus combined, work in Xi'an's aviation industries, supervised by a Chinese engineer in his fifties who has a bust of George Washington in his office.

The Chinese industrial sector as a whole was inefficient and poorly designed, by world standards, during the Mao era, and the same was true of its aerospace factories. "A major structural weakness and a legacy of the Maoist past is the widespread duplication and balkanization of industrial and research facilities," Tai Ming Cheung, of the University of California, San Diego, said at a U.S. government hearing on "China's Emergent Military Aerospace and Commercial Aviation Capabilities" in 2010.[7] He pointed out that technically backward, underfunded Mao-era China had well over a hundred separate airplane-related factories or research centers all across the country. Far from pooling their limited resources or coordinating their efforts, they were active rivals for funding and prominence, meaning that together they made even less progress than they might otherwise have done.

Until the late 1970s, the operations of China's domestic airlines were similarly state-controlled and sheltered from market forces. The few airlines in existence sent the few airplanes they had to a few cities along a limited number of state-mandated routes. The few passengers were not allowed to buy tickets unless they had authorization from their *danwei,* the Party-led business or work unit that controlled most aspects of their lives. During the most totalitarian periods under Mao, authorization from the *danwei* was needed before members could marry, have children, consider different jobs, or travel inside or (rarely) outside the country. The whole air-travel network operated more or less the way military air travel does in the United States, without the efficiency or the scale. Thus its transformation into a system that had to compete with, or at least coexist alongside, established international carriers, while expanding domestically on pace with the new era's growth, was as difficult as for any other Chinese industry—if not more so.

How other countries did it

Economists use the term "path dependence" to convey the simple idea that choices you made yesterday affect the choices available to you today. It is easier for the Seattle area to maintain an aerospace industry, since one has grown there over the past century, than it would be for New Orleans to start one from scratch. The same applies to New York with finance, greater Boston with higher education and medicine, Houston with the energy business, and so on. Nations, regions, cities, and companies can of course change from one path to another—that's why we speak of historic rises and declines. China's development strategy over the past thirty years can be seen as one mammoth attempt to will itself onto the path of modern industrial development.

Through the half century after the Wright brothers' first flight, aerospace developments in most of the world followed a path that was more or less similar from one country to another, but quite different from what China is attempting now. We naturally think of aviation as being a huge, concentrated enterprise that only a few global megafirms can afford to compete in. But in its early days, airplane inventors, designers, and entrepreneurs were at work on almost every continent, including those who started their own small companies before Bill Boeing did.

Many countries had nascent aerospace tech-business centers. Apart from the United States, they included Australia, Brazil,

Canada, Czechoslovakia, England, France, Germany, Italy, Japan, Poland, Russia, Sweden, and more. In most of them the sequence that eventually led to an aircraft industry was more or less the same. First there was the rapid spread of a hobbyist approach to aviation, typified by the barnstorming culture of daredevil pilots and air shows. Everything about flying in those days was hazardous. Orville Wright himself was nearly killed in a crash at Fort Myer, just outside Washington, D.C., in 1908, when the Wrights were demonstrating their airplane to the U.S. Army in order to qualify for military contracts. His passenger, the young army lieutenant Thomas Selfridge, who died in the crash and was later buried in Arlington Cemetery, is generally considered to be the first person ever killed in an airplane accident.

But even as the barnstorming era sustained public excitement about aviation, three longer-term "real" markets for airplanes and air services began to emerge: the military; airmail transport; and the bare beginnings of a passenger-airline business. The sagas of those early decades are very much like recent accounts of the evolution of computer and Internet start-ups: Entrepreneurs across the United States, Europe, South America, and elsewhere founded their small aircraft companies in a warehouse or a barn. Most failed in the short run—or, if they survived, were taken over by competitors. Even so, to a large extent these companies, reflecting their founders' energies and ambitions, managed to push the technological or commercial frontiers of aerospace at least slightly forward while they were around. Although Bill Boeing's name is now the best known of those early innovators, through aviation's early decades he was a small player in a field that attracted people already well known for other successes. Henry Ford branched out from cars to make the popular Ford Tri-Motor, which was a refinement of a Fokker design from the Netherlands. During World War II, Ford's Willow Run assembly plant became the world's largest aircraft-production facility. Howard Hughes, of course, built his *Spruce Goose*. Geoffrey De Havilland founded and led what became Britain's most important aircraft company. Ryan, Northrop, Grumman, Sikorsky, McDonnell, Douglas, Fairchild, Vought, Curtiss, and many others had names that for a while were synonymous with aircraft—as did the Loughead brothers of California, with their Lockheed company.[8] They had their counterparts across Europe. In the Soviet Union, where the state made all the airplanes, the famous names were of the designers: Antonov, Ilyushin, Tupolev.

Aircraft made their combat debut during World War I. Despite the celebrated exploits of aces like Germany's Manfred von Richthofen, known as the Red Baron, and America's Eddie Rickenbacker, air power was not a decisive factor for either side. Yet even by that stage military contracts had become crucial to keeping the Wrights and their emulators in business. The Navy ordered fifty of Boeing's Model-C planes, the ones designed by Wong Tsu, which represented the new Boeing company's most important early sale. In the 1930s, the first instrument navigation systems were developed in the United States and England. These allowed pilots to keep airplanes under control and on course even when flying through clouds or at night, rather than crashing as they frequently did if trying to "fly blind"—without instrument guidance. In the last two years of World War II, the first practical jet engines were developed, by German engineers who produced the Messerschmitt 262. The combination of instrument guidance and jet propulsion gave aircraft lasting military and economic importance. Part of America's "arsenal of democracy"—a surge in the building of military matériel that wore down the Axis powers—was its increase from producing four thousand airplanes in 1940 to a hundred thousand in 1944.

A nationwide airmail network was in place across the United States by the mid-1920s,[9] with mail sacks and small parcels carried on airplanes that the U.S. Post Office owned and operated. In 1925, the right to carry mail was transferred to commercial carriers, where it formed a significant stream of dependable income as these carriers began building passenger-travel networks. Two years later, Charles Lindbergh's flight across the Atlantic increased international excitement about aviation so much that, within the two years after that, worldwide investment in airplane and airline companies tripled. Even through the Depression of the 1930s, the improvements in speed, safety, and comfort of passenger planes made the airlines one of the few growing industries in the United States. It was during the 1930s that coast-to-coast travel first became faster by air than by rail. After this came the airpower-heavy combat of World War II; the commercialization of jet travel in the late 1950s; and the subsequent revolution in business, leisure, and family patterns around the world made possible by ever-safer and, for a while, ever-cheaper airline travel.

While so much was happening in so many parts of the world in the decades after the Wright brothers' flight, almost nothing of the sort was happening in China. China had warfare, revolution, and turmoil through nearly the first eighty years of the twentieth century. It was cut off, by design and by circumstances, from the mainstreams of technical competition and innovation everywhere else.[10] Despite the efforts of people like Wong Tsu and Feng Ru, it fell steadily further behind.

The first airplane flew in China in 1909, only six years after the Wright brothers' first flight at Kitty Hawk, but the gap between China's standards and the world's widened from that point on. The war, revolution, and tumult of the first half of the twentieth century made it hard for Chinese authorities to maintain roads and railroads, let alone invest in a new air-travel infrastructure. In principle, for an underdeveloped country with difficult geography, creating a network of airports can be a more economical and attractive way to link far-flung regions than trying to build railroads. To get supplies or travelers to Tibet or Qinghai, you need only pave a few square miles for airports and their support structures, not lay thousands of miles of track.

But building even those few airports was hard, given the chaos and poverty of the country at that state of development. As the main academic historian of Chinese aviation during this period has pointed out, aircraft need their own sort of land support, "a system of terrestrial navigation and communication facilities spread out along the route to provide navigation assistance and weather reports."[11] No one had the time, patience, money, or security to produce these systems in China. By the time of the Japanese invasion in the 1930s and China's subsequent engulfment in revolution and war, there were only a handful of passenger flights operating in the country, and most were run by foreign companies like Pan Am.

Why China did it differently

By the time Mao's government turned its attention to aviation, in the late 1950s, the path dependence of China's transportation system made its choices different from those available in most other countries.

In Europe as in the United States, private flying, by hobby-ists, tinkerers, and adventurers, came first. By the time of World War I the military was emerging as an important source of funding; and through the 1920s there was a diverse and quickly changing ecology of people who one way or another made a liv-ing through aviation: amateur flyers, crop dusters and air-show performers, military flyers, government airmail systems, and the early private airlines (an important one of which, United Air Lines, was spun off from Boeing in the 1930s).

The regulatory system in North America and Europe was also diverse, and reflected a belief in a checks-and-balances system with divided responsibilities and powers. In the United States, a Civil Aeronautics Board was established to oversee—and promote—the business of air travel and to regulate routes and fares; the Federal Aviation Administration (FAA) worked on improving safety and procedures, while also working on naviga-tion systems and weather forecasting; what was eventually the National Transportation Safety Board had an independent role in investigating crashes; and NASA, the military, and other groups played significant parts as sponsors. As the country with the largest and fastest-growing aerospace business, the United States also set an international lead in how regulatory systems should be designed.

Even the training of pilots was diversified. In Europe and North America, the military directly trained a number of pilots (many of whom eventually left to join the civilian airline fleets), and specialized "aeronautical universities"[12] were created to train others, along with mechanics and air-traffic controllers. By the 1950s, the United States had built more than four thou-sand airfields, large and small, across the country. Some were military bases, some big commercial airports, some rural or pri-vate landing strips; some were civic booster projects to attract businesses to remote communities or make it easier for residents to reach big-city services. There were a lot of them, and the great majority offered small flying schools or repair shops too. Only a handful have been built since then, the most notable being Washington Dulles in the 1960s, Dallas–Fort Worth in the 1970s, and Denver International in the 1990s. Meanwhile hundreds of smaller airports have been closed.

Thus, in most of the flying world, the military propelled a business that civilians had started and still dominated. China's reentry into aviation in the communist era was under military control from the start. There was practically no tradition of civil aviation in China. At the dawn of World War II and again for the Korean War and Vietnam, the United States could call on hundreds of thousands of young men and women who had been exposed to airplanes or air shows in some way. They had no counterpart in China, and don't even now. If you look at airspace maps of Europe or North America, the portions that are still controlled by the military are relatively small (except over the desert areas of Nevada, Utah, and Southern California, where they are very large). All the rest is for business, recreational, or commercial-airline use. If you look at an airspace map of China—well, that is an achievement in itself, since generally they have been controlled by the military and are viewed as too sensitive for foreigners to see. But if you could look, you'd see at once that the areas *not* controlled by the military are relatively thin, crabbed corridors connecting the biggest cities. All the rest has been off limits to everyone except the People's Liberation Army (PLA).

There was another important structural difference in China's approach: the centralized power of the Civil Aviation Administration of China, or CAAC, which played nearly all of the varied and sometimes conflicting roles that Western countries kept carefully divided among different official and agencies. In China, the reins were in one set of hands.

The CAAC decided—with the military—what kind of airplanes could and should be built. (In the United States, this "certificating" role lies with the FAA, and the aircraft companies work with their customers, the airlines, to decide what kinds of planes to build.) CAAC and military engineers and designers planned the planes. CAAC inspectors certified the designs as being "airworthy." Its factories built the planes and set the internal "transfer prices" at which they would be sold—to the flight-operations divisions of the CAAC.

The CAAC's flight schools trained the pilots. Its airline division set the routes, sold the tickets, and trained the flight attendants for the trips. Its maintenance people took care of the planes between flights. Its airport operators built and ran the airports. Its fuel division kept the supply tanks full. When there was a crash, as happened very often, its safety division would try to find out what had happened. It ran the airports, it ran the airlines, it ran the regulatory functions. It was like one huge military operation, with the inefficiencies that arise in such a structure.

Through the beginning of the reform era, the Chinese system had airplanes that were mainly built and designed by the military as knockoffs of Soviet and occasionally Western models; it had a rudimentary system of internal routes; its planes did not undertake long overseas routes, because as the Australian analyst Mark Dougan pointed out[13] in his history of Chinese aviation, the planes couldn't make overseas trips without refueling, and the very act of stopping at refueling sites would have constituted a humiliating display of how poor the equipment

was. The heavy industrial base that would be involved in aviation was in the protected hinterland, rather than on the coast,
where the big market reforms would start; the whole operation
was run by a central ministry, which itself was answerable to
the military; and this was part of China's presentation of itself
to the world.

And the airplanes . . .

3 ★ The Men from Boeing

I first saw airplanes from China's old fleet in 1986, when my wife and our then young children traveled by CAAC planes from Beijing to Shanghai and Guangdong. We went by CAAC because there was no alternative; foreign carriers didn't service domestic routes in China, and private Chinese airlines had not been allowed to emerge. What my wife swears she remembers— that we could *see* parts of the ground through holes in the airplane's fuselage—probably can't be true, since it would have kept the plane from being pressurized. And yet in those days the airlines might have stayed at low enough altitudes to make a plane with holes technically flyable.

Tickets were written out by hand, as throngs of passengers crowded around the few airline clerks. Seats were assigned as if you were loading up a packing crate—first every seat in the very last row was filled, then the row in front of that, and then the next one, working forward, so that on any given flight every seat in the last twenty rows in a cabin could be jammed, and the first ten entirely empty.

The planes were mainly old Soviet junkers, just beginning to be replaced by the first Boeings that the opening to the United States had made available. Through the 1970s, not long after delivery of the Boeing 707s whose sale was agreed during Richard Nixon's visit to China, the Shanghai Aircraft Research Institute developed the Y-10. This was a four-engine jetliner that closely resembled the 707 and was powered by Pratt & Whitney engines that China had bought as part of the 707 deal. The plane's first flight, in 1980, was a point of national pride, but it proved to be inefficient and the project was scrapped after only three aircraft were built. In the mid-1980s, by the time of our visit, the CAAC fleet also included a few Tridents from Hawker Siddley in Britain, but we only ever flew in the old Ilyushin and Tupolev models from the Soviet days. The seats lacked seat belts—or, if the belts had once been there, they had long since disappeared from the planes we took, on internal flights from Beijing to Shanghai, and later Shanghai to Guangzhou. As we walked past the First Class section on one of the flights to our seats in the very back, we saw that the luxury seats were the squat, thickly cushioned armchairs familiar from any formal Chinese meeting room, seemingly just hauled into the airplane and bolted onto the floor. Passengers moved around at all stages of flight, from takeoff to landing, as if they were on a bus or a train. Flight attendants passed sugar-wafer cookies to the passengers during the flight. The safety record in those years was terrible, as we would have guessed from looking at the equipment. But news of crashes was hushed up, so we didn't know enough to worry.

However challenging air travelers of the mid-1980s, like us, found the Chinese aviation system, it was nothing compared with what the first international representatives of modern aerospace had found only a few years earlier. The best known of them is E. E. Bauer, who came to Beijing in 1980 as Boeing's first official representative in China. "We had expected cold weather in Beijing, but were unprepared for the sub-freezing temperature inside the terminal," he wrote in his memoir, *China Takes Off*.[1] I often had the book with me when traveling in China and would thumb through it as a token of how much the circumstances truly had changed. And also as a reminder of how often China's technological growth and success have confounded those who assumed that practical and cultural obstacles were too great to overcome. Even Bauer felt this way early in his stay, when he contemplated the way air travel operated in the CAAC era: "As I sat in the barnlike room facing a long counter with small, teller-windowed openings in the solid plywood wall that extended to the ceiling, one for each city destination, watching the customers massed in tight groups, jockeying for positions in front of the windows, everyone shouting and gesticulating, I feared with certainty that the Chinese would never break out of the cocoon that has inexorably bound them for so many centuries."[2]

I emphasize Bauer not just for his observations but because of the central and, relative to its reality, underpublicized role that Boeing has played as a third party to interactions between the U.S. and Chinese governments. E. E. Bauer exemplified an early part of that interaction; his successors illustrate it now.

E. E. Bauer and the early days

Bauer was a veteran Boeing engineer and manager with little experience outside the United States. He got to Beijing soon after Deng Xiaoping's 1979 state visit to Jimmy Carter at the White House had cemented China's new opening to the West. At the time, six different U.S. airlines had, each on its own, a fleet larger than the entire Chinese inventory of passenger airliners. The CAAC was about to receive its first three Boeing 747s. This purchase—like all major airline sales in the modern age—was as much a diplomatic gesture as a commercial transaction, constituting a big and noticeable U.S. export to China. After Richard Nixon's visit to China, Zhou Enlai had approved the purchase of ten Boeing 707s as a goodwill gesture in U.S.-Chinese relations, and with little regard to what markets they would serve or how they might pay their way.[3]

On his arrival in Beijing, E. E. Bauer found that every safeguard that made for reliability in an air-transport system was at odds with the Chinese model of the time.

For instance: By Boeing procedures, certain materials or pieces of equipment had the equivalent of an operational "use by" date. Once they had been in service for a given period of time or a stated number of "flight cycles" (takeoffs and landings), they had to be replaced—whether or not they were actually used up or worn out. Fixed replacement schedules for parts and supplies were an important protection against planes taking off with defective equipment.

After their years of privation, making-do, and duct-taping their way around shortages, the Chinese maintenance staff found the concept of scheduled obsolescence to be wasteful and offensive. They wanted to recycle tires that still had tread on them, reuse engine oil if it still looked clean, put washers back on if they looked okay. "The all-saving society, where even scraps of newspapers were culled out of garbage for reclamation"—a process anyone who has walked through Chinese cities can witness even today—"did not accept the idea of discarding anything remotely reusable," Bauer wrote.[4] Mechanics liked to rinse out the filters in the airplanes' hydraulic systems, rather than replacing them at the set service-life intervals. After the filters were washed, they looked perfectly clean! The problem, as Bauer pointed out,[5] was that invisibly small metal fragments were still embedded in the filters—and after the filters had gone through enough cycles of being subject to three thousand pounds per square inch of pressure, the metal particles would begin seeping out the other end, into the engine works, and promptly destroy a multimillion-dollar engine.

He also warred constantly against the overhang of the state and of military style rather than market-minded thinking and planning. One morning in April 1982, as the 747s were being integrated into the fleet of 707s and Soviet legacy planes, Bauer steamed in frustration watching a lineup on the taxiway at Beijing's airport. Two months earlier, the airport had opened a second runway, capable of handling the biggest and most modern aircraft in the world. But some days the central authorities forgot about the new runway or neglected to approve its use. "No on-the-scene initiative could be undertaken by the controllers" who were actually at the airport, Bauer wrote. "They had their orders."

Bauer watched ruefully as six full-sized airliners—two Ilyushins, two Tridents, a 707, and a 747—waited with engines running on a taxiway, while another airplane used the same runway for the routine landing practice known as touch-and-goes. "The 747, with its four 50,000-pound thrust engines gobbling fuel, was still waiting in line, followed by the four-jet IL-62" and the other airplanes, Bauer wrote. "All this in a society which prided itself on saving scarce resources, particularly energy. . . ."[6]

Remnants of the same mentality can still be found all across China, and other poor countries; but the world Bauer operated in has been transformed. Part of the responsibility lay with his successors, like "Joe T."

Joe T becomes "half Chinese"

Joe T's full name is Joseph Tymczyszyn, pronounced *tim-chih-zin*. His father's family was from Poland. His name is a mouthful even for Americans, and in China no one tries. There he is known to Chinese-speaking friends as Ding Zhou—a major decision for a foreigner is the choice of the right Chinese name—and often to non-Chinese as Joe T, which is also the name printed on his business card.

Early in his career Joe T had done regulatory and engineering work at the FAA and had worked briefly in politics, as a staff assistant to Representative Barry Goldwater in Washington. In the early 1980s, he joined Boeing in Seattle. He spoke good French, and much of his work involved regulatory coordination with airlines and agencies in Europe. Then a supervisor told him that his next project would be in China.

"At first I was upset," he told me, when I first met him in Beijing in 2008. "I was grumbling until I looked at the sales forecasts, which changed my mind. In Boeing you are always looking at layoffs, and China was going to be Boeing's number one international customer." He knew that the people who survived layoffs through the ups and downs of Boeing's employment cycles were those who, as he put it, were "the very top guys in an area where they're not going to eliminate the whole group." He threw himself and his family into learning spoken Mandarin, starting the same way my family had when we were first learning Japanese a few years before: He bought a *Chinese in Ten Minutes a Day* book, which like ours for Japanese included little stickers to put on the refrigerator, the front door, the TV and radio, and the bookcase with reminders of the names for those objects in the new language.

He was assigned to Chinese projects in 1992; he made his first trip to China in 1993; and he commuted there regularly over the next ten years. In 2002, he retired from Boeing and moved to Beijing, where he has lived ever since. He initially worked again for the FAA as their representative at the U.S. embassy in Beijing. He has since held other jobs, all involving U.S.-China aviation projects. Some days he works at a Chinese aviation university, where he speaks Mandarin with his coworkers. He jokes that they tell him he has become "half Chinese." His two sons, now in their early thirties, studied Mandarin at the Beijing Language and Culture University; his wife has learned the language too. "Not all Americans will have the opportunities my sons did," he told me recently. "But I feel that young people today really need to know China in order to have the tools needed to succeed in what will be a tougher environment for Americans."

As E. E. Bauer was part of Boeing's effort to introduce China to the modern aviation age, Joe T has witnessed the rapid next steps forward. In the early 1990s, a major challenge for Chinese aviation, and also for Boeing in its hopes to sell large numbers of airplanes, was the unsafe nature of flying there.

Boeing officials knew that their success in the China market depended on several factors beyond their control, and several others they could hope to influence. Boeing could not affect the plans of economic development inside China, nor the pace of its opening to the outside world. But it could play some role in the overall climate of relations between the countries, which, given the political symbolism of aircraft sales, could make a difference in how many Boeings the Chinese decided to buy. When Hu Jintao came to the United States in 2006, his first stop was not Washington, D.C., or anyplace in the vicinity (unlike the 2011 trip, when he flew straight to Andrews Air Force Base). President George W. Bush had offered him only a business lunch at the White House, not a formal state dinner, so on his first visit to America as China's President, Hu touched down at Paine Field, north of Seattle in Everett, Washington, which adjoins Boeing's 747-assembly plant. There he toured the factory and saw some aircraft destined for service in China being completed, before attending a dinner that evening at the home of Bill Gates. "Boeing is a household name in my country," Hu told five thousand Boeing workers at the factory, plus an assortment of Chinese-Americans from the area.[7] "When Chinese people fly, it is mostly in a Boeing plane. I am happy to tell you that I came to the United States on a Boeing plane."[8] In 1993, then-President Jiang Zemin had also begun his trip to the United States with a stop at Boeing.

In addition to these indirect efforts to foster good feelings with an important customer country, Boeing had a direct stake in improving the safety record of Chinese airlines, and felt it had a responsibility to do what it could. If commercial airliners kept crashing—as five of them did within a four-month span in 1992, including an accident in southern China in which more than 140 people aboard a Boeing 737 died—neither Chinese nor foreigner passengers would ride on them, and Boeing's prospects would be limited. Thus, making Chinese airlines safer became Boeing's job, which meant that it was the job of all members of its China team.

Rule of man and rule of law

As with air travel in most other parts of the world, the majority of crashes in China occurred either on takeoff or on landing. This makes sense as soon as you think about it: That's when the aircraft is in the most vulnerable position, since it is closest to the ground. But other aspects of Chinese procedure were out of sync with standards anywhere else.

Many of the problems stemmed from the centralized, Soviet-style model of China's aerospace organization, in which the all-powerful CAAC controlled everything from ticket prices to safety standards. Moreover, inspections procedures and other steps toward safer operations reflected the spirit so prevalent in China then and even now—"the rule of man"—versus "the rule of law." This mattered more in aviation than in some other fields because standardized procedures—checklists, inspections, mandatory minimums for training and operations—have been the foundations of safe operations elsewhere.

On an early visit to the control tower at Beijing's main airport, one foreign adviser was taken aback by problems he had barely envisioned. Controllers in the tower could not even see the airplanes they were supposed to be directing. The glass was dirty; shades were pulled down; controllers might be shuffling papers at their desks even when they were telling airplanes where to move along the taxiways. Moreover, the obsessive adherence to rules and procedures that had made civil aviation so safe in the outside world was still unfamiliar in Chinese organizational life, despite the changes since E. E. Bauer's time.

One example was the Minimum Equipment List (MEL). Before a pilot can operate a certified airplane of any sort, especially one certified for commercial flight, he or she must be familiar with the MEL. This is the list of parts that must be present and properly functioning before a plane is allowed to take off. Pilots take quizzes for each type of plane. If the red and green navigation lights on the wings don't work, are you allowed to make a flight? What about if it's clear weather? Do you need to carry extra fuses to fly that plane? Are the standards different for daytime and at night? The idea is that there is a list, and the list is law. If the MEL says that a plane can fly without its red and green lights—but only during the day—then you can take off, assuming that your planned route will let you land before dark. Otherwise, you can't. In private-plane flight or charter operations, pilots are responsible for observing the MELs and similar regulations. For the airlines, there are multiple redundant checks: flight crew, airline dispatches, mechanics, along with regulators all have to agree that every requirement has been met before a flight can take off. The most junior inspector, armed with a rule book, can overrule a senior airline official and say it is not safe to fly.

Under the Soviet-style Chinese system, the MEL existed but—like other standardized procedures—was applied in a subjective way. If a gauge was broken or a part missing, an airline executive could say, Looks all right to me. Let's fly! Strict inspection schedules could also be made more lenient. In the world of international aviation, airplanes were inspected according to rigid schedules. After a certain number of days, or flight hours, or takeoffs, an aircraft could not legally make another trip until it had had crucial parts checked. This scrutiny pays off—think how often buses, cars, trains, and subways fail, and how rarely commercial airliners do. But as of the early 1990s China's inspection schedule was still slapdash and largely subject to "the rule of man."

Perhaps the most important safety-related problem, as the efforts began, was the "check airman" system. In the United States and elsewhere, airlines have evolved the "check airman" system of continuing competency exams for which it is hard to imagine a full counterpart in medicine, the law, academics, or publishing. No matter how experienced and veteran the captain, he must periodically satisfy a specially trained pilot known as the check airman that he is still proficient. And the check airman, in his or her turn, must prove his continued competence through the check airmen's records, as examiners are also subject to scrutiny by the FAA, to see how the percentage of passes and failures they are awarding compares with national norms.

Much as with MELs and scheduled inspections, the need for

check airmen and check rides was observed more in form than in reality in China. (For airliners the check rides are conducted in simulators rather than real airplanes, in order to present pilots with a wider range of emergencies and stressful situations than would be practical or safe to undergo in real airplanes.) Check rides are meaningful only if pilots are held to consistent, objective standards—and, in practice, if some of them fail. But in China the standards varied widely, and often all pilots passed. In 1997, a Chinese airliner plane crashed in Shenzhen, just north of Hong Kong, killing thirty-five people and injuring dozens more.[9] The crash investigation indicated basic errors by both the pilots aboard, who made two landing attempts in the middle of a thunderstorm rather than diverting to a safer landing site. Things like this happen elsewhere—for example, the Colgan Air crash in Buffalo, in 2009, led to a reevaluation of how regional airlines trained and supervised their pilots. But within the Chinese system it highlighted existing concerns that the system was not doing enough to ensure that planes—or pilots—were safe to fly.

"The check airman system was a problem," Joe T told me, not long after the Colgan incident. "The check airmen lived with all the other pilots, their wives were friends, their kids went to the same schools, they had the same housing." If a check airman judged one of his neighbors on a test flight, and failed him, he knew that the unfortunate pilot would lose face, would be subject to remedial training, and might possibly lose his job— all very disruptive consequences within a tight-knit community.

Through the late 1990s, the shared imperative of reducing crashes created an improbable alliance of Chinese, American, and international businesses and organizations. In 1997, two Chinese airlines—Air China and China Eastern—had already been approved for prestigious and strategically important routes to the United States. China Southern had applied for approval to be the third, and had taken delivery of new Boeing 777s in anticipation of launching service from Guangzhou to Los Angeles. Because Guangzhou was a center of the outsourcing business, direct service there was expected to be attractive to business travelers and be lucrative for the airline.

But routes to the United States required approval from the U.S. Department of Transportation, parent body of the FAA. At the urging of the FAA, the department decided to use the application as leverage to force—or encourage—a broader improvement in Chinese safety standards. The FAA had no direct regulatory power over China Southern or any other foreign airline. But it could ask for confirmation that China's regulatory standards, as applied by the CAAC, conformed to the worldwide guidelines laid out by international agreements. The message came back from the U.S. government to China: Before any more airlines get routes to the United States, we'd like to know more about how Chinese regulators do their business.

The Chinese airlines were naturally flummoxed. Boeing, an American company, had sold them the planes in expectation that they would be used on flights to the United States. Why would the American government get in the way of this transaction? Was this some kind of double-cross? The Chinese government would not interfere with commerce in this way! China Southern had more planes on order from Boeing, but its officials were in no mood to receive—or pay for—those planes unless this mess with the regulators got straightened out.

Boeing was not the cause of the safety problems with Chinese airlines, but Boeing decided that resolving them was partly its responsibility. In collaboration with the FAA, it began preparing a series of seminars, tours, training sessions, and briefings to

connect Chinese regulators and inspectors with their counterparts in the United States. Boeing could not legally hire current
FAA employees to come to China to provide safety briefings.
But it could hire recent retirees—and it contracted with several
of them to come to China to size up the situation and then brief
and train CAAC officials in several major cities. Joe T—who
knew the FAA, Boeing, and China—was involved in coordinating this project.

Because of careful warnings by Joe T and others, the U.S.
training team was hyper-sensitive about two aspects of this
training exercise for their Chinese colleagues. One was to present all their recommendations in terms of meeting *international* standards for air safety and airline procedures, rather than
seeming to say, This is how we do it in the U.S. of A. Presenting
the challenge this way made it far more palatable to the Chinese
side. Learning to comply with international standards was one
more sign of modernization in China; doing things the "American way" could seem like a sign of continued subservience. The
examples were, of course, from American practices at the FAA
or the operational details of Boeing and United Airlines, but
the leitmotif was that Americans had learned how to make their
practices meet international standards, and they could help the
Chinese do the same thing.

The other sign of cultural sophistication by the U.S. team
was its awareness of "Chinese characteristics." Even as the Chinese government and business officials felt they were moving
toward international practices, they highly valued the idea that
they were doing so in a distinctively Chinese way. Deng Xiaoping's famous description of the country's post-1979 market
system as "socialism with Chinese characteristics" set the pattern. The term illustrated not only the flexibility of names for

the fast-moving contradictions of modern China—a "socialist" system with room for Lamborghini dealerships and the world's starkest extremes between rich and poor—but also the importance of "Chinese characteristics," known as *Zhongguo tese,* or 中国特色. Because of China's scale, its unusual speed and pattern of development, its low labor costs and other unusual cultural or historic features, systems developed in Tokyo or Los Angeles usually need adjustment to work properly when they are applied in Tianjin or Shenzhen. Even when they don't need any changes, leaders of Chinese organizations value the idea that systems have been changed to reflect Chinese characteristics. This is their version of what Americans have come to call "American exceptionalism." In the case of the air-safety briefing teams, this meant, for instance, that FAA and Boeing officials would explain how they wrote safety manuals and regulatory codes, leaving it to the Chinese to apply those principles in their own circumstances.

"Early on, some Chinese people pulled me aside and said, 'We're not really sure this will ever work in China,'" Joe T said to me, ten years after he began the project. "They were worried about losing face, disrupting the culture of 'human relationships.'" One of his crucial allies was a pilot named Rao Xiaowu, who had flown MD-11s for China Eastern Airlines and gone on to become a senior flight-standards official at the CAAC. (The MD-11 was an even larger version of the familiar DC-10, an airplane with one engine under each wing and a third in the vertical stabilizer, just above the tail.) Rao had experience overseas and understood how profoundly Chinese airlines had to change if they hoped to reach international standards. The second champion was another pilot, Yang Yuanyuan,[10] who had joined the PLA at age sixteen during the Cultural Revolution, graduated from flight school at age nineteen, and joined

China Southern Airlines, for which he eventually became chief pilot. In the late 1990s, as the cooperative Chinese-U.S. safety efforts were beginning, Yang had gone to CAAC as head of flight standards.

"Yang and Rao made clear that they really did expect this to work," Joe T said. "They went to meetings and told people at all the airlines, 'We want you to pay attention, because we want a system that is run to international standards.' They told their colleagues, 'If we stick to regulation by "human relations," we're going to keep having dead people. It has to be run the international way.'" Yang had the authority at CAAC to place key allies in the airlines' safety department, which he used. "The Chinese have a term, 'air-drop soldier,' for someone who is dropped in because of high-level connections but doesn't know what to do," Joe T said. "Yang did just the opposite, making sure he had the right people in these roles."

Neither the Chinese nor the U.S. government had a big budget for the training efforts, so Boeing continued underwriting much of the cost. United Airlines helped as well. In Seattle, visiting teams of Chinese regulators and check pilots watched Boeing train pilots in its simulators. In a special demonstration at United's simulator center in Denver, they watched a pilot mimic the mistakes and rash judgments of an incompetent airman—mainly to observe how the United check pilot handled the situation and corrected his errors.

"Those exchanges started in 1997, and they have never stopped," Joe T told me in Beijing in 2011. It was the beginning of the underpublicized but thoroughgoing near-integration of the U.S. and Chinese aviation establishments in safety measures. In 1999, Yang Yuanyuan became vice minister of the CAAC. Three years later, he became minister, and thus the single most influential person in China's aerospace establishment. Did their efforts make any difference? Through the next decade, Chinese commercial aviation, while expanding faster than any other country's, was statistically among the world's very safest. And it prepared for the surprising next transition the government authorities had in mind.

4 ⋆ The Chinese Master Plan

How aerospace fits into the larger vision

When Deng Xiaoping met Jimmy Carter in 1979 to formalize the new era in U.S.-China relations, which in turn helped provide markets for the new enterprises that were possible under Deng's reforms, the per capita annual income throughout China was about a thousand dollars. Over the next thirty years, that went up almost fivefold, a sustained increase unprecedented in world economic history. Most of what has made the country steadily richer through that period has arisen from the following sequence: *farm to factory to bulldozer.*

First came improvements in *agriculture,* through a shift from inefficient collective farms to smaller private plots, plus very heavy use of insecticide and fertilizer (with subsidized water as well). The subsidies meant that Chinese farmers often used even more fertilizer, pesticide, and water per bushel of output than their European or American counterparts. But the boost in productivity allowed a densely populated nation to feed itself, so that the famines that had been its recurring historical calamity—including the disastrous politically induced famine during the Great Leap Forward—were no more. The same improvement also marked the beginning of many modern farm-based fortunes—some of today's famous rich families in China made their money in the cattle and dairy business in Inner Mongolia or with pig farms in central China—and reduced the manpower needed to tend the fields, freeing family members to go to the cities for factory jobs.

Then came the *low-cost manufacturing* boom whose effects began to be noticed throughout the world in the early 1990s. This was different from Japan's modern manufacturing boom, which had started in the 1960s, in that China's was largely driven by foreign firms. Dell, Walmart, Apple, Siemens, GM, GE—they and hundreds of others shifted and outsourced operations to China, whereas the most important steps in Japan's development were taken mainly by their own big companies. Because it started its industrialization almost a century before China did, even by the 1960s Japan had big, mature corporate groups—like Mitsubishi, Toyota, Matsushita, Fuji, NEC, Toshiba, plus postwar upstarts like Sony and Honda—that could compete internationally with American and European firms. China still has no counterparts and indeed virtually no globally known brand names.

China's low-wage industrial boom differed from India's development through the same period in that it depended much less on an educated workforce, like the software engineers working in Bangalore and Hyderabad, and more on hardworking young men and women straight from the countryside. China's boom also depended on the roads, shipping docks, and other elements of infrastructure that could get the products to their customers in big Chinese cities and overseas.

Creating this *infrastructure* was itself the third element in the sequence of Chinese development, and a subset of the fourth element, *construction* in general.

Visitors from anywhere, and with special piquancy those from the United States, have to notice how new—how smooth, how capacious, how modern—the recently finished parts of China's infrastructure are. Roads, subways, train lines, power stations—they are, in fact, new compared with most of the U.S. and European infrastructure.

It is true that buildings and facilities tend to age quickly in China, because of pollution and, sometimes, shortcuts in construction standards. Early in my time in China, I'd see buildings that I thought were from the 1960s or earlier, and then be surprised to learn that they were only four or five years old. After a while, I learned to apply an "accelerated aging" factor to any structure I saw. For instance, the mammoth and uniquely styled CCTV tower near our apartment in Beijing, which was designed by Rem Koolhaas and which has two slanting black legs connected by an angled upper story, was rushed to completion in time for the Olympic Games in 2008. Three years later, its harshly weathered look made it appear as if it had been there for decades—even before the CCTV news operations had moved in. It is true as well that successive public disasters in China have repeatedly led to outrage over "surprising" defects in construction materials, safety standards, honest inspections, and so on. This was especially so after the Sichuan earthquake in 2008, when thousands of children died in the collapse of shoddy school buildings, and after a high-speed rail crash in 2011.

Still, on average, China's infrastructure looks much newer, and is often better, than its counterparts in North America and Europe built fifty or one hundred years ago. The heavy infrastructure of U.S. cities on the East Coast was laid down in the decades after the Civil War; that of the Midwest at the beginning of the twentieth century; and that of the West Coast and the Sunbelt in the decades after World War II. The freeways of

Southern California looked wide and new when I was growing up there in the Boomer era. That is how the freeways of China look now.

Simply keeping its existing bridges, freeways, and water-works from falling apart is the infrastructure challenge for the United States. For China, the heavy investment in roads, ports, power stations, train lines, and so on has been, like many of its other growth strategies, so successful that it has bred a different kind of problem. The consequences of more than a decade's worth of *over*investment are as important in shaping China's choices, and its outlook on new industries like aerospace, as the consequences of long-term underinvestment are for the United States.

Addicted to growth

Part of the success of China's infrastructure strategy is that it has made every other kind of growth more attainable. When factory wages go up in the Shenzhen area north of Hong Kong, outsourcing businesses might think about relocating to Viet-nam or India. But they are more likely to end up heading to Sichuan or Gansu province in inland China, because the Chi-nese roads and facilities are likely to be so much better than those of any country that has not been building at such a frantic pace through recent years.

Also, infrastructure efforts and the larger construction indus-try remain powerful growth engines on their own. Charts of the components of China's growth since the early 2000s con-sistently show one element that is higher than its counterparts in any other major economy: "capital formation"—essentially, investment of all sorts. New factories, new houses, new roads, new bridges, new sewer systems, new subways. New everything, with the caveat that these are not goods for immediate consumer use. The advantage for China is that this investment builds future productive capacity, a better life, a richer society, and so on—and in the meantime, it creates jobs for people who are doing the building, and markets for companies that sell structural steel, cement, and every other ingredient.

The problem for the Chinese economy has become its *dependence* on stimulus through investment. If by the early 2000s the American economy had become addicted to cycles of borrowing, overconsumption, and further borrowing to propel its expansion, China's was addicted in the opposite way, through cycles of overinvestment and the resulting need to export. Once a new factory is built, the construction jobs are over—and people can keep working and getting paid only if there's a market for what they make. Or if new construction projects begin, which eventually add even more to the nation's productive capacity. In 2007, before the world financial crisis began, investment and capital projects of all sorts, including construction, represented 39 percent of China's economy. By 2010, that share had risen to 46 percent—an astonishing increase, even as investment was being cut back in most of the rest of the world. But a *Wall Street Journal* analysis in 2011, which noted this change, pointed out that China could use this tactic to sustain employment only so many times.[1] The country had become more and more reliant on build, build, build as a way of keeping its people at work, and the longer that strategy went on, the harder it would be to maintain.

Any trend that can't continue won't, and at some point the Chinese juggernaut will have to "rebalance" itself with the rest of the world. The typical economist's scenario for this transition is as follows: As China's own people get richer, they will buy more of what their own factories make, plus more of what foreigners provide as well. China's growth will be more self-sustaining, and less dependent on chronic trade surpluses with the Americans and new roads in every corner of the country.

That's where China is headed, at least in theory. But for now, it keeps people at work through a heavier reliance on "capital formation"—new factories, roads, shopping centers, power plants,[2] and government and corporate projects—than any other economy, ever;[3] and infrastructure projects, including airports, are an important part of that drive. The construction of a hundred airports at once is a classic illustration of Chinese stimulus through massive investment. The aspirations to match Boeing and Airbus in airplanes, Sikorsky and Robinson in helicopters, Rolls-Royce and GE and Pratt & Whitney in engines, Honeywell and Avidyne in avionics, symbolize the direction in which many Chinese leaders hope the economy will go in order to break its reliance on farms, factories, and construction sites.

China as the new America, in a bad way

By the time of the Beijing Olympics, even as China was increasingly seen around the world as the rising economic model of the age, economists inside and outside the country said, in various forms, *this cannot go on.* This—the Chinese boom—could not go on environmentally, because of the costs to people and the pressure on resources. It could not go on strategically, because of the aberrant relationship in which Americans kept borrowing Chinese money to buy Chinese goods. And it could not go on for reasons within China, because of the social tensions and dislocations it was creating.

There is one particular aspect of *this can't go on* that got much less attention outside the country than it deserved. That is probably because it was a weakness that looked like a strength: It was China's huge "success" in selling so much more to the world than it bought.

In politics, press coverage, and barroom talk, it's natural to consider exports and the resulting trade surpluses as proxies for individual and national merit. And there's some truth to that: The broken-down economies of the old Soviet bloc could barely export anything to customers who had any choice about what to buy. Boeing's, Intel's, and Apple's victories in world markets are generally points of pride for Americans. The same is true for Siemens and Mercedes in Germany and for their counterparts all around the world. But too one-sided a reliance on exports can ultimately be as destructive and destabilizing as too little success in selling overseas. To illustrate why, think about the similarity between China around the time of the Olympics and the United States eighty years before. That would, of course, be 1928, which few people outside Holland identify as the time of the Amsterdam Olympics but which many people recognize as the eve of the great worldwide depression and subsequent world war.

An economist and financial-markets expert named Michael Pettis, who was trained in the United States and Europe but has taught since the early 2000s at Peking University, drew out this comparison for me during one of several interviews I had with him in Beijing around the time of the Olympics, this one in 2009. When people say that China is like "what America used to be," he told me, it's often meant as a compliment to China and a criticism of the United States. But there was an important opposite side to the story.

Through the early 1900s, he said, the United States played a role in the world economy surprisingly similar to China's since about 2000. Until the start of World War I, the United States had long been a "net debtor" country—as premodernized China had also been. Through its first century-plus of development, the young United States had relied on foreign loans and investments to build the factories and lay the railroads that ultimately made it an industrial titan. By the end of World War I, it had become a "net creditor," as its undamaged industrial base supplied European combatants and the former customers of ruined European companies.

In the 1920s, its farms and industries made America the workshop of the world. It ran trade surpluses with most other economies, which meant that a disproportionate share of the world's jobs were in America (that is, it was doing work to create products that other people consumed). By the same logic, a disproportionate share of what it made went for other people's use. Foreigners paid the difference by transferring gold reserves—the economist John Maynard Keynes complained in the 1920s that the United States was amassing "all the bullion in the world"—or taking on loans and investments from Americans. So far, this is like China's story. And so far, apparently, so good.

But its very role as global exporter made the United States unusually vulnerable when global demand collapsed in the 1930s. Having had more than its "fair" share of the world's jobs to begin with, it had more of them to lose. This doesn't mean that Americans suffered more deeply than Europeans, overall. Americans got Franklin Roosevelt; Europeans got Hitler, Stalin, Franco, and Mussolini. But as a matter of plain economics, the layoffs and unemployment of the Depression years were worse in the United States.

That was the prospect for China, as the world economies began their series of shocks and contractions soon after the triumphant Beijing Olympic Games. China's several-trillion-dollar war chest of foreign holdings, built up from its long string of trade surpluses, gives it advantages. But China's reliance on foreign customers is a serious vulnerability.

Pettis wrote in 2009 that China's worldwide trade surplus, "the cleanest measure of overcapacity"—factories that are running and workers who are employed *only* because of foreign customers—was by one measure about as large as America's had been in 1929. China today, like America then, has a trade surplus equal to about 0.5 percent of *global* economic output. But as a proportion of its own economic output, China's trade surplus has been much bigger than America's ever was. In proportional terms, China has in recent years been five times as reliant on foreign customers to create domestic jobs as America was in 1929. So unless China can find a sustainable way to keep selling when its customers have stopped buying, it will face proportionately greater employment shock.

China's response to that shock in 2008 and 2009 was to ramp up its public-spending surge even further. That buffered the shock of this recession but didn't change the reality that China was still too dependent on customers everywhere else to provide markets that would keep its own people at work. As of 2010, net exports still represented more than one quarter of China's total economic output, an astonishingly high number. (That manufacturing powerhouse Germany, in comparison, had net exports of less than 4 percent of its GDP at the same time.)

"The next decade for China is arguably just as important, if not more so, than the last three combined," the analyst Damien Ma, of the Eurasia Group, wrote in 2011, about the overall efforts to shift the economy from its infrastructure-and-export frenzy. "The curtains on the era of easy 'catch-up' growth are being closed, and a transition to a prosperous and equal society is the fundamental issue facing Beijing. It's not that the Chinese leaders don't get what's at stake—they know such a reckoning must be had. But recognizing what must be done is quite different from summoning the political chutzpah to achieve it."[4]

The word "chutzpah" might seem odd in this context. Mustering the kind of cheek and daring it suggests is only part of the Chinese central government's challenge. The rest involves incentives to governors, mayors, managers, bureaucrats, to pull in the direction the government wants—plus the means of figuring out whether they are doing what they say. The system has to keep growing fast enough that most people continue to feel that things are overall getting better rather than worse, and that the disadvantages of a one-party system are outweighed by its effectiveness. All the evidence suggests that, despite their complaints, most Chinese people have felt this way through the country's decades of growth. But it has to change course enough to accommodate all the tensions that growth itself has created: a radically unequal income distribution (some people are buying jets with cash, while others pull oxcarts down the streets) and a perception of life being rigged, chronic trade frictions with the Americans and others, a devastated environment, and a steady demand for the daily liberties increasingly prosperous people would like to enjoy.

The way ahead for the economy

How could the Chinese model "change" or "rebalance" to address these concerns? Although reckoning time in units of Five-Year Plans seems strange outside China, the shifting emphasis from the Tenth plan, released in 2001, to the Eleventh, in 2006, to the Twelfth in 2011, does help illustrate a significant shift in strategy, and sets the context for ambitious projects like the dream of aerospace preeminence.

The Tenth plan, still in effect when Hu Jintao assumed power,[5] emphasized economic growth at the highest speed possible. Then, starting in 2006, as Hu and his premier Wen Jiabao solidified their hold on the government, and as much of the country prepared for the Beijing Olympics and the Shanghai World Expo, the Eleventh Five-Year Plan was supposed to reflect the spirit of the "Harmonious Society" (in Chinese 和谐社会, or *hexie shehui*). In practice, a more harmonious China was supposed to be one that paid more attention to the devastated environment and took better care of the hundreds of millions of farmers and migrant workers left behind by the Chinese miracle. That aspiration was reflected in a variety of social-welfare measures—for instance, relaxing the *hukou,* or residence-permit, system that had made it near-impossible for migrant workers to enroll their children in schools outside the family's officially "registered" home or to be eligible for medical treatment without trekking hundreds of miles back to their home villages. It also lay behind a number of "Green China" initiatives, from funding wind- and solar-energy projects to judging provincial bureaucrats in part on their environmental record, to allowing and even encouraging journalistic exposés of environmental problems.

By the end of the Eleventh Plan, the major imbalances remained: a huge trade surplus with the United States, an infrastructure and construction boom that was gaining rather than losing momentum, an ever more extreme gulf between rich and poor. Anything the Chinese or others said about "rebalancing" or "harmony" would be a mockery, as long as the economy kept racking up huge trade surpluses and relying on foreign markets, as long as the building and industrial boom kept ravaging the country's own environment, as long as Chinese society kept indulging the most extreme Gilded Age excess with little sign of correction or balm on social unease.

The Twelfth Five-Year Plan included very long lists of strategic initiatives and "areas of focus," but the ideas for "rebalancing" and "harmonizing" the economy fell into a few main categories. Aerospace is affected by each of these, and its progress will be an indication of the Chinese planners' overall success in realizing their new goals:

1. "Apex industries" and escaping the "smiley curve"

Will it be possible to move from assembly factories, which capture a small share of the value, to the brand names that get most of the profit? And therefore to convert China from a workhouse of the world to one of its sources of innovation? Few politicians or outside observers dwell on such questions. They obsess economists and business leaders within China.

In the mid-2000s, I heard a way of thinking about these questions that has stayed with me ever since. It is the concept of the "smiley curve," and I heard about it from Liam Casey, an Irish businessman who had lived and worked for nearly ten years in Southern China.[6]

The smiley curve is a U-shaped graph (named after the smiley-face symbols of the 1970s) that covers the different stages of a product's development. On one end of the curve, at the highest point on the left side, are corporate brands, with the extra market value they bring—Apple, Mercedes, GE, Samsung, all of which command a premium compared with their generic counterparts. Next comes product concept and industrial design—thinking up the iPad, the S-class car, GE's new turbine engines. Then, moving down the curve, come high-value components—turbine blades, graphics chips, advanced displays.

Then the commodity components, like simple memory chips. At the bottom of the curve comes assembly—the process of combining the elements into a finished product. Moving up the other side of the curve, as it rises, are transportation—DHL or FedEx—and then retailer's margin, and then after-sale service.

The height of the curve indicates the relative profitability of each stage of the process. The highest values are at its two extremes—the extra profit that goes to an Apple- or Mercedes-branded product, and the margin from retail sales and service. The lowest value is at the bottom of the curve, where the actual manufacturing takes place. And that lowest niche is the one that China has occupied throughout the first thirty years of its growth. The work was done in China, and the money went everyplace else.

The smiley curve and its implications became so famous that Wen Jiabao began mentioning them in speeches and negotiations with U.S. officials. Of an iPhone costing four hundred dollars or a computer costing a thousand, at most one tenth of the total profits stayed with anyone in China—even though every iPhone and iPad in the world, and most computers of any brand, are produced in Chinese factories. Much larger shares of the profit stayed with Apple, Philips, or the other international brand holders, or with the Japanese, Korean, or German chip-makers who produced the advanced components, or the retailers and deal-makers in North America and Europe, or with others. The curve also accounted for distortion in trade figures: While the entire value of an iPad or iPhone is treated as a Chinese "export" and thus a component of China's trade surplus, nearly ten times as much of its value comes from Japan or Germany as from China. An Asian Development Bank study released late in 2010[7] used the example of an iPhone, with a wholesale cost of $178.96 and a retail cost of as much as twice that. A total of $6.50 of the value of each phone went to workers in China, according to the report, even though all the phones were physically assembled in China, in plants from the Foxconn company.[8] Twenty-five to thirty times that much could go to wholesalers, distributors, and retailers. The biggest surprise of the Asian Development Bank analysis was what it illustrated about the fallibility in normal trade statistics. While every penny of the wholesale cost of an iPhone was listed as a Chinese "export" to the United States—which together made iPhones seem to account for more than 1 percent of China's total trade surplus with America—in reality, when all the components were traced to their source, each iPhone represented a small but net *export* from the United States to China. The ingredients of each iPhone that came from U.S. suppliers to China were worth considerably more than the small value added from Chinese assembly. Statistical artifacts like this made the American trade situation look more hopeless than it really was, and made the Chinese economic model seem unrealistically triumphant.

This pattern is generally not known outside China (except by the corporations doing the outsourcing) but is very well understood by China's political and economic leadership. "In the United States and Europe, the manufacturing industry *was created* due to technology innovation," Helen Wang, author of a book about China's middle class, wrote in 2010. "In China, the manufacturing industry is *being created in response* to global demand. Chinese manufacturers take orders from Western companies that have designed products for their home markets. They have no involvement with product development, innovation, market research, and even packaging."[9] Yet those factories churning out goods for foreign markets are miracles of high-value productivity, compared with much of the rest of China's vast workforce in stores, offices, and government bureaus. Even the slightest exposure to China anywhere outside a high-output factory leaves foreigners (and well-traveled Chinese people) asking, Why does it take so many people to do this job?

An American teacher who had lived for years in a second-tier city in China began cataloguing the make-work jobs of modern China, in order of superfluousness. First came the "bus line monitors," who walk around and observe as snarls of passengers struggle to get on buses but who have no apparent influence over the process. Then the "receipt stampers," who stand by the exits of even fancy Western stores and add an extra stamp, in red ink, to receipts as people leave, certifying the sale as official. Then the separate staffs of ticket-sellers and ticket-takers at museums and other public buildings, usually with several people assigned to each role. And on through a list that any foreign—or Chinese person—could match, or top. Yet as the teacher noted, in the end the reason for this countrywide featherbedding was really no mystery at all. It mainly indicated how low prevailing wages still were, and how important it was to keep everyone on someone's payroll.[10] With a more ruthlessly efficient approach to output-per-man-hour, many Chinese enterprises could get twice the results with half the staff, and could afford to pay the remaining staffers much better. But what would those laid-off receipt-stampers and ticket-takers do?

These patterns are changing, with more of the innovation coming from inside China, and with the average value of Chinese factory output (and therefore average wage) going up. But they are not changing fast enough, from the Chinese planners' point of view. Every policy paper, every speech, just about every conference or newspaper editorial since the mid-2000s has stressed China's "need to move up the value chain" or "create a high-value economic base" or "switch to high-margin industries for a better life."[11]

This push and logic have obvious application to aerospace, as one of the mainstays of the U.S. economy for nearly a century and as a symbol of advanced technological status. As Joe T told me one afternoon when I met him at his office at a Chinese aviation university, "This industry is a perfect test case of economic maturity in general, since there's no shortcut to success."

In biology there is the concept of the "apex predator"—the lion on the savanna, the wolf or puma in the forest, the hawk or eagle in the air, the marlin or salmon in the sea. Their existence depends on many tiers of prey beneath them. If they survive, it suggests that the ecosystem as a whole is robust. Aerospace provides that same capping symbolism for an economic and technological establishment, Joe T suggested. "You have to do everything in consonance," he said. In the design and construction of the airplanes themselves, that meant research, design, engineering, testing, manufacturing, and very large-scale and complex project management. In the creation and maintenance of an air-transport system, it meant certification, training and education, route design, inspection, enforcement, weather-and-navigation research, air-traffic control, airport design, accident investigation, and more. And then for airline companies come all the vagaries of dealing with often dissatisfied customers, at vast scale, while also buying and maintaining aircraft, setting route schedules and prices, training and scheduling crews, and such nightmares as dealing with baggage and security. So if Chinese companies could succeed in aviation, that would be an "apex" indicator that they could succeed at anything.

2. A green economy

Different people have different assessments of the main threat to China's continued economic success. For me the easy choice is environmental devastation. "The environmental situation is still grave in China, though with some positive development," the Chinese central government itself said shortly before the Beijing Olympics, in a surprisingly candid white paper that accompanied its Eleventh Five-Year Plan for Environmental Protection. While the "positive developments" part is true—efforts are being made everywhere to insulate buildings, purify water, install clean-energy plants—the "still grave" part is more evident by the day. "The emissions of major pollutants far exceed environmental capacity with serious environmental pollution," that white paper said. "Environmental problems at different stages of [the] industrialization process of developed countries over the past several hundred years [are now] concentrated in China."[12] The problem is so deep and widespread that for now the point is simply to mention that it affects every aspect of China's development. In 2011, the Chinese health ministry announced that cancer had become the nation's leading cause of death. This is an unfortunate distinction. In poorer countries, infectious diseases and malnutrition are the leading killers; in richer countries, heart diseases and the consequences of obesity. China's cancer epidemics, and the "cancer villages" found near a number of factories or mines in the countryside, are consequences of decades of uncontrolled industrial emissions. The reported air-pollution levels in major cities are routinely in the "hazardous" level, by international standards, and until 2012 the Chinese government did not even measure or report on particulate matter that the rest of the world considers the most dangerous form of air pollution.[13]

Despite its investment in conservation and clean-energy projects, China's growth is still energy-intensive.[14] As fast as the economy grows, its energy consumption grows faster still. Each percentage-point increase in economic output leads to a more than proportional increase in demand for energy. Although it is harder to be sure whether this energy consumption leads to a corresponding rise in pollution and reliance on ever-greater water use, overall China is clearly in a race between how bad this problem is and how fast the system can regear itself to cope.

China's aviation dreams are right in the center of this tension. Air travel inevitably creates disproportionate environmental stress. For the foreseeable future, airplanes will be able to operate only on liquid fuel—oil, in one form or another. Battery-powered planes have made test flights, mainly in Europe. A Swiss design team has even created a plane that flies with no energy source other than the solar panels across its wings. But those are small, experimental models. Batteries must become much lighter, and solar-panel efficiency much greater, before they will be able to keep passenger planes in the air. Modern turbine engines are a great deal cleaner and more efficient than their kerosene-guzzling predecessors of a generation ago. Nonetheless, they inject their emissions into a layer of the upper atmosphere that magnifies their potential "greenhouse" effect, so one airplane traveling at 35,000 feet can do two to three times as much damage, in global-warming terms, as the same engines burning the same amount of fuel at ground level would.

Chinese engineers and environmentalists know this. They also know that more aircraft will be flying to more cities, more frequently, carrying more passengers, every year in China than they did the year before. So they work on their plans for expansion fully aware that everything about their efforts will be subject to increasing scrutiny and pressure. One sign of that

pressure is the competition between China's heralded investment in high-speed rail projects and its simultaneous construction of airports by the dozens across the country. Foreign reports
often present these projects as carefully coordinated expressions
of China's larger ambitions for a modern transportation system,
and to an extent they are. But there are also bitter bureaucratic
and commercial rivalries between the airline and railroad interests within China, each seizing any opportunity to argue that
it reflected the wiser and more farsighted use of the country's
resources. In reality, Chinese designers are likely to push ahead
on both fronts.

3. Megacity China

What drives Chinese people away from their rural homes is
the same force that has propelled urbanization for centuries:
the bleak, unrelenting lack of opportunity in the countryside.
When interviewing factory workers in Shenzhen or Dongguan,
men and women in their late teens through their early thirties, I frequently heard about the gap between China's rural
and urban economies. Back on the farm, their entire family's
cash income might be $150 to $200 per year. In the city, one
worker might earn that much in a month, or every few weeks.
Chinese working-age people by the tens of millions have come
from their family homes in the countryside to the factories and
dormitories or apartments of the big cites. They have replicated
at much faster speed and larger scale the social history of Europe
and North America through their eras of industrialization.

In 2009, the McKinsey Global Institute released a five-
hundred-plus-page survey of the scale and likely effects of the
increasing movement of Chinese people to the cities. It was
called "Preparing for China's Urban Billion," and it described
a phenomenon with no precedent in economic or urban his-

tory. According to the study, within a twenty-year period, from 2005 to 2025, more people will be *added* to China's major cities than now live in the entire United States. In 2005, about 575 million people, or just under 40 percent of the whole Chinese population, lived in big cities rather than agricultural areas. By 2025, about 925 million are expected to, an increase of 350 million. The rural-to-urban shifts that transformed the culture and economy of Europe through the course of the nineteenth century and North America through the twentieth will be compressed in China into a span of a relatively few years.

This shift is expected to give China some 221 cities with populations of over a million by 2025, versus 35 in all of Europe as of 2010 and only 9 in the United States. Time and again in China, I would have the exciting but disorienting experience of coming to a city I had never heard of before and finding out that it was larger than most cities in the United States. For example: Yueyang, which is the second-largest city in Hunan province, behind the capital, Changsha (which is also the home of the environmentally minded mogul Zhang Yue and was the departure point for my Cirrus flight to Zhuhai). Until I spent several days in Yueyang, at the Hunan Institute of Science and Technology, I had never heard of it. But if Yueyang were in the United States, with a population that could be as high as 5 million people (counts vary), it would be a major metropolis.

The heavily urbanized future China would also have fifteen "megacity" complexes, like Shanghai-Hangzhou, of more than 25 million people. The Guangzhou-Shenzhen-Zhuhai complex of the Pearl River Delta would by itself have 80 million to 100 million inhabitants. The only way to amass comparable population totals in the United States would be to combine the multi-hundred-mile stretches from San Francisco to San Diego on the West Coast, or from Boston to Washington in the east, each of which includes 25 million people or more.

As the McKinsey report put it, simply building China's new cities "will account for around 20 percent of global energy consumption and up to one-quarter of growth in oil demand" over the next decade. By 2025, as many as 170 Chinese cities could have subway systems or other capital-intensive mass-transit projects—twice as many as in all the countries of Europe combined.[15]

Everything about China's development and its presence on the world stage will be affected by these shifts. Environmentally, it creates both problems and opportunities. Hundreds of millions of people who had been living without air-conditioning, elevators, dishwashers, street lights, neon lights, and other energy-intensive urban amenities right down to espresso machines will now demand them. "When I was a child, it was incredible for my father to have even one cold beer," a Chinese friend of mine named Sean Wang told me in Beijing not long after the Olympics. "Now people want twenty-four-hour heating, hot water, refrigerators. It is not sustainable unless we make a change." The opportunity, as with almost every physical and technological aspect of modern China, comes from the chance to start from scratch. Unlike the United States and Europe, China largely skipped the landline era and went straight to mobile phones. It similarly has the chance to skip the suburban-sprawl model of mid-twentieth-century America and go straight to the higher-density urban patterns that made subway and streetcar lines efficient for cities like Paris, London, and New York.

Decisions being made right now will affect China's look, livability, sustainability, and environmental and cultural effect on the world for decades to come. The early twenty-first century is, for Shenzhen and Xi'an and Nanjing and a hundred other cities, what the late nineteenth and early twentieth centuries were for New York, or the whole of the Victorian era for London, or the Imperial period for Rome: the age in which big and lasting choices are made about how and where people will live, where they will work, how they will move about, and what identity and spirit their city will be known for.

Chinese city planners do not lack for grandiosity. One of the dependable joys of even a modest-size Chinese city is seeing the dioramas of how it will look when it is all done. Beijing and Shanghai have set a model for other cities in creating "building museums" that present scale-model replicas of the entire urban sprawl, with tiny representations of every structure.

What is happening in Chinese cities is two centuries' worth of development compressed into ten or twenty years. And as with previous episodes of high-speed expansion, this one has already been characterized by waste, fraud, extravagance, and scandal. Starting in 2010, both Chinese and Western journalists chronicled the construction of "ghost cities" mainly in the Chinese hinterland. These were huge tracts of factory zones, apartment buildings, civic centers, and shopping malls, all built to accommodate populations of a million or more, and all standing virtually empty. They had been built on free or nearly free land from provincial governments, with free or nearly free loans. While they were going up, they had enriched construction companies, kept workers on the job, and boosted GDP figures for the local Party officials. What would become of them afterward no one could say.[16]

One night in 2007, while my wife and I were living in Shanghai, we looked out our twenty-second-floor apartment window and saw a worker fall from a nearby forty-story scaffolding where welding was going on around the clock. The blue glare of welding torches kept the night lit in Shanghai, even when many of the neon billboards around People's Square were shut off each night at 10. We could not see where the worker landed, nor did we see any follow-up Chinese or English news coverage, but it seemed impossible that he could have survived. An average of two hundred people die each day in China in accidents at construction sites, coal mines, factories, or other industrial sites. Soon after we left Shanghai, an unoccupied thirteen-story apartment building fell over onto its side, intact, because it had been put up so quickly with such shoddy foundations.[17]

Until recently, aesthetics, like safety, have been a distant concern in the development of Chinese cities. Buildings left over from the Mao era are squat, Stalinist-looking, and now in terrible repair. Their successors from the late 1970s through the 1980s, when construction was still done quickly and very much on the cheap, are not much of an improvement. The opening words of a recent noir thriller set in Beijing, *Rock Paper Tiger*, by Lisa Brackmann, accurately evoke the feeling of much of late-twentieth-century urban China. "I'm living in this dump in Haidian Qu, close to Wudaokou, on the twenty-first floor of a decaying high-rise." She is writing about the university district in the northwest of Beijing, but she could be describing much of urban China. "The lights have been out in the lobby since I moved in; they never finished the interior walls in the foyers outside the elevators; and the windows are boarded up, so every time I step outside the apartment door I'm in a weird twilight world of bare cement and blue fluorescent light."

The next stage of China's growth and advancement rests on the assumption that its population will be more and more concentrated in cities. Transportation within those cities, and among them, naturally becomes an important focus for government investment and therefore private profit. Especially if—consistent with the other goals—better transportation can help China's industries move to a higher "value level," and deal with environmental problems at the same time.

4. Modern transport for China

Objects in motion have been the secret to China's economic boom. Materials and supplies are in motion—steel brought to factories; cement from the plants where it is created to the construction sites where it is used; above all, coal, nearly ten million tons per day, hauled from the mines to power stations where it is burned to keep everything else going. Finished products have been in motion to their customers, within China and overseas. And *people* have had to move, by the tens of millions, from villages all across the countryside to the few dozen major cities where most of China's industrial growth has occurred.

Each of these flows takes place in China on a scale matched nowhere else on earth, which makes the interlocking transportation networks—road, rail, boat, air—as important to China's development as the transcontinental railroad, the interstate highways, and the airline network have been for the United States. But even China's constantly expanded transportation networks have just barely kept up with the challenge of movement at this scale. For example:

- Late in 2010, there was a three-week-long dead-gridlock traffic jam on the roads that led hundreds of miles north from Beijing toward the coal-mining zones of Inner Mongolia. Most of the traffic that had overwhelmed the roads was private trucks carrying coal and avoiding bigger, newer roads on which they would have had to pay tolls. Indeed, one of the big pushes for the country's high-speed rail system is to get the people off the "normal" trains so there is more space for coal and other goods.[18]

- In the sprawl of the Pearl River Delta factory zone, where so many of the world's electronic products—and toys, clothes, and housewares—are made, the production system in many electronic companies is built around the daily pickup schedules for the big international carriers. The factories work overnight or very early in the morning, all based on when the collection trucks from FedEx, UPS, and DHL will arrive to get shipments for the Hong Kong airport, where they will go off to customers in North America and around the world. At an aerospace conference in 2010, I met a FedEx official who was brimming with excitement about an announcement that he said would change outsourcing: cargo planes that could go efficiently nonstop from Hong Kong to Los Angeles. This would cut several hours off the existing cycle, with flights through Anchorage, Tokyo, or San Francisco. That in turn would make it easier for Apple, for example, to have Chinese-made products delivered in America the day after a customer pressed the "buy now" button on a Web site.
- The big freeways around port cities in China are not only newer and better than those in North America or Europe. Many are also less crowded, because they have modest tolls, equivalent to a few cents a mile. This is high enough to keep ordinary Chinese pleasure traffic off the roads—but low enough to be a worthwhile investment for companies moving goods straight to the airport, the seaport, or the railhead.
- And of course there is the largest movement of people in human history, the billion or so trips made each year at Spring Festival time, or lunar new year, which usually occurs between mid-January and early February. The 2009 documentary *Last Train Home* captured the predictable crisis and drama of the migrations: there are not enough seats, and train tickets are generally *not sold for round trips*. You have to wait in line at one station to get the outbound ticket, and then wait in line at the other station, in the other city, to get a ticket for the trip back. Think for a moment about the stress and inconvenience this creates.

The Spring Festival train and bus rides are events of surprising sociological, economic, logistic, and emotional consequence. Sociological, in that the holiday is the one time each year when families are reunited—if the journey is impossible for some reason, the opportunity is lost. Economic, not just because the industrial engine halts for a period but also because many employees use this time to shop for better work offers, or they decide not to return to the factories at all. It also is an obvious blip in China's export and import behavior. The variable calendar date of the Spring Festival, like that of Easter or Passover in the West, explains why January or February will show abnormal statistics one year or another. It is of logistic importance because each year's journey is a gamble on whether people will be able to get home and then back again. And it is emotional on an epic scale matched mainly by visits during wartime. Will the family still be there? Will my child still know me? Will my parents think I have changed, or gone wrong?

There are other complications too, affecting China's drive to modernize and the role of simple physical movement in that process. They involve the special role of western China, especially the autonomous regions of Tibet and Xinjiang, and the uneasy balance between the Chinese military—weak in international terms, strong as an internal factor—in allowing the country to move ever more freely.

5 ★ An Airport in the Wilderness

"The emperor is far away . . ."

One day in June 2009, I had a longer discussion than normal with a taxi driver outside our apartment building in Beijing. I was trying to convince him, in Chinese, that when I said I wanted to go to "the airport"—*dao jichang qu*—I wasn't talking about the main international airport, Beijing Capital, where every foreigner he'd ever carried had wanted to go.

Instead my destination was the small, almost rural-seeming Nanyuan Airport on the south edge of town. Pedal-cart drivers lazed outside under trees along the narrow road into this airport, waiting for customers but not appearing to expect any very soon. Passengers who were departing went from the terminal to their airplanes not through enclosed jetways but across the open tarmac, which was edged with trees. From Nanyuan, one of China's odder minor airlines—China United, owned and operated by the People's Liberation Army—ran flights to small inland destinations, in my case, the relatively large inland destination of Xi'an.

This would be my first-ever trip on China United Airlines, which, as with many other domestic carriers, filled its seats up from the back. There were only thirty or so passengers for a Boeing 737 that could have held more than a hundred, and we were sent back to fully occupy the last few rows in the plane.

(Once the door was closed, the passengers scrambled around to take empty seats.) I stayed in the rear, in a window seat, and settled down to watch the scenery on the two-hour flight to Xi'an.

To the world, Xi'an is, of course, known for its army of terra-cotta warriors. In China, it is known as the capital of the arid western coal-and-farming province of Shaanxi (not to be confused with the neighboring and also coal-producing province of Shanxi—the difference is more obvious in Chinese: 陕西 versus 山西) and as the modern site of the ancient Imperial capital of Chang'an. Many of the city walls from the Imperial era remain, enclosing among other features a mosque in the city's Muslim quarter.

To the aspiring Chinese aviation community, Xi'an is known as one of several potential seats of a new aerospace boom, a combination of Kitty Hawk, Aspen, Teterboro Airport, and Everett, Washington: a place where important things will be born; where elite travelers will fly in on holiday; where business jets will congregate; and where airliners will be built for customers around the world. Each of these goals reflects an aspect of the ones that China has set for its development. The question is how did they all strangely come together in the place on the far outskirts of Xi'an called the Luyanghu Integrated General Aviation Development Zone, near a provincial center called Weinan?

Francis Chao and Gao Yuanyang

The trip of a number of international aviation enthusiasts to Weinan was part of the Fourth Annual China General Aviation Forum. I had come along at the invitation of its organizer and impresario, Francis Chao, a Taiwanese-American in his fifties.

Around the beginning of the twenty-first century, Chao had begun to think that sooner or later a business-aviation boom was destined to come to China. The people then just starting to consider BMWs and Mercedeses would eventually be looking to Lamborghinis and Bentleys, and after that to Gulfstreams and Learjets and fancy personal helicopters from brands like Robinson. As China's road and rail networks improved, so eventually would its airports and aviation infrastructure. Chao had worked in the 1990s as a contractor for the U.S. Department of Defense, the FAA, and other federal agencies, providing interpretation and other support in their dealings with China and Taiwan. Early in the George W. Bush Administration, when a People's Liberation Army naval fighter plane collided with a U.S. Navy EP-3 electronic-surveillance plane over the South China Sea, he worked with the Pentagon negotiating team to calm a potentially volatile confrontation. A few months earlier, in a project for the FAA, he escorted a delegation from the CAAC to the AirVenture summer air show in Oshkosh, Wisconsin, so they could have a sense of the scale of general aviation in the United States and its potential for China. He sensed the potential too and decided that he could play a role in connecting an emerging aviation community in China with its established counterparts in the United States. The connections would include commercial ties, since many of the goods and services that Chinese customers would be looking for would come, at least initially, from companies and experts in the United States.

The first time I met Chao, at an aerospace expo in Beijing in the fall of 2006, I didn't fully appreciate how emblematic his chosen role was. As I traveled over the next few years to more parts of the country and watched more businesses in their high-speed and often unplanned process of development, I saw again and again the importance of the cultural interpreter, or middleman, playing the Mr. China role. "Mr. China" was a term given jokey immortality by the British writer and businessman Tim Clissold, in his book of the same name. It referred to the crucial niche in the business ecology occupied by the Chinese or foreign intermediary who becomes an indispensable guide for outsiders hoping to do business in modern China. On one side are international companies large or small who sense that somehow they have to "get into" China because of its vast potential. On the other side are the complexities, confusions, and constant changes of customers and operating rules on the Chinese side.

The people who know how to make the connections are enormously valuable—and a large number of them, for natural linguistic and cultural reasons, are ethnically Chinese people like Chao from mainland China or Taiwan who had immigrated to or studied in the West. The middleman role naturally attracts its share of charlatans, and foreign companies often have to rely on hunch or trial and error to determine whether someone who is good at languages and claims to "understand the real China" really has any business skills or knows what he is talking about.

Francis Chao does in fact have entrepreneurial and organizational skills, and he knows about aviation, and over the years he had cultivated contacts in China that would, he hoped, pay off whenever the aerospace boom finally came. In 1998, he published the first edition of the *China Civil Aviation Report,* which came out quarterly from his offices in Northern California. Each summer starting in 2001 he organized a China General Aviation Forum, at which a rotating cast of Western businesspeople met their Chinese counterparts and discussed prospects for aviation in China. In the late 2000s, Chao also produced and distributed some forty thousand copies of a glossy 130-page Chinese-language booklet called *What Is General Aviation?* ("什么是通用航空?") as part of an effort to convince Chinese regulators of the benefits of opening up their airspace to private flight.

By 2009, he felt he had made a breakthrough of sorts. It was not at the national level of high politics or policy but with a modest, soft-spoken, local academic-technocrat. The man in question, Gao Yuanyang, was officially the assistant mayor of Weinan Town but unofficially was one of the many idealistic dreamers in the provinces of China.

Gao, who was born in the remote southern province of Guizhou in 1963 and therefore was too young to be affected by much of the tumult of the Cultural Revolution years, had been trained in Beijing as an aeronautical engineer. Through the first ten years of his career he worked as a technician at the Guizhou Aviation Industry Group, near his original hometown. In 1999, he got an appointment teaching at his prestigious alma mater, BeiHang University—the name, 北航, is a "Caltech"-type shorthand for Beijing Hangkong Hangtian Daxue, the Beijing University of Aeronautics and Astronautics. In 2005, as a sign of his success and as part of his professional development, he was sent for a year as a visiting scholar to the Haas School of Business at U.C. Berkeley.

"I was sponsored by the government, so of course I had to do what they wanted when I came back," Gao told me in English when I first met him, with Francis Chao, in Beijing, shortly before the GA Forum. What the government wanted was for him to go spend a few years in Weinan, which was roughly comparable to a New Yorker's being assigned to a small city in Kansas, while his wife and child stayed back in Beijing. In

Weinan he was assigned his post as assistant mayor—since elec-
tions apply only up to the village level in China, mayor and
governor are appointed Party positions.

Rather than just wait out his posting, Gao decided to embrace
a dream: to make this remote part of Shaanxi province into
an international center for aviation research, sport flying, eco-
tourism, and luxury vacation sites. If his plans succeeded, the
Weinan environs would attract high-end tourists from China
and the rest of the world, and, meanwhile, would be an international center of aerospace development.The starting points
for the dream were the elements that Weinan and its boosters
considered its natural assets. These included a nearby marsh-
land that in principle could become a tourist-attracting wildlife
refuge; a local musical culture that featured a historic sort of
Chinese folk-blues singing; and one of the country's bona fide
and established tourist draws, a towering granite peak called
Huashan. (Imagine a less stark version of Yosemite's El Capitan,
with steep walkways, and bearers carrying heavy loads—small
refrigerators, five-gallon water bottles, full cases of beer—up the
thousand-plus steps to the cafés at the top.) With its location on
the edge of Xi'an's vast aerospace-industrial complex, which was
sited in keeping with Mao's concern of staying as far as possible
out of enemy bomber range, greater Weinan had potential that
was almost too obvious.

"We will make history!" Gao said. "Weinan is the dead center
of China. This can be a plus! For charters, for UPS, for FedEx.
You can get anywhere in an hour and a half"—this was the logic
that led to the choice of Memphis as the hub for FedEx—"and
you've got the huge aviation base in Xi'an."

Since this was China, would their next step be lobbying for a
grant from the national government in Beijing? That approach

would fit outside views of a centrally guided Chinese juggernaut, with dictates being handed down from on high, with funding too. Some big projects do operate that way, from the Olympic development to parts of the high-speed rail system. But in reality Gao and his Weinan team knew that, as with most Chinese development projects, the money would come mainly from city and county sources. The local governments' contributions might come in the form of free or low-cost leases for land; new roads, factory buildings, or other facilities built at public cost; tax holidays; favorable loans from banks allied with the local governments; investments from local tycoons; or all of these and more.

"They have given their blessing," Gao told me before our trip to Weinan, meaning that the development of local resorts and high-tech zones fit the larger scheme of a richer, more sophisticated China laid out in the revered Eleventh Five-Year Plan. It had been several years since he had spoken English regularly as a student at Berkeley, and he seemed both proud to be trying it out again on me and tentative in looking for words. "But . . ." at this point Francis Chao, the former interpreter, stepped in to say, "If this was going to be top-down, the government would step in to build the airport and buy the planes. With bottom-up, we have the local government involved."

Gao had arranged for eight other people from BeiHang to be put on semipermanent assignment to Weinan. Through Chao and others, city officials were in constant touch with investors, customers, and partners from around the world to work on projects. Their ambitions were practically unlimited and went in more hopeful directions than I can begin to recount here.

"We have the pilots," Gao said. "And we can have the mechanics. We need to learn the modern aviation mechanical skills! So why not bring in all the old abandoned airplanes from the U.S.? The ones they store in the desert. They might give them to us for free! Or for a low fee.

"We could bring them to China. We could upgrade and refit them. We could buy the spare parts and then learn how to build them. Our mechanics could touch the planes, and tear them apart, and put them back together again. Once we can fix it, then we can sell it! Maybe the U.S. won't take the planes back after we fix them. But there are other purchasers. There might be people who would be glad to have an airplane just for fun. This kind of airplane would be easy to register.

"We will have a flying school. We would have all the ingredients for an aerospace industry. We would be using aircraft in our everyday life!" At this first meeting, Assistant Mayor Gao saw where it all could lead. And Francis Chao expanded on the vision. "In China, we know that everyone tries to jump in on the same thing once it seems to work," he said. "So many people would want to copy this model of success! Our goal is not just to build the program but to build a model. Like a franchise! Connect the dots all around the country, and we would have a little piece of each dot."

Big-man politics, big dreams

This was the prospect that drew us to Weinan. Each time I went to some new corner of China I was startled by details I had not previously made mental space for before. That was the case in Weinan—I had not previously seen a huge runway surrounded by nothingness in the Chinese interior. But in other ways the fundamentals of this boosterish project resembled many others I had seen over the years.

The effort depended not simply on visionaries and dreamers, as represented in their different ways by the middleman Francis Chao and the aerospace bureaucrat Gao Yuanyang. It also depended on the support or at least thumbs-up verdict of the charismatic local Big Man, in this case the Communist Party boss for the Weinan area, a man in his late forties named Liang Fengmin.

If the phrase "regional Communist Party boss in China" calls up any image it might be of the laughably stiff figures seen on the commercial screen or stage. But Chairman Liang, like many of his counterparts whom I met in other provinces, was anything but reserved or formal. The instant I laid eyes on him, it became apparent what dramatic role he had cast himself in. He bore a strong resemblance to Chairman Mao in his prime, and he seemed to play up the similarities. His hair was slicked back, Mao style. He struck poses, cocked his head, and held his cigarette in ways immediately familiar from photos of Mao.

Twelve hours after starting out from my apartment in Beijing, I was toasting the Weinan Party leaders at an introductory reception and banquet. Through the following day of meetings and briefings the chairman said very little but nodded appreciatively as he took in the presentations about how much money the city would have to commit, and how glorious the payoff might be for the future of Weinan. When reading academic studies of how China ended up spending so incredibly much on infrastructure projects, I had seen countless reminders that the driving force was often a local booster effort. Businesses in a city or county—land developers, construction-firm owners, bankers, the equivalent of the Chamber of Commerce—convinced the local government or the Party boss that a new road, bridge, or shopping mall would be good for business all around. From the Party boss's point of view, every new project could mean an extra point in his area's GDP growth rate, which until recently had been by far the most important measure of success and grounds for promotion. (In the late 2000s, environmental measures were added to the report card for communist cadres, and of course maintaining order and containing dissent was obligatory.) The meetings in Weinan are what that prospect looked like up close. This was one element of the Weinan story that struck me as emblematic of much of recent Chinese hyper-development: the crucial role of local developers, officeholders, bankers, and boosters, rather than central-government planners directing development from afar.

As is usual in Chinese business gatherings, the daytime discussions were followed by a celebratory sealing-the-deal banquet. As the toasts went on and the new rounds of delicacies appeared, Chairman Liang dropped his reserve and seemed to take more and more kindly to the plan. It looked as if the project could proceed.

The second familiar and representative element in Weinan was the sheer scale of the investment in infrastructure, beyond what any "normal" reckoning of risks and opportunities might support. The day after the crucial bonding dinner with Chairman Liang, Assistant Mayor Gao, and other big men of the town, the visiting delegation rolled through the countryside to what was . . . an enormous new runway and paved area, with nothing around it but construction equipment. The idea behind this "trial zone" was that the Weinan area could have three small airports within a few dozen miles of each other. Planes could fly back and forth among them and eventually create an aerospace infrastructure! Tourists would come, and economic growth would follow.

There were some blank spots in this outline, but the Weinan team could worry about those concerns later. Meanwhile, the local authorities had gone ahead and paved what looked like the main runway at Dallas–Fort Worth airport, minus either Dallas or Fort Worth on the horizon, or any of the other sprawling developed tracts in between. The foreign visitors were stunned to walk around the tarmac in the baking heat, distracted mainly by posters showing an idealized version of how the scene might someday look.

Through the rest of the day I filled notebooks with the local planners' dreams and visions of what would become of these vacant zones in the bright sunshine. "Our runway apron is one hundred thousand square meters—very large!" a young English-speaking woman from the city government said. "We will have hangars, hotels, some aerospace-tech incubators."

It could happen. Similarly, the now-empty cities being built in western China's frontier districts might soon be populated, and the Armani stores and Maserati dealerships in Chengdu or Wuhan might pay off. All across China, I kept running into people determined to plow ahead despite all obstacles.

This led to a third familiar note in Weinan: a determination just to plow ahead, and to worry about obstacles later. We spent the rest of the day being entertained by musical and dancing troupes costumed in "authentic" village garb from the area. And then a few of the visitors asked about the problems no one had mentioned.

Great plans. But . . .

There were a lot of them. A constellation of obstacles made the gap between vision and the reality larger in aerospace than in many of the other high-tech or high-luxury schemes being cooked up at the same time elsewhere in China. Among the smaller problems: The country had very few pilots (fewer than three thousand, versus more than half a million with active pilot certificates in the United States and sixty thousand in Brazil). It still had very few airplanes, and the network of supply bases, fueling facilities, repair-and-maintenance shops, and other unglamorous but essential parts of the aerospace infrastructure were also undeveloped.

Flight schools were a particular problem for Chinese aviation. Flight training is a boom industry across China, as the airlines scramble to find crews for the steadily increasing schedule of flights. Chinese passenger airlines and freight-haul operations place "pilots wanted!" ads in North American and European aviation magazines.* At every flight school or airport I visited across the country, I met young foreign pilots and flight instructors who had come to China because they thought it was the land of opportunity in flight.

For instance, in a "small" town in eastern China with a population of about four million, in 2009 I met a North American

---

* Just to give a flavor, here is a sample ad I saw on a Western aviation site in 2011:

Sichuan Airlines—A320 Captains
(UPGRADED Package!)—Now the BEST OPPORTUNITY in China!
Domiciles: Chengdu, China
Requires: 600 hrs PIC [Pilot in Command] in type, 5,000 hours total time, Age under 55 years old
Compensation: $13,500 USD/month + $162.50 USD/hour for hours over 80
45 days paid personal leave per year
Approximately $162,000 USD/year
$18,000/USD bonus at the end of the first two years
$24,000/USD bonus at the end of the next two years
Contract Term: 2 years (renewable)

woman in her early thirties, and her slightly older European husband—they asked me to conceal their identities. Her job was to teach "aviation English" to young Chinese pilots; his was to teach them how to fly. While stuck in jobs they didn't like in North America, they had seen an ad in a flight magazine promising the great opportunities available in China.

From this couple I heard the same complaints I had heard at flight schools in several other locations in China. The students were poorly motivated, since in many cases they had been chosen for having good eyesight rather than for any particular interest in the skies. Their curriculum had the overemphasis on rote memorization and tests that was the bane of Chinese schools more generally. "I find that my 'textbook' for teaching English is the Boeing technical manual of the 747," the young American woman told me. "So rather than real English I am supposed to explain to them what a 'sugar-scoop air inlet' means." All training flights would be grounded for thirty minutes before and after the arrival of any commercial flight—no controller wanted to take a chance on a conflict or error. But during that time, as I saw in two regional airports myself, the instructors would keep the engines running on the grounded training planes. This burned out the engines (which overheat if they don't have air rushing through them at more than 100 mph for cooling) but counted as "training time" for their payroll purposes and for the students' instruction.[1]

But all these were incidental compared with the awkward fact that the kind of flying that the Weinan pioneers hoped to promote was still illegal in most of China. The Chinese military still "owns" most of the airspace in the country. Even the major airlines working from the big international airports had to humor, cajole, and wait out the PLA authorities for permission to fly. Compared with the flight corridors in and out of any other major world airport, those from Shanghai and Beijing were narrow, cramped outlets, which snaked through military-controlled airspace and made chronic delay and congestion almost inevitable. On the afternoon of December 1, 2006, all flights in and out of Shanghai's Pudong International Airport, at the time the second-busiest in China, were canceled without warning. Planes headed into Shanghai were rerouted elsewhere. The weather was fine, and none of the airport's equipment had malfunctioned, nor was there a terrorist threat. For hours there was no official explanation of what was happening; eventually, terse press accounts said only that the Central Military Commission had ordered the airport closed for several hours. Normal operations finally resumed that night. "Imagine if in the United States the U.S. Air Force decided to close Los Angeles' LAX airport for an afternoon, without any explanation or apparent reason," Christopher Jackson, an aviation analyst based in Hong Kong, wrote about the incident. "Imagine being shrugged at by airport ground staff, and told that 'military exercises' had caused your flight to be cancelled. This sort of thing has long been accepted as standard operating procedure in China."[2]

At smaller airports, I have seen civilian airport managers present local PLA officials with "red envelopes," including cash, at holiday time, or build "goodwill" in similar ways. "Very rarely will a military official say, 'I won't let you fly unless you pay me,'" a Western aviation expert who has worked for years in China told me. "Instead they'll say, 'I understand your problems! And if only our office had more modern computers or if our fax machine worked, we might be able to concentrate and do a better job.' Or they will point out the window and say,

'Yes, I would like to help, but right now I am worried about the terrible condition of my car.'" Another official told me that through the first decade of the twenty-first century, China's civilian aviation authorities "kept having to buy airspace from the PLA, mainly the little corner zones that allowed them to straighten out the main commercial routes and that can make a big difference in scheduling."

As wealth spread through the country, I heard more and more reports of people just deciding to fly despite the PLA. They went very low over roadways, in helicopters, in the flat southern parts of China—and in the mountainous west, they could fly at safer altitudes in airplanes, knowing that most of the region was beyond radar coverage. (Radar works on line-of-sight principles. If a hillside or other barrier shields a "rogue" plane from beams sent from the radar station, the radar operators have no idea that it is there.) But the new airparks couldn't operate sub rosa, and the question across the Chinese aviation world was when the PLA would back off.

The Chamber of Commerce meets the PLA

By 2010, the PLA was beginning to do so, and again for a reason practically never mentioned in the Chinese or U.S. press. Years earlier, both Boeing and the FAA had played a crucial, discreet role in bringing Chinese airlines up to acceptable safety standards. Something similar was about to happen with the business jets and private planes that both Chinese and foreign enterprises viewed as an upcoming bonanza.

Within the United States, the name Chamber of Commerce implies either a booster operation at the local level or a mainly conservative political lobby in Washington, D.C. But within

China, the two main "AmCham" organizations—the American Chambers of Commerce in Shanghai and Beijing—have proven to be tough, technically sophisticated, nonpartisan organizations that have often served as a necessary go-between and third party to ease dealings between the two governments. In the early days of the Obama Administration, American officials talked up the importance of joint Chinese-U.S. energy projects of various kinds. They did so both as a way of dealing with climate problems and in hopes of giving American firms a bigger share (compared with their technically advanced European, Japanese, and Korean rivals) of China's rapidly expanding market for clean-energy installations. But the Chinese government research institutes and the huge state-owned enterprises that dominated China's coal, electricity, and nuclear businesses found it awkward or confusing to deal with disparate American firms. Thus the AmCham of Beijing created the Energy Cooperation Program, or ECP, which was paid for by its members, and which provided a way for several dozen U.S. firms to coordinate their dealings with large Chinese counterparts. The firms were as sizable and established as GE and Honeywell, and as small as some electric-car and solar-power start-ups. "We're like one of those chemical agents, where you place one little drop in the water and suddenly it makes the crystals form," Sabina Brady, a long-time resident of Beijing who was the ECP's first director, told me in 2010. "The catalyzing process starts early, before you even talk to the Chinese, because it forces the industries to talk with each other. And then the Chinese are much more comfortable feeling there is one place where they can talk with 'the American side.'"

The ECP was modeled on the Aviation Cooperation Program, or ACP, sometimes known more grandly as the Wright Brothers Partnership, which the AmCham of Beijing had created late in 2003. It brought together United States–based companies that are ordinarily rivals—the main engine makers, GE and Pratt & Whitney; both Textron, which makes Cessna jets, and its competitors from Hawker Beechcraft; avionics makers like Honeywell and Rockwell Collins; both FedEx and UPS; United Air Lines along with American, Delta, and Northwest; architects and airport-equipment companies; plus others as large as Boeing and as small as the fledgling Cirrus—and put them under the public-private umbrella of the American Chamber of Commerce and the U.S. Department of Commerce's own Trade Development Administration. As its executive director, it chose the obvious candidate: Joe T, who had worked for both the FAA and Boeing and was a familiar figure to the Chinese from his visits and training sessions with CAAC.

The Aviation Cooperation Program soon became an important vehicle for connecting Chinese and U.S. companies, agencies, and individuals, and bringing Chinese institutions into ever greater conformity with international norms.[3] The ACP has arranged regular meetings between officials of the FAA and the CAAC. It has operated programs to train Chinese air-traffic controllers and airworthiness inspectors for Chinese airliners. Every year it sends a team of CAAC administrators and rule-makers to the United States for several weeks, where they receive executive management-development courses at air-traffic-control centers, at pilot-training sites for the major airlines, and at Boeing's assembly plant.

In the fall of 2006, a group of Chinese officials had come to Washington for a meeting of the every-other-year U.S.-China Aviation Summit, sponsored by the U.S. Trade Development Agency. During the day, many of them went to the FAA's Air Traffic Control System Command Center outside Washington. There they saw military officials working alongside civilian regulators, and in constant contact with representatives from the airlines and business-aviation organizations, to reroute flights and open corridors through military airspace as weather and traffic conditions demanded. It was a complete contrast to the norm in China, in which the military fiercely kept its airspace separate from civilian use. At twilight, the group went for cocktails to a rooftop restaurant at the Kennedy Center in downtown Washington. The wind was from the south, so flights landing at National Airport wound their way down the Potomac River, passing alongside the Kennedy Center at less than 1,000 feet elevation. "No one in Beijing had seen aircraft above the city," he told me several years later; airline flights were far out of town, and helicopters were very rare. "They got very excited and could hardly believe what they were seeing. They said, There's the Pentagon! And the White House! It is four years after 9/11, and the flights just kept coming in." The evening experience was, Joe T thought, more dramatic than any number of briefings in demonstrating what a liberalized air-traffic system might mean.

Through exchanges and experiences like these, American officials hoped to persuade Chinese regulators to view aerospace in all aspects as a natural part of the country's development, rather than as a security threat that needed to be fenced off carefully from the rest of life. For now let's set aside the irony of U.S. government officials talking a less rather than more security-minded view of air travel. From the Chinese perspective, the U.S. air-travel system as a whole still seemed a marvel of making police and soldier interests take second place to commercial and recreational interests. Business and private aircraft could go virtually anywhere they wanted in the United States, with little or no advance clearance or permission needed. Hence the standard scene in corporate-intrigue movies, where the passengers on a corporate jet tell the pilot that there's been a change in plans and they're heading for New Orleans now, not Little Rock. Nonmilitary aircraft in China could go virtually nowhere in China without submitting flight plans for approval several days in advance.

All this would have to change for the Weinan aerospace-utopia dreams to come true, along with their counterparts in other provinces across the country. Starting in 2007, the American members of the Aviation Cooperation Program began drawing up a United States–based manifesto for the transformation of China's airspace rules.

A manifesto for growth

By the summer of 2008, the consulting firm Booz & Company completed its draft of a 160-page study called "Catalyzing Growth in China's Regional and General Aviation Sectors," which had been commissioned by the Aviation Cooperation Program. With dozens of charts showing trends in Chinese transportation needs, and with extensive descriptions of the history and importance of aviation not just in America but in the other big, continental-scale countries where aviation played a major business role (Australia, Brazil, Canada), the report skillfully played on a twinned fear and hope often found among Chinese economic planners. The fear was that China would remain in a backward condition relative to other modern developed economies; the hope was that China could leap ahead and, by virtue of its scale, become a leader in yet another field. The "fear" charts showed where China stood now; the "hopes" showed what it could become.

The report also had an extensive road map for the regulatory steps China could take toward a phased and orderly opening of its airspace. First, it could create several trial zones to see what would happen if the controls came off. This proposal reflected a shrewd awareness of the steps Chinese leaders had actually taken in liberalizing their economy since 1979. Despite the image of the great monolith, China had in fact operated through the reform era as a patchwork of citywide or province-wide trials. If an approach—say, allowing more direct foreign investment—worked in its first trial near Shenzhen, then it might be expanded to Xiamen or Dalian. If it failed or didn't work as planned, it could be closed down and some other approach would be tried elsewhere. The Booz/ACP report suggested three initial trial zones.

One, in the bleak northeast of the country, would drop regulations so as to allow much freer use of planes and helicopters for agricultural and forestry use—crop-dusting, firefighting, transportation among far-flung sites. A second, in the industrialized southern areas of Guangdong province, would allow freer use of helicopters for business and personal transportation. In practice, this also meant legalizing a lot of the surreptitious chopper travel that was already going on. And the third proposed test zone would be . . . around Xi'an! This was where the proposal's writers thought conditions would be most promising for an aerospace-industrial-resort-educational complex, very much like the one the dreamers of Weinan hoped to create.

The report had other suggestions too, notably an experiment that would be nationwide rather than confined to one trial zone. In this proposed scheme, the military would give up control on "low level" airspace—roughly, the space between ground level and 1,000 meters above sea level—and watch to see what happened. This was a highly limited form of liberalization. In much of the country, ground level itself was more than 1,000 meters above sea level, so there would be no flying space at all.

Even in the low, flat coastal areas, only helicopters and small propeller planes could operate efficiently at such low altitudes. Still, it was a start.

Although the authors of the report could not have known or foreseen this, the Chinese government's willingness to listen suddenly increased after the devastating Sichuan earthquake, when thousands of survivors died of blood loss, shock, and exposure in the following two or three days, as rescuers tried to reach them on foot through steep terrain where existing roads had been wiped out. Because China's total helicopter fleet was smaller than, say, Portugal's, and barely one thousandth as large as that of the United States, there was simply no way to get supplies in or survivors out in time. Japan had suffered a serious though not catastrophic earthquake at about the same time; rescue helicopters were overhead in less than five minutes. In many devastated areas of Sichuan, it was five days before rescuers appeared.

The Chinese central government can ignore public opinion in many areas, but the appearance of delay, incompetence, or neglect in responding to tragedy is something it works hard to avoid. The potential to trigger popular outrage is too great. For the first few weeks after each of China's recent earthquakes, floods, or other great natural disasters, popular mood has been stoic and supportive of the government's efforts to save lives. But soon thereafter, bitter protests have broken out, led by parents asking why shoddily built schools collapsed onto their children, or homeless families asking who had vouched for the safety of a dam that broke. The central government took extra time examining the risks of expanded small-plane flight. But by the time the Aviation Cooperation Program held its U.S.-China Aviation Summit in the summer of 2009, the head of the CAAC made an announcement. There would be three "experimental" zones for freer flight rules: In the northeast, for agricultural flight; in the south, for helicopters; and near Xi'an, for an aerospace-industrial complex. A few months later, the Chinese government announced that the airspace from the ground to 1,000 meters above sea level would be opened for uncontrolled flight. In practice this of course created possibilities mainly for helicopters, which unlike most airplanes can operate effectively at altitudes that low. But rules for the next tier of airspace, up to 4,000 meters in elevation, were also relaxed. Pilots would still have to file flight plans in advance, but mere filing would be sufficient. They would no longer have to wait hours or days for government approval before departing. As part of the liberalization, the range of new test sites for freer flight was also expanded.

American officials limited themselves to saying that the moves seemed to make good sense and would enhance the promise of China's aviation future, rather than spelling out how closely the plans followed the recommendations of the ACP report.

The airspace seemed to be opening. The next step was to prepare Chinese companies to take advantage of this opportunity.

6 ★ An American Dream, Turned Chinese

Cirrus comes to China

I watched the effort to open China's skies from the perspective of the foreign flight instructors, the Chinese visionaries, and the veteran China-America hands like Joe T and Francis Chao who coördinated developments between the countries. But I saw it with particular interest and poignance through the course of the three-stage drama of the Cirrus Design Corporation and its ambitions in China. Compared with Boeing and Airbus, Pratt & Whitney, or GE, Cirrus is a niche player in the world's aerospace industry. But it has unexpectedly been at the center of important decisions about China's aviation future.

In the mid-1990s, while still in the United States, I began noticing in the aviation press increasingly excited reports concerning the young Klapmeier brothers, then of Baraboo, Wisconsin. In the inward-looking world of aerospace, they were inescapably likened to the Wright brothers a century before. Indeed, there were parallels: Like the Wrights they were Midwestern inventors and tinkerers, who could not be dissuaded from pursuing what seemed an impossible dream. Alan and Dale Klapmeier were born into an entrepreneurial family in small-town Illinois in the early 1960s, whose operations ranged from fiberglass-boat making to nursing homes. "Ours was not the kind of family where you ever assumed that you'd finish college and then just get a job," Dale Klapmeier told me when I first met him, in the late 1990s. "The idea was always that you'd start a business of your own." As teenagers both Alan and Dale had learned to fly and become airplane-design enthusiasts. While Alan was in college and Dale was still in high school, they would spend the summers building mock-ups of planes with spaceship shapes and futuristic propulsion systems.

In 1984, the brothers began working together full time on their airplane designs. By 1987 they had incorporated their grandly named Cirrus Design Corporation, based in a barn in rural Baraboo. Its first product, which was a technical success but a market failure, was the VK-30, an odd-looking but very fast plane that used a "pusher" propulsion system, with its engine and propellers at the rear. It was sold as an experimental aircraft, one that didn't have to go through rigorous FAA certification and that customers would fly at their own risk; also, it was a kit plane. Cirrus would ship off a huge crate containing the engine, major airframe parts, and all the internal controls and instrumentation, and then a customer would spend hundreds of hours of skilled labor assembling and testing the craft before it would fly. Not many of them sold. "We were looking for people who had hundreds of thousands of dollars to spend on the airplane, and the skill and time to put years of work into it," Dale Klapmeier told me in the late 1990s, long after market reality had set in. "Those people were not there."

The brothers borrowed money from parents and friends. They persevered in developing other models, all with a radically more streamlined, modern shape than had ever been seen on small-airport tarmacs accustomed to Cessnas and Pipers. Their ST50, another very high-speed "pusher" airplane, went into production as a joint venture with Israviation, an Israeli government-sponsored aerospace firm. Then Israeli politics turned against Israviation and its funding, and the project died after only two of the ST50s had been built.

Nearing the end of their spouses' and their family's patience (Alan got divorced around this time), nearing the end of their ability to borrow, nearing despair about their *Jetsons*-style dream of producing a plane that was safe, inexpensive, and convenient enough to make flying mainstream, the Klapmeiers and their team gave it one more try, with the airplane that was known as the SR20 and became the most famous small airplane in half a century. It was sleek-looking inside and out, like a leather-appointed Mercedes or BMW rather than a Jeep. It was intended to be a huge step forward in safety, with its built-in parachute for the whole plane and with computer-age graphics and navigation tools that were far more informative, intuitive, and advanced than what was available in the cockpits of most airliners. At least initially it was inexpensive, by aerospace standards. It was, in its way, the Macintosh of the small-airplane world; Cirrus, in its new headquarters along Lake Superior in Duluth, was the Apple. In 2001, I wrote a book about the Klapmeier brothers and other modern aerospace innovators, *Free Flight*. I also bought an early model Cirrus SR20 and flew it frequently, before selling it when we moved to China.

When the Cirrus SR20 came onto the market in 1999 it was an immediate hit. It was followed late in 2000 by a faster, more powerful model called the SR22. By 2003, the SR22 overtook various well-established Cessna models to become the best-selling small propeller aircraft in the world, a title it has held ever since. By the mid-2000s, Cirrus had silenced most marketing, business, and technology doubters and was extending its sales network worldwide.

Developing and certifying airplanes, especially new models from a brand-new company, takes an almost limitless amount of up-front capital. The kinds of well-heeled clients who might consider being early customers are notably demanding and fickle. The business was terribly vulnerable to any surprising bad news—surprises in this field usually coming in the form of a fatal airplane crash. Cirrus's entire existence was called into question by a crash in 1999, just before the first SR20 customers were due to receive their planes. That crash killed Scott Anderson, a local hero from Duluth who had gone to Stanford and then returned as an Air National Guard fighter pilot and early member of the Cirrus team. Anderson had flown most of the tests in the southwestern desert that led to development of the famous Cirrus whole-airplane parachute. But for this final test flight before the SR20 went out to customers, he was in an airplane that had not yet had its parachute installed. Because of an aileron problem, he could not control the plane. He attempted to guide it back to the main Duluth airport but instead crashed into a federal prison facility less than a mile from the airport and Cirrus's headquarters. The company, in mourning, survived commercially only by reminding customers and the press that every Cirrus delivered to a customer would come equipped with a parachute—the parachute that Anderson had helped develop and that could presumably have saved him.

The Klapmeiers never had quite enough money for the next round of production equipment, the next increase in sales staff, the next set of computers to design the next generation of airplanes. So in 2001, just before the shock to business in general and the aviation business in particular that followed the 9/11 attacks, they sold a controlling interest in the company—58 percent of a firm their family had tightly controlled—for $100 million, to Crescent Capital. Crescent was based in Atlanta and staffed by Americans, but it was the business arm of First Islamic Investment Bank of Bahrain, that country's sovereign investment fund. After the sale there was a flurry of concern and criticism in the aviation world about the significance of selling this gem of American innovation to an "Islamic interest." The real significance, as would become clear a few years later in China, was the Klapmeiers' loss of control to a company that, as they knew from the start, hoped to get its money back out within six or seven years.

Stage one of the Cirrus drama, then, was the company's debut as the innovative darling of the industry. Like other start-ups it was always looking for money—but it managed to keep finding it. As it was introduced into each new market—Brazil, France, England, Australia—its planes soon became best-sellers there as they had been elsewhere.

From a Chinese point of view, in 2006, when I saw Peter Claeys undertake his sales attempts from his office in Shanghai, a small airplane was purely a conspicuous-consumption luxury good. Almost no one in China who was qualified to fly an airplane could afford to buy one. Almost no part of Chinese airspace was open to legal flight by anything other than airliners or military planes. So Claeys was in the business of trying to ride China's early luxury boom. I saw him propose to coal millionaires from Inner Mongolia the advantages of having an airplane (even though there was no place to fly it), in addition to the yachts they had bought (that they had no place to sail). At an aviation conference that I attended with Claeys, I chatted with a potential Cirrus customer from southern China who had no intention of flying the plane but thought it would be impressive if parked in front of the company's headquarters. In the end, he didn't buy.

Claeys spent his days in endless frustration with the realities of trying to fly a plane inside China—where to get fuel, how to get flight-plan clearance, how to train mechanics to serve the demo planes he operated inside the country. Cirrus's market position was unique. Less expensive airplanes, from Cessna or Piper, were far less glamorous and therefore had little value as status symbols. More capable airplanes, like Gulfstreams or Falcons, cost from ten to one hundred times as much as a Cirrus and were too expensive for mere display.

Cirrus tries "reform from within"

At this time, Cirrus's prospects in China were always promising but never actually profitable. Claeys would court a rich customer, close a deal to sell a plane—only to have delivery held up for months by Chinese customs inspectors, at which point the Chinese multimillionaire might lose interest and think of buying a villa or a vineyard instead. Sometimes a purchaser would back out when a shift in exchange rates made this luxury seem too expensive, or when the tumultuous changes in the Chinese economy meant that a thriving business had suddenly failed. As of early 2008, a total of five Cirrus SR22s had reached customers within mainland China.

Rather than working strictly within the constraints of a boutique Chinese market, Cirrus decided to place more emphasis on trying to remove those constraints. In cooperation with other foreign aerospace firms, it attempted to speed China's transformation into a society where more people could legally fly small airplanes, and thus in which more people and companies would have a rational incentive to buy them. Around the time of the Beijing Olympics the company's public face in China changed from Peter Claeys—fluent Mandarin speaker, European cosmopolite, expert in Asian cultures, and scholar of Buddhism who happened to work for an airplane company—to

Paul Fiduccia, a lifelong aviation buff from America whose new assignment happened to be China.

Peter Claeys had been based in Shanghai and had concentrated mainly on the Chinese nouveau riche in the southern half of the country. Paul Fiduccia commuted between Cirrus's headquarters in Duluth and Beijing, where for days on end he met with the bureaucrats and administrators who would eventually decide whether to open Chinese airspace to civilian small-airplane flight.

Fiduccia, in his late fifties, was a longtime friend of the Klapmeier brothers and, like them, he had been in and around airplanes since he was a teenager. Through the 1980s he was a consultant on projects for the FAA and NASA, mainly for changing their regulations to reflect technical advances in navigation systems, weather forecasting, and safety devices. He spent his days in China talking to government officials about why they should change their policies, and providing specific suggestions of how the new policies should look.

When he was in Beijing, Fiduccia explained to CAAC officials how they might coordinate their safety or inspection practices with international standards. When he visited Zhuhai or Xi'an or Badaling, he spoke with local airport authorities about the practicalities of setting up a flight school, or how airspace could be more efficiently configured, or how to develop an emergency-rescue service to airlift accident victims to hospitals. Cirrus was paying him for the same reason Ford or General Motors might have sent road-safety experts on tour in the 1920s to give advice on engineering better highways.

I often had dinner with Fiduccia during his stays in Beijing. "I like you fine, Jim," he told me one time, "but no offense, the main reason I look forward to seeing you is to hear some English." The rest of his days and weeks in China were spent inside Chinese organizations, working through interpreters. At each of our meetings, he was disgruntled and frustrated, like most foreigners—and for that matter like most Chinese people—trying to pick their way through the country's modern bureaucracy. "I figure the only reason we use the word 'Byzantine' is that at the time Western people didn't have enough experience with Chinese bureaucracy," he told me after one particularly frustrating siege. "If they had, we'd use 'Chinese.'"

There were signs of change, particularly the three new "general aviation test zones." The reliance on test zones was entirely consistent with the pattern of Chinese liberalization through the previous thirty years. Rules were lifted in a variety of ways at a variety of test sites. If all went well, the government would extend the new approach to another set of provinces or towns. That is how economic liberalization had spread from the original "Special Economic Zones" like Zhuhai and Xiamen to most of the country, and Fiduccia and his allies within the CAAC assumed it could work in similar fashion in aviation.

By the end of 2009, when CAAC officially promulgated its "Notice of Issuance of Relevant Measures for Accelerating the Development of General Aviation," Fiduccia and other foreigners who had been working to transform China's approach to airspace and aviation thought that their work was at last paying off. The deceptively dull-sounding "Relevant Measures" document contained a number of statements with potential. The ingredients were all there: An emphasis on taking a scientific approach to the development of general aviation, "scientific approach" being shorthand in Chinese communist officialese for "doing it the right way." A promise of government funding of $25 million per year to build and maintain new airports. An emergency emphasis on new small airports that could be used to support disaster-relief efforts. The establishment of test zones

with relaxed flight rules. A profession of belief in the importance of private aviation to China's emergence as a fully modern
business culture and economy. A reminder that aerospace technology would be the arena for China's next breakthroughs and
successes.

Fiduccia was cheerier than normal at our dinner at a Thai restaurant in the Sanlitun district of Beijing just before the report
came out, because he sensed the direction it was heading. "So
far, everyone is saying the right thing," he said. He reeled off a
list of cities where officials seemed interested in Weinan-type
projects. "There are lots of wealthy people all around," he said.
"With just a few of them, you can make this work." The global
aircraft industry was in another slump just then, because of the
global financial crash of 2008, and Cirrus was confronting the
worst sales downturn in its history. "It's never easy here," Fiduccia said, "but China can be what keeps our production lines
open."

From Zhuhai to Duluth

He turned out to be right. Cirrus became more fully integrated
into China's aerospace ambitions in a way few would have foreseen when the optimistic young Klapmeier brothers were first
bringing their revolutionary new designs to the market. As markets plunged and trillons of dollars' worth of paper wealth disappeared in the economic collapse, orders for Cirrus airplanes
"dropped off a cliff," as one company official told me at the time.
The company had produced 721 airplanes in 2007; by 2010, its
output had fallen to 264. Something similar, though milder, had
happened in the aftermath of the 2001 terror attacks. But back
then Cirrus was still a small, very low-overhead, start-up-phase

company with only a few hundred of its planes in service around the world. Its relative handful of employees were accustomed to belt-tightening. The small size of the delivered fleet meant that it did not need an extensive network to stock spare parts or answer questions and complaints from customers.

Cirrus was in a very different position when sales collapsed again in early 2009. By then its design and manufacturing workforce was over a thousand. It had a large customer-service division to take care of the thousands of airplanes flying on every continent but Antarctica. It was investing heavily in the Klapmeier brothers' next dream project, a small, fast, safe, relatively inexpensive "personal jet." As new orders disappeared, it could not lay off the service staff; they were "fixed overhead," the long-term obligation created by its previous success in selling airplanes. Alan Klapmeier did not want to delay or cancel work on the jet, which the company had publicized heavily as the key to its commercial and technological future. Also, since announcing the jet project in 2007, the company had taken deposits of $100,000 apiece from customers eager to get an early place in the delivery line a few years hence. Those deposits provided some of the working capital for R & D on the jet, and they were spent as soon as they came in. But in a confident (or extravagant) gesture during the boom times of 2007, the company had made those deposits fully refundable. If word got out that the jet was being scrapped, depositors would inevitably rush to get their cash back, and Cirrus would be in even more serious trouble trying to cover this counterpart to a run on the bank.

At the request of the Klapmeiers, the managerial staff of Cirrus took a 10-percent pay cut in 2008 and again in 2009, but as sales continued to fall there was no alternative to laying off production staff. From its peak employment of fifteen hundred in

2007, Cirrus was down to six hundred employees by the beginning of 2009. That reflected the results of two big layoff waves, and a third was apparently in store.

At that point, everything about Cirrus's story changed, when Alan Klapmeier was forced out of the company. In the aviation business, this was instantly likened to what had happened at Apple twenty-five years before, when Steve Jobs was ousted from the company he had helped found. Like Jobs before him, Alan Klapmeier lost the crucial struggle between his view of what the company "should" do and the financiers' judgment of what it "had to" do to survive.

The majority owners from Crescent Capital, having invested in 2001 in hopes of a relatively quick payout, had started looking for purchasers during the flush times before the 2008 financial collapse. They had considered a range of private-equity offers but not nailed down a deal. They did not want to put in any more of their own money—but further investment was what Alan Klapmeier was asking for. He said it would be a costly error to postpone work on the jet. In the short term, the company had no way to cover the inevitable demand for refunded deposits, and in the longer run, without a jet it would have no way really to broaden its business whenever customers began buying again.

Crescent Capital was looking to cut its losses rather than deepen them. It had an ally in Brent Wouters, a consulting-firm veteran who had come to Cirrus a year earlier as its CFO. The contrast between him and Alan Klapmeier was stark. Klapmeier had pictures and models of airplanes not just at his office but all over his home; inside the front door of his house was a glass display case holding hundreds of small airplane models. Wouters had no apparent passion for aviation and in presentations referred to Cirrus aircraft as "our product" rather than as air-

planes. As an aviation enthusiast who had become a businessman, Klapmeier wanted to keep spending on future airplanes.
Wouters, a financial-management expert who happened to
work at an airplane company, wanted to hold down the payroll
to let the company survive the tough times. In a family drama
that became the talk of Duluth, but whose details none of the
participants has fully disclosed, Dale Klapmeier—the younger,
less extroverted and outspoken, operations-rather-than-vision
member of the family—sided with Wouters and Crescent Capital. In February 2009 they voted Alan Klapmeier out as CEO,
and Brent Wouters in.

Wouters had two crucial objectives, only one of which was
publicly discussed. The first was to lower the company's "burn
rate," or fixed operating costs, through whatever means it took,
so that it could get by on its reduced sales levels in worldwide
hard times. More layoffs ensued, bringing the workforce to four
hundred fifty. The aviation press was full of grumbles from Cirrus suppliers who waited months for payment; two of them
sued. The company said that jet work was proceeding at full
speed, but many of the crucial engineers and designers on that
project had left or been laid off. Jet depositors who asked for
their money back waited six months or more before they saw
the cash.

The company did survive, and long enough for Wouters to
realize the other goal Crescent Capital had set: to sell the company to the only apparent source of ready cash during a crisis, the Chinese government. In the spring of 2009, soon after
his ascent as CEO, Wouters began negotiations with China's
AVIC, working through an overseas middleman whose specialty
was brokering this kind of deal. Despite their own problems in
coping with the aftermath of the financial crisis in 2009, big
Chinese corporations and state agencies recognized that their

relative position in the world economy continued to improve. Businesses and governments in the rest of the world needed cash. Chinese businesses and government interests had it. So their deliberations, as I heard in many interviews with Chinese officials at the time, concerned how to manage their international expansion deftly rather than clumsily. The businesspeople laying out this strategy had typically worked or studied extensively outside China. They understood—as the little-traveled leaders of China's political hierarchy did not—why a sudden influx of Chinese cash, Chinese control, and Chinese faces might create resistance in countries that received this influx.

Many of the Chinese authorities also understood that the situation would be all the more delicate with an aerospace company like Cirrus. It was a prime example of American innovation and enterprise. Its takeover by the rising Chinese might be perceived as a symbol of American decline. The jobs it provided, though reduced in number, were high-paying factory jobs in the hard-pressed Midwest. Would they too be shipped to China? Even though Cirrus planes were in non-American hands all around the world, and even though Cirrus was actively bidding to sell its planes to the People's Liberation Army Air Force as trainers (the U.S. Air Force Academy in Colorado Springs had already bought some for that purpose), a sale to "the Chinese" would require Federal clearance[1] to be sure U.S. national security was not at risk.

For these reasons and others, negotiations remained secret through 2009 and 2010. When the deal was announced, at a press conference in Duluth on February 27, 2011, all involved in the transaction did what they could to assuage both local and national concerns about what this transaction might signify. The mayor of Duluth, Don Ness, said that the Chinese officials had assured him that they would keep jobs there rather than transfer them to China. "They've made every indication that it is their intent not only to maintain their local operations but to grow jobs here in Duluth," he said.

Promises, promises—but the city signed on as a party to the deal, offering forgiveness on rent paid for city property, if and only if Cirrus employment in Duluth went up rather than down under Chinese ownership. Two months later, Mayor Ness got what he considered a more tangible commitment. After Minnesota's two senators, Al Franken and Amy Klobuchar, sent a letter to the new Chinese parent company of Cirrus, asking for more details about its employment plans, the head of that company came to Duluth for another signing ceremony. President Meng Xiangkai, an aerospace engineer who had risen to become head of the China Aviation Industry General Aircraft group, or CAIGA, invited Ness to the Cirrus plant. Ness presented him with a carefully negotiated one-page memorandum saying that CAIGA intended to keep the manufacturing plant in Duluth, and to maintain or increase employment levels, even as it expanded sales and eventually production elsewhere. Meng, with a smile on his face, signed.

There was an extra safeguard for jobs in Duluth that most news reports left undiscussed. If the new Chinese owners wanted to make the planes in China and have them sold in any market except their own, they would need to receive a new production certificate from the FAA and its international counterparts. Certification is a time-consuming and extremely painstaking process, the prospect of which would presumably keep jobs in Duluth for the foreseeable future. If the Chinese owners did take this step, it would be a sign that they were serious about building up their own Chinese abilities in aerospace, rather than just buying foreign assets. The acquisition, while the most heralded, was only one in a continuing series that Meng Xiangkai had overseen. His CAIGA group, designed to produce future rivals to Cessna, Hawker Beechcroft, Gulfstream, and—if it didn't already own it—Cirrus, was one of several subsidiaries of the catch-all Chinese aviation consortium AVIC. Before coming to CAIGA, Meng had been head of another subsidiary, the Xi'an Aircraft Industry (Group) Company (which for some reason goes by the English acronym XAC). In 2009, he signed a deal by which XAC bought an Austrian company called FACC, a component supplier to Boeing and Airbus.

In an interview with the Chinese press after that sale, he explained why he thought it so important to look for further takeover targets: "If we remain at the low end of the aviation industry chain, it will do us no good in the international division of labour and we will never be able to find an equal partnership," he said. "If we want to survive in the aircraft manufacturing industry, we must keep an open mind and have an international vision."[2] Toward that end, after his move to CAIGA early in 2010, Meng had arranged the purchase of Epic, a small-jet company based in Oregon, in March, 2010, and in September the purchase of Teledyne Continental, in Mobile, the main manufacturer of piston engines for small airplanes including Cirrus.

In July, 2011, the Cirrus sale passed government security reviews in both the United States and China. On behalf of CAIGA, Meng Xiangkai issued a congratulatory statement. "We are very impressed with Cirrus' performance in the global general aviation industry," he said, in Chinese ceremonial hortatory style. "It has a very strong record of consistent product excellence, comprehensive safety features, an outstanding management team, and a highly skilled workforce who operate from advanced production facilities."[3] To mark the occasion and to welcome a team of engineers, trainee pilots, service representatives, and other CAIGA staff members who were coming to Duluth for familiarization and training, Cirrus officials draped a huge banner across the hangar where officials from both companies would speak. It expressed greetings and hearty welcome to the new partners arriving from CAIGA.

Just before the ceremony, one of the CAIGA officials asked his Cirrus counterpart please to take the banner down before the speaking began. What was the problem? "The banner says 'partners.' But we are not partners. We are the owners." The concept of ownership had survived the communist era intact.

7 ★ China's Own Boeing

The Chinese airliner of the future

The world's established aircraft-makers have one big question about China. It is their specific version of the question the rest of the world has about China as a whole. In its simplest form: Is China more of a threat? Or an opportunity? If it's both, is it more of one or the other? If the answer to that question is uncertain, when will outsiders know which is more likely? And is there anything they can do to bend the result in the direction they would prefer?

In the special world of airplanes, the question takes the form of balancing the opportunities of the world's fastest-growing market with the challenges posed by the world's most rapidly expanding industrial base. The great promise for Boeing and Airbus, and for their smaller brethren like Embraer and Gulfstream, Cessna and Beech, is to sell more of their products in the one country likely to increase its fleet dramatically in the next ten years. The great nightmare for these same companies is that the price of entering the Chinese market will be joint ventures, technology transfers, potential theft of intellectual property, and local-content requirements that in effect force them to create and foster the Chinese competitors who will one day unseat them. Even if a resurgent China does not create competitive aerospace companies of its own, it might use its always growing financial reserves simply to buy up whatever firms have become world leaders, as it began doing in 2010 in the helicopter, engine, and small-aircraft ends of the market.

The balance between opportunity and threat will depend on decisions being made now and in the next few years by companies, financiers, and governments in North America, Europe, South America, India, and elsewhere, of course including China. The obstacles the Chinese face are different from what is generally assumed outside the aerospace industry, and more imposing than many people inside or outside China might guess.

The Chinese efforts in this regard are significant in their own right, because of the importance of the aerospace industry to American exports and general high-tech success. They also offer a near-perfect distillation of the strengths and limitations of China's larger attempts to will its way up the ladder of high-tech industrial economic value. That is, they illustrate very clearly the unusual combination of traits that have characterized China's efforts in other fields: openness to foreign efforts combined with a determined effort to increase the Chinese share; a powerful role for state ownership and government guidance combined with room for private initiative. So far, the Chinese efforts look more like an expensive way to pursue national grandeur than a real step toward economic, technological, military, or strategic power. But that could change.

Trying to build an aircraft industry

Through the Mao era, aviation was backward, mainly military, and strictly government-controlled. Through the first twenty-plus years of the opening under Deng Xiaoping, it remained backward, and also remained more government-controlled than most of the rest of the economy, which was gradually being liberalized. In the early 1990s, under President Jiang Zemin, the giant conglomerate called AVIC, the Aviation Industry Corporation of China, was created from the diverse aerospace factories and organizations that had been part of the military or other government ministries. In the late 1990s, AVIC was split into two groups: AVIC 1, dealing with large airplanes and military aircraft, and AVIC 2, for smaller airplanes and helicopters. And in 2008, it was all reorganized once again, this time in the reconsolidated Commercial Aircraft Group of China, or COMAC. That is the main institution now pursuing China's airplane-building plans.

COMAC and its subsidiary groups are theoretically independent businesses but in reality are part of the great penumbra of state-influenced organizations in China. The influence, as we have seen in the cases of Weinan and Zhuhai, comes not just from national officials but also from provincial and city officials hoping to be part of a new boom, or to somehow make it happen in their hometowns. As with so many aspects of modern China's tech-based industries, the organizations share both corporate and governmental traits. As Tai Ming Cheung, of U.C. San Diego, pointed out in a 2010 report on Chinese aerospace prepared for the United States–China Economic and Security Review Commission, a group that keeps a watchful eye on signs of Chinese military and technical predation, the creation of AVIC and COMAC signaled several steps toward more market-minded operation of a still government-guided operation.[1] This reorganization, Cheung wrote, was a necessary corrective for the legacies of the Mao era, including "the widespread duplication and balkanization of industrial and research facilities."

What do the resulting entities make, and do? In principle,

COMAC and its allied Chinese subunits represent nearly the entire range of aerospace activity.[2] At the most sophisticated end, Chinese companies are near completion of one "regional jet" competitor, known as the ARJ21, which would compete with Embraer and Bombardier models (and in U.S. terms might be used for, say, the Washington–Charlotte or Seattle–Spokane routes). It would hold about ninety passengers, it has been in development since 2008, and nearly all of the orders that have been placed are from "captive" airlines—the state-controlled Chinese domestic lines. COMAC is also beginning development of its C919, a "single-aisle" airliner comparable to—and, its developers hope, eventually competitive with—the Airbus A320 or the Boeing 737. At the bottom end, Chinese companies have for years made a number of Soviet-style, antique-looking planes used mainly for crop-dusting and similar chores.

COMAC and some still military-controlled companies are also planning to build almost any other flying-related product you can think of. Rockets to launch satellites. Satellites themselves, including a system to rival the existing United States–run GPS network. (And since the current GPS system is not just "United States–run" but managed by the United States Air Force, it is hard to blame the Chinese military for recommending this step. War between the United States and China is unlikely, but if it happened, the PLA would not want to have its navigation systems vulnerable to disruption by the other side.) Apart from the large-scale commercial airliners to compete with Boeing and Airbus, there will be smaller regional planes to compete with Embraer and Dassault, and private aircraft to compete with Cessna and Hawker Beechcroft. Helicopters to fill what seems to be an enormous market void. And behind all of these is the same integration in the global supply chain that has made

China a low-wage, low-value power in many electronic projects, and that makes Japan and Germany high-value-component producers now.

How Chinese manufacturers would prevail

If you were going to write the script by which Chinese aerospace interests convert their current plans into eventual world dominance, the steps might be described as follows:

1. *Political pressure.* All around the world, but even more so in China, the market for airplanes depends on political as much as commercial factors. The central government of China, when it does not directly approve or determine airlines' purchasing plans, heavily influences them. It is in the government's interest to play Boeing and Airbus against each other, so neither will be allowed a fully dominant share—and both will be affected by larger political relations between their home base and the Chinese government. Through the early 1990s, before Airbus had really gotten going, Boeing provided nearly all the new airliners for China, and Boeing officials were de facto liaisons between the Chinese and American aviation establishments. By 2010, Boeing's share stood at 55 percent, and Airbus's at 43 percent. Each of them knew that future changes would depend on their commercial improvements—but also on the government's decisions about the right balance to set. The more heavily the balance eventually shifts in favor of China's own emerging producers, the less will obviously remain for either Airbus or Boeing.

2. *Shifts of production.* Among the criteria the Chinese government obviously watches very closely are foreign companies'

willingness to teach local Chinese firms and workers to do
what the foreigners did. Thus Airbus set up its only assembly plant outside Europe in Tianjin, not far from Beijing, in
the late 2000s, where it assembled most of the Airbuses that
China agreed to buy. Similarly, GE agreed in 2011 to share
engine technology with a COMAC subsidary, as part of
an arrangement to supply engines for the C919; Boeing
increased its reliance on Chinese suppliers; the small-plane
manufacturers Cessna and Diamond set up production
plants in China; and others in the business shifted their
production to where they hoped the market would be.

3. *Transfer of knowledge.* By legitimate learning or unauthorized copying, Chinese firms quickly learn what the foreigners know, leading to:

4. *The natural conclusion.* Lower-cost production at higher
volumes from Chinese factories, with bigger shares of the
market inside China, which in turn becomes a platform for
exports around the world. Former Western industry leaders
must find another business.

That's the model, which with variations has shown up in
other industries from light electronics to clean-energy products
to cars. And there are many people who argue that it will inescapably apply in aerospace as well. In 2001, when the prospect
of Chinese-made airliners was largely speculative, a Boeing engineer laid out a trenchant internal case that the company's reliance on outsourcing would send it into a cycle of self-inflicted
decline, opening the door to aspirants from China and elsewhere. The engineer, an Australian named L. J. Hart-Smith,
argued that outsourcing would undermine Boeing's ability
to create succeeding generations of high-value aircraft, since
insights about those future offerings often came from the
hands-on experience of making and tinkering with the current

product line. He also showed the perverse conflict between the pressures and incentives on each of the component parts of the system. For example, a company that produced struts or other small but crucial components of an airplane would optimize its profit for that strut. But in doing so it would have no incentive to worry about Boeing's larger efficiency and quality control as it matched that strut to components coming from a variety of other sources.[3]

In principle, Boeing or other outsourcers would foresee and allow for all these variations, and coordinate instructions to its suppliers so that they all served Boeing's larger goal. Companies from Walmart to Dell and Apple have used worldwide supply chains to their evident advantage. But subcontractors make computers for Dell and clothes or toys for Walmart in batches of millions per year. They have daily opportunities to refine any part of the process that isn't working, and at relatively small cost if a few days' production goes bad. It is different for airliners, which are produced in small quantities and at very high unit costs. The multiyear delay and huge cost increases of Boeing's 787 "Dreamliner" seemed, by the time of its introduction, in 2011, to illustrate all of the concerns Hart-Smith—and the Machinists' Union, which naturally opposed outsourcing—had raised within Boeing a decade before.

The marketplace and technological concepts behind the Dreamliner were the direct opposites of those applied by Airbus in its development of the world's largest airliner, the A380. Plans for both airplanes were first sketched out in the late 1990s, with engineering, development, and testing stretching out over most of the next decade. The A380, which, depending on seating layout, could hold between 500 and an appalling 825 passengers, was intended for very heavily trafficked hub-to-hub routes in airline "hub-and-spoke" systems. It would carry people from London to Dubai, from New York to Frankfurt, from Singapore to Shanghai. Once at those hubs, passengers would switch to smaller airplanes for "spoke" flights to their real destinations.

The Dreamliner was designed for lower-capacity "point-to-point" flights. Depending on its seating layout, it would hold between 210 and 290 passengers. But it would do so with lower fuel costs and emissions, and with more attention to interior comfort and layout, than previous Boeing or Airbus models. Boeing's market planners believed that the world's hub-and-spoke networks were becoming unsustainably clogged. An airplane that could operate profitably with smaller passenger loads would allow airlines to offer more of the point-to-point routes—Singapore direct to Seoul rather than through Tokyo, Rome to New York nonstop rather than through Heathrow—that most travelers preferred.

In addition to this shift from prevailing practice in market concept, the Dreamliner also represented a change in Boeing's manufacturing strategy. Starting as far back as the 1960s with the 747, Boeing had successfully outsourced parts of each aircraft model's production. The 747's fuselage was outsourced to Northrop; then Japanese and Italian companies produced major components of the 777, which was a technological and commercial triumph. The difference with the 787 was that Boeing went much further in its outsourcing, in what one industry analyst described to me as a "big, dumb, costly mistake."

With the 787, Boeing outsourced not simply specific components but much of the design and integration of the aircraft, which had been its distinguishing advantage. A larger share of the plane's components and subassemblies would be contracted out to suppliers, including many in Japan and some in China.

Less of the work would be done start-to-finish under Boeing's own control. This was economically rational, in that many contractors could beat Boeing's internal price. But in a larger business sense it proved problematic, since delays from the contractors and difficulties in combining and coordinating their work caused a rippling series of postponements in the Dreamliner's delivery date.

"Boeing's goal, it seems, was to convert its storied aircraft factory near Seattle to a mere assembly plant, bolting together modules designed and produced elsewhere as though from kits," Michael Hiltzik, of the *Los Angeles Times,* wrote in early 2011, as the plane's delivery was postponed yet again.[4] "But it ended up costing more and slowing the plane, and reducing the company's control over the technologies that would be the longer run sources of value. . . . As a result of this whole setup, a plane that was designed to be a breakthrough in many ways—longer ranged, more efficient, quieter, dominant in its market share, a smarter approach for point-to-point travel than Airbus's giant A380—this plane missed its opportunity in being at least three years later and grievously over cost."

The many obstacles in COMAC's way

It would seem logical enough to fear, therefore, that the combination of forces set up in China would almost certainly lead to the rise of COMAC, the C919, and the rest of the Chinese aerospace lineup—and the consequent eclipse of Boeing, Airbus, Embraer, and the other foreign competitors. So many factors are working in China's favor: scale, finance, control of the market, control of supply chains, lower-cost labor, ability to make the foreign companies with the advanced systems do its bidding. So many corresponding perils endanger those foreign firms.

So it could well be that the aerospace industry rankings of 2030 will start with COMAC, and maybe include other private Chinese firms before they get to shrunken versions of Boeing, Airbus, and Embraer. Or perhaps, like Cirrus and Epic, those companies will by then have been absorbed into the Chinese production system.

Since that seems so obvious a conclusion, it is worth considering just the opposite possibility. Perhaps the aerospace industry will reveal the limits of the Chinese model, rather than its limitless power. In other words, a China capable of creating its own Boeing, its own Airbus, would have to be a transformed China from the one we know now.

According to Richard Aboulafia, an aviation expert with the Teal Group, a market-analysis firm, in Washington, "There are two ways to build an aviation industry. Smart and dumb. The way China is doing it is not the smart way."

Aboulafia is not the only analyst who has made the case that the spend-first, think-later approach that has kept the Chinese economy humming but has led to such overbuilding of apartments, toll roads, railways, and even airports, will not succeed when it comes to building modern airlines and airliners. But he makes the case more vividly than most.

"An awful lot of China's aviation effort has been simple boosterism on a massive scale," Aboulafia told me in Washington in the summer of 2010. "You've got a lot of 'activity' related to this plane." He was talking in specific about the new Chinese regional jet, the ARJ21, but he meant the larger C919 as well.

"People are getting paid. People are getting rich. It's all adding points to the growth rate of the GDP. The question is whether it's going to *lead* anywhere at all." And his argument is that, on current evidence, it will not.

Aboulafia has a larger theory about the circumstances in which state-guided catch-up industrial policies, like what China is trying to apply in aerospace, can and cannot pay off. In brief: world industrial history is full of examples of successful government sponsorship of industry, especially in high-tech fields. But it contains even more examples of wasteful, misdirected, ill-timed, or corrupt undertakings. Governments, Aboulafia argues, should be very selective about what they back, with a bias toward keeping hands off, since they are so likely to be wrong. And he concludes that most of the signals about China's aerospace ambitions are highly discouraging—if, that is, their purpose really is to foster internationally competitive aerospace companies rather than just keeping people on payrolls now.[5]

Aboulafia's analysis also turns on the peculiar circumstances that make building and selling a $100-million airliner so different from building a $20,000 car or a $50 electronic device, or even a $100-million dam, all activities in which China has proven to excel. Those special circumstances include:

- The sheer impossibility of becoming successful in aviation *quickly*. Anyone stepping on a Boeing airplane knows that other passengers have gotten on Boeing planes—and, in a statistically overwhelming majority of cases, have gotten off safely at the other end—for most of a century. Anyone getting on an Airbus knows that they have been in comparably safe operation, by the thousands, for several decades. Bombardier, Embraer, and Fokker have been increasingly familiar factors in travel.

  By definition, it would be decades before Chinese-made

planes could rack up as long a safe-operating history as the
established companies already have—even if those first few
decades were completely accident-free. (And even if the
background reputation for low-defect production from Chinese factories was a match for Airbus's or Boeing's, which
it now is not.) Moreover, operating an airline and maintaining airplanes requires a constellation of skills found in
few other industries. Repair facilities, with spare parts and
trained engineers, have to be ready wherever the planes
might fly. Companies must learn to deal with highly—and
properly!—intrusive safety inspectors, for both aircraft and
crew.

- The world's aircraft-certifying agencies work closely with
one another, and the U.S. FAA and its European counterpart, the European Aviation Safety Agency (EASA), in effect
set standards for the world. Unless a Chinese-built—or
Brazilian- or Japanese-built commercial airplane—can pass
the onerous steps necessary for a "certificate of airworthiness" from the FAA, it won't even be considered on the
high-end international market. (AVIC and its predecessors
have exported small numbers of Soviet-designed airliners
over the years, but only to developing countries, mainly in
Africa, that don't care about international certification and
have bought the planes as part of larger trade or aid deals
arranged by China.) An aircraft company's reputation—like
that of a university or a medical center—can be built only
over a span of many years, and depends both on single huge
events (is there a crash?) and the accumulation of millions of
customer experiences day by day.

In short, challenging as it may be to set up a factory in
southern China capable of producing defect-free iPads, that
is nothing compared with the cost, complexity, and multi-
decade commitment necessary for making airplanes that
the world's airlines will base their financial and operating
plans on.

- The surprising economics of the airplane-building business, in which all of the glamour goes to the final assembly process, in those enormous Boeing or Airbus or COMAC hangars, but much of the profit comes from supplying the components that go into the plane. Engines, electronics, avionics systems—these are the expensive elements for which the airframe itself can in business terms be a kind of delivery system, or shell. "Aircraft are being eaten by their own value chains," Aboulafia told me in 2011. "The real value goes to the GE or Rockwell Collins"—GE, like Rolls-Royce and Pratt & Whitney, makes jet turbine engines; Rockwell Collins, like Honeywell, makes avionics systems. "They're going for a tube with the national flag on the back," Aboulafia told a Seattle newspaper about the Chinese projects.[6] "They're just developing a chunk of metal onto which all the real value added is inserted by Western suppliers."
- The most important elements in developing better airplanes are all skills or technologies in which Chinese companies currently lag. These areas are better engines, more advanced avionics, design and construction of wing surfaces, and the "systems integration" of the literally millions of components that go into a modern airplane. They are fields in which a North American, European, or Japanese firm dominates, Russian firms are active, but no Chinese institution is yet competitive.

The combination of these problems showed up most acutely in the ARJ21. It was meant to be a standard-bearer for Chinese aerospace development, but because so little of the high-value work has been done in China or by Chinese firms, so far it has essentially been an elaborate container for expensive components made by European, North American, and Japanese companies.

As a product that commercial airlines might consider, it was

barely plausible or competitive. It has about the same number
of seats as models from Embraer or Fokker—seventy-eight in a
normal configuration—but because of various inelegant aspects
of design and manufacture, it weighs about *ten thousand pounds*
more. In aviation, this is a crippling disadvantage. The "operating empty weight per passenger," essentially the deadweight
burden of operations per paying seat, was 705 pounds for the
Chinese plane, versus 597 for an equivalent Embraer. This is
a huge handicap for the heavier plane, or advantage for the
lighter plane, in a business where every ounce matters. Indeed,
if the ARJ21 receives international certification—for which
the original target date of 2007 will be missed by at least five
years—the most likely markets for the plane will be forced purchases by some of China's own domestic airlines and the same
developing-country customers who have bought previous Chinese products.[7]

"We know that this plane, the ARJ21, is completely useless,"
Richard Aboulafia told me in 2010. "It amounts to a random
collection of imported technologies and design features flying
together in loose formation. The question it makes me ask is,
How much of China's growth is just like this? How much of it
is genuinely productive? And how much is just misinvestment
on a colossal scale by state owned enterprises?"

"Tell me where you want to go"

If the same standards are applied to the ARJ21's big brother,
the large C919 that is meant to compete not with Embraer or
Dassault but with Boeing and Airbus themselves, many of the
same concerns arise. To explain them, I'll turn to the pilot and
businessman Shane Tedjarati, whom I met in Beijing in 2011.

From childhood in Tehran he had been fascinated by aviation. When he was about ten years old, his father, a pilot, took him on a flight in a small Cessna, and Tedjarati says that "a spark was ignited" in his heart. When he was in college in Montreal, he wanted to start flight training but didn't know how he would pay for it. His father gave him a rare Persian carpet, then worth about $3,500, as a "flying carpet" to be used toward his training costs. With his father's help and encouragement, he earned his certificate as a private pilot while still a teenager. He was determined to continue the tradition with his own son, who earned his private-pilot certificate in Canada and the United States at age seventeen, the third generation of pilots in his family.

Tedjarati is a person of linguistic as well as technical abilities. When I told him about a mutual friend whom I'd recently heard doing business near-simultaneously in four languages—English, French, Chinese, and Dutch—Tedjarati smiled politely. I asked about his language skills, and he said that he felt business-comfortable in six languages: Persian; English, which we were speaking; Chinese, in which I heard him operate several times when taking calls on his mobile phone; French, from his student years in Montreal; Arabic; and Turkish.

Tedjarati began working for Air Canada after graduation, including a stint measuring satellite reception in the Canadian Arctic. He later joined Oracle and eventually started his own consulting firm. In 1992, while still in his twenties, he came to China to be part of what he called "this dramatic human transformation." After working for Unisys he became head of Deloitte Consulting in Greater China, where his projects included helping large state-owned enterprises make the transition to a market economy. In 2004, he was appointed head of Honeywell China and now runs the company's operations in both China and India, its two largest growth markets.

In the United States, Honeywell was generally known for home thermostats, but for the past two decades its most important businesses have been large-scale high-tech monitoring and control systems. These are used in the energy business, at large medical centers, and—crucially and profitably—in modern airliners. It was in this capacity, while bidding for shares in China's aerospace projects, that Tedjarati has come to know the C919 project from the inside and to be aware of its limits as well as its potential. Simultaneously through these ambitious days of China's aircraft-building plans, Shane Tedjarati had joined Joe T, Paul Fiduccia, Francis Chao, and the other outside tribunes, agents, and agitators for aviation reform within China.

Like those other Westerners, he believes in the explanatory power of showing Chinese officials how a liberalized air-traffic system really worked. He took one CAAC official with him on a trip to the hangar in Leesburg, Virginia, outside Washington, D.C., where Tedjarati stored a small, sleek Cessna 400 airplane. "I pulled the plane out of the hangar and asked him, 'Where do you want to go?'" Tedjarati said. "I told him: You are Chinese, I am Canadian, we're both foreign nationals. It's less than twenty-five miles to the White House, and this is the most restricted commercial airspace in America. This is as tough as it gets! So just put your finger on the map and tell me where you want to go!"

His claim was partly bluff, because if the Chinese official had said, "Okay, let's fly right over the Lincoln Memorial and down the Mall," Tedjarati would have had to inform him that in the years since 9/11 the Special Flight Rules over Washington had made that impossible. But they could head almost anywhere out of town, toward the west, as they did—down through the Virginia tidewater to Jamestown and Williamsburg, where they landed at a little airport about three miles from the historic district. The airport had no control tower, which meant they could fly right in without talking to any air-traffic controllers or asking anyone's permission. Pilots at these little airports (which make up the great majority of the landing sites in America) just "self-announce" on the local frequency, to let any other nearby aircraft know what they have in mind. "He was sure that the Air Force jets were going to be scrambled to come after us," Tedjarati told me. "Then I took him for a similar tour in New York, circling around the Statue of Liberty and going right over Central Park. I told him, 'We are doing this as two foreigners, with no previous flight planning or permissions, within the immediate precincts of the 9/11 tragedy. Yet, it is safe and secure. This is how it can be in China!' I explained how it was all much safer than their system, and people got their clearances in a few minutes rather than days in advance."

While doing missionary work for the larger growth of aviation, Tedjarati's real work was increasing Honeywell's share of the big Chinese aerospace projects. These efforts were almost ridiculously successful with the C919. All the crucial components of the new airplane—engines, electronics, landing gear, and so on—were sent out for international bid. Honeywell won the contracts to provide four systems, from the wheels and braking system to the flight controls and inertial-navigation electronics, for a total value of $16 billion. No other company wound up with more than one such contract, and few outsiders understood the C919 as thoroughly as Tedjarati did.

Why building an airliner is harder
than going to the moon

"In some ways, the Chinese can go to the moon long before they build an airliner that global carriers will buy in large numbers," Tedjarati told me early in 2011, even as COMAC was showing mock-ups of the C919 at air shows and the Chinese press was reporting weekly on its progress. Beyond Richard Aboulafia's skepticism in principle about state guidance for high-tech projects, Shane Tedjarati was concerned about the practical realities of managing projects as complex and on as large a scale as aircraft production. Could the Chinese system master huge, moonshot-style challenges? Of course! But "building a certified commercial aircraft is *much* more difficult than going to the moon," he said. "A moon shot is a single mission. You're sending four or five people. If the people die they become national heroes. This is so much more complicated, because you're making something for the public that they're going to be using around the world, and nothing can go wrong."

Even aviation buffs, he said, can barely imagine the scale or complexity of large-airframe construction, or the potential for small imperfections or missed connections to create major delays and problems. For instance, the dull-sounding challenge of "cockpit integration." This would be like designing high-end computer software—for a computer that must simultaneously monitor and control high-temperature power plants; operate and test electrical systems with thousands of connectors and many miles of cable; give pilots the data they need to control a vehicle that can weigh nearly a million pounds and travel at nearly the speed of sound; and do countless other functions, all with triple redundancy or more, and with the constant potential of having to switch to emergency-rescue mode. "Building and certifying a commercial aircraft is one of the most complex tasks in the world," Tedjarati said. "It takes a continental economy with a determined national will to attempt such a monumental undertaking. In almost all cases, it would require participation by internationally recognized suppliers for various components and systems. Managing and integrating all these systems into one workable, certifiable aircraft with traceable documentation is especially challenging. Many manufacturers with decades of experience get it wrong and often there are many program delays."

He pointed out that in the entire world there are relatively few engineers experienced in the complex work of integrating software for avionics and flight controls, and most of them already work for a handful of companies, like his own. Expanding their number is not a quick or easy matter. "And what about program managers?" he asked. "They are particularly difficult to come by. The trick in these huge projects, the tiny difference between success and catastrophic failure, lay in the subtlety and perfection of program management and systems integration.

Tedjarati was careful always to make clear his confidence in China's long-term prospects with the C919. "I believe it will succeed," he said, "but to build a reputable, globally recognized commercial aircraft industry with a solid brand will take many years, perhaps more than one generation." The difficulties might seem enormous, but he had learned never to underrate the Chinese capacity to cope and succeed: "I am a big believer that this will eventually come to pass and that's what excites me about being here in China."

Two airplanes do not an industry make

How will we know whether this situation is changing, and Chinese competitors are succeeding in this complex industry? The most significant indicator would be progress against what is now by far the greatest obstacle to Chinese preeminence in the world aircraft industry: the inability of Chinese companies to produce jet engines that are anywhere close in power, efficiency, or reliability to the top-line offerings from GE, Rolls-Royce, and Pratt & Whitney.

It is obviously in hopes of closing that gap that Chinese aerospace firms have been pushing for partnerships or local-content requirements with the foreign engine-makers. Unless Chinese companies develop their own engine-making technology, or can copy or absorb techniques already devised by the market leaders, any Chinese aircraft business will be in a situation roughly like that of today's Chinese computer-making industries. They will "make" airplanes in China, as most of the world's computers are now Chinese-made. But the expensive components will come from overseas, for a bolting-together process on Chinese soil, and from China's perspective the gap that separates them from a "real" aerospace industry will close slowly if at all.

Every element in an airplane's design affects its final performance: the overall contour and smoothness, for airflow; the wings, for efficiency; the weight of every single rivet, strut, and seat cushion, which ripples through the whole design, since each extra ounce that must be carried requires stronger (and thus heavier) structures through the rest of the plane. But the big advances all depend on the engine. That is why we speak of the "jet age": the invention of turbine jet engines allowed planes to fly fast enough that continent-crossing travel was possible in North America or Europe, and it allowed them to fly high enough to avoid the great majority of weather problems except when taking off or descending to land. Thunderstorms, which can tower 40,000 to 50,000 feet or above, are the exception; even the largest airliners have no safe alternative than simply to fly around them.

The fundamental science of jet engines is well known; the steady improvement that has made planes quieter and ever more efficient comes from constant refinements in engineering and in manufacturing techniques. The tolerances within the engine become tighter; they are built with greater precision to withstand greater temperatures and pressures and to convert fuel into propulsion with ever less waste. These advancements don't make planes faster, because of the physics of wind resistance. As planes near the sound barrier, each extra knot of speed meets more and more wind resistance, which requires more and more fuel to surmount.

I have around me dozens of technical reports totaling thousands of pages about why, exactly, Chinese-made engines have done so poorly. Part of the explanation is historical: Americans and Western Europeans have been steadily refining airplane engines for more than a century, and jet engines for sixty-plus years. The Chinese are only recently in the business. Partly it is because the traits that have been so valuable during China's infrastructure-and-export boom—high volume, quick turnaround, low cost, a "happy with crappy" tolerance for product defects—are the opposite of what is required for the high-precision work of engine development. A "threat assessment" of the Chinese Air Force, prepared for the U.S. government in 2010,[8] reported that "one of the biggest Achilles' heels is the aero-engine sector, which has struggled mightily to develop and produce state-of-the-art high performance power plants." (Instead, the PLA Air Force still uses Russian engines in most of its planes, although it is trying hard to change that.)

The requirements for military and civilian jet engines are somewhat different, but if anything, China's engine development for airliners lags behind what its military is trying to do. In September, 2011, Gabe Collins and Andrew Erickson of *China SignPost* released an extremely detailed study of this very question—the title was "A Chinese 'Heart' for Large Civilian and Military Aircraft: Strategic and Commercial Implications of China's Campaign to Develop High-Bypass Turbofan Jet Engines"—and the most surprising of its many assertions was that the Chinese aerospace establishment simply wasn't spending enough money to keep up with developments in the West. GE is investing about $2 billion per year in research and development of new engines; Pratt & Whitney and Rolls-Royce together invest about $3 billion more. By comparison with this annual research total from the companies that already have a large technical lead, the Chinese engine-building entity known as ACAE has budgeted only about $300 million per year through the next Five-Year Plan. Research is cheaper in China, but not by that much. As Collins and Erickson drily observe, "ACAE's lower investment level may not enable it to catch up and develop a competitive commercial (and military) jet engine construction capability." And, they go on, "jet engine production involves exceedingly complex supply chains and ACAE will face significant challenges in creating a sufficiently large and flexible supplier base when it becomes capable of producing its own commercial engines."

What happens next, like so much about China, is unknowable. The engine-makers are under constant pressure to shift their production to China, to form joint ventures with local partners, to show that they deserve a place in the Chinese market by making themselves ever more fully Chinese. In 2011, GE announced a deal to share avionics technology with an AVIC subsidiary, on top of a similar engine-making deal. The potential long-term risk to the company and its U.S. production base was evident.[9] "Joint ventures with jet engine market leaders like General Electric (GE) have the potential to give the Chinese aerospace industry a 100 piece puzzle with 90 of the pieces already assembled," Collins and Erickson said of that deal.[10] In a familiar pattern, destructively different time scales are also in play here. The U.S. corporation can look ahead a quarter or two; its executives operate under pay schemes that encourage them to maximize profits while they can. Their state-guided Chinese business partners have the handicaps but also the advantages of being under less short-term profit pressure. Where might this lead? Collins and Erickson spell it out: "The imperative to prioritize quarterly profits today over long-term profits and strategic concerns may be exacerbated as long-term military spending constraints in Europe, Japan, and now even the U.S. may drive Western aero-engine manufacturers even further into Chinese joint ventures to replace revenue."

So much is possible. China's ACAE could become the new GE or Pratt & Whitney. COMAC could become the new Airbus or Boeing. Honeywell, Rockwell Collins, Siemens, and others could come to regret the factories and research centers they have built inside China. But the point of this long review is that such an outcome is not fated, and perhaps not even likely. And whatever their Chinese competitors do, the American, Canadian, British, German, French, Japanese, Brazilian, and other players with established businesses will have only themselves to blame if they do not keep innovating as fast as they can.

When people within China say that the low-wage, low-tech industrial model may be hitting a limit, or that a China capable of high-end, high-tech innovation would be different in basic ways from today's society, building modern airliners is the sort of challenge they are referring to. A different industrial organization, built upon a different research base, bolstered by different intellectual property laws, and run with a different management approach, might close all the gaps that keep China from the all-fronts aerospace achievement that is part of its announced plan. But a lot more than aviation would need to change to realize that version of China.

8 ★ The Environmental Consequences of Aviation

The environmental crisis of aviation

Through the summer of 2011 and into early 2012, the main trade battles between China and the European Union were not the familiar ones over subsidies or trade barriers. Instead they concerned the E.U.'s proposal to make all airlines flying into European destinations pay an emissions tax for each ton of carbon dioxide they produced.

Chinese representatives complained that the tax was "unfair."[1] The carbon calculations, and fees, would be based on the length of the entire flight, from point of departure to destination—so long hauls from Asia would pay much more than European carriers on their short regional flights. A Chinese airline company threatened to cancel a gigantic $3.8-billion order with Airbus in protest.[2] "China's actions show it is ready to use its economic muscle to pressure EU policies," an Asian-based environmental news service observed after the postponement of the Airbus deal in 2011. U.S. companies also opposed the E.U. program, but naturally they expressed their disagreements by filing lawsuits.

The importance of this issue can only grow. How can China possibly entertain these ambitions, from opening new airports to doubling the volume of air traffic to building its own airliners, in the face of certain environmental constraints on polluting activities in general and on aviation in particular?

In any discussions of environmental issues in China, it's a toss-up as to which deserves more emphasis: how dire the situation is, or how hard Chinese authorities are trying to cope with it. The immediate threat posed by airline emissions in China is less obviously dire than, say, the particulate pollution that so often makes big-city air opaque, or the heavy-metal tainting of food and groundwater supplies that has contributed to China's current cancer epidemic. But airplane emissions are significant, and will become more so, especially as aerospace grows faster than other parts of China's economy.

A reminder of the scale and nature of the problem:

As of 2010, all human activity together put roughly 37 billion tons (37 gigatons) of carbon dioxide into the atmosphere each year. Twenty years earlier, it was less than 25 billion tons. Twenty years later, it could well be 50 billion tons. Carbon dioxide is not the only greenhouse gas, but it is important because we produce so much of it, and because its effects are so long-lasting. Carbon dioxide persists in the atmosphere for many decades, even centuries—unlike methane, which has a more powerful greenhouse effect but can disperse within a single decade.

Before James Watt invented the modern condensing steam engine in the late 1700s—that is, before we had much incentive to burn coal and, later, oil in large quantities—the concentration of carbon dioxide in the atmosphere was around 280 parts per million. By 1900, as Europe and North America were industrializing, it had reached about 300 ppm. By 2010, the carbon-dioxide concentration was at or above 390 ppm, which was probably the highest level in many millions of years, and was rising by about two ppm a year. It is estimated that it will pass 400 ppm by 2015, and 420 by 2025.[3] Of those 37 billion to 40 billion tons emitted in 2010, aviation in all forms accounted for about 2 percent in sheer quantity—and perhaps twice that in climate-change potential, because the pollutants are more damaging when injected into the atmosphere at high altitude. The world's entire shipping fleet, which together with aviation ties the globalized economy together, contributes about the same total of carbon emissions.[4] Electric-power generation is the largest source of carbon emissions, followed by transportation in all forms.

What drew the international airlines' attention to the emissions problem was the likelihood that as world CO_2 emissions keep going up, those from aviation will be going up even more, and might double by 2030.[5] A study sponsored by an airline industry consortium found that between 1990 and 2003, aviation's output of greenhouse-gas emissions in Europe had gone up by 80 percent, whereas transportation as a whole was up only 20 percent, and many other sectors (including power generation, agriculture, and manufacturing) had actually declined.

By 2010, when climate talks in Copenhagen were going nowhere, the aviation industry was long past the point of denial on emissions issues. Its European and U.S. leaders realized that for reasons of appearance, and because of impending legislation, and to forestall reaction from customers, they needed to act. They also had particular economic incentives. Fuel represents the largest single expense for airline companies. Each gallon they did not burn made their flights more profitable.

What could they do about it? In China, the answers are routing, and algae.

Detours and gas-guzzlers

In the spring of 2011, my wife and I went with a young Chinese friend, River Lu, and a friend of hers to a concert by the Eagles in Beijing. The Eagles, as they say, are big in China and drew an enormous crowd of a wide range of ages to what in 2008 had been the Wukesong Olympic Basketball Arena and is now the MasterCard Center.

The concert lasted three hours, with the crowd on its feet from the halfway point onward, once Don Henley began singing "Hotel California." When it was all over, it took another few hours to travel what would have been at most a ten-mile straight shot from the arena back to our apartment. My wife and I had no car (or driver) in China and usually traveled by subway, but our friend wanted to show off her new Chinese-made Audi and had given us a ride. Apart from the jam in the parking lot, which had only two narrow exits for several thousand cars, our routing across town was the problem. Because of Beijing's numerous one-way streets and freeway-like "ring road" layout, we had to circle far around the city before we could head back in the right direction. In addition to taking extra time, of course we used far more gas in those hours of idling and indirect routing than if our friend had been able to drive right down Chang'An Road.

Those wasted hours were an analogue for why air travel in China has been exceptionally inefficient. The military's control of the airspace around even the biggest commercial airports is the equivalent of having only a few narrow exits for a jammed parking lot. (That is, planes have to line up for chances to pass through the narrow military-authorized corridors.) And the military's control of nearly all the airspace between Chinese destinations means that flights within China, even by the favored national carriers, fly indirect routes that are the equivalent of going all around the city on a ring road.

These inefficiencies in air-traffic control are the main reason flights are more often delayed in China than in other major aviation countries; why their scheduled travel time, per mile flown, is much slower than in North America or Europe; and why they burn up to *twice as much fuel* per passenger mile as their counterparts in Europe or North America.

Let me say that again: For reasons of sheer pointless inefficiency in routing, airlines in China are now burning twice as much fuel and emitting twice as much carbon as they would "have" to if they could fly more directly, with fewer delays. Or, put in terms that more closely match the planned expansion of Chinese aviation, commercial air travel in China could double, with no increase in emissions, if the air-traffic system worked the way it does in the rest of the world. The situation is similar to the burden created by China's "legacy" building stock—the architectural remnants of the Mao era and the early reform years that were so cheaply built and poorly insulated that they take twice as much energy to heat and cool as their Western counterparts. Replacing all those old buildings with greener modern structures will take decades, and billions of dollars. Relatively speaking, wasteful airline routing could be corrected almost overnight.

There is one more fuel penalty imposed by military control of the airspace. Modern airliners work more efficiently the higher they fly. With their high speed and great mass, they generate disproportionate drag if they fly through the relatively thick atmosphere below about 20,000 feet. More of their fuel goes simply to overcoming wind resistance. Everywhere else in the world, commercial jetliners spend their cruise time at 30,000 feet or above. In China, military restrictions sometimes keep jets at 10,000 or 15,000 feet for extended periods, where they become the equivalent of gas-guzzlers.

Ending this sheer waste will require the cooperation of the Chinese military, but it will also be speeded up through a new technology for navigation based on a particular application of GPS guidance.

GPS as fuel saver

For cars, GPS simply means that we no longer have to get lost—even if people who know a neighborhood can often improve on the suggestions from the voice in the device. For air travel, GPS means a number of related improvements. An obvious one is more direct routing—cutting the corners off the indirect, jagged course marked by the older aviation guidance system called VOR,[6] with consequent savings in time, fuel, and pollution.

Another is reduction of the airport nuisance factor in big cities. The combination of very precise real-time GPS readings, which can locate even a fast-moving airliner within a space of a few feet, and sophisticated new computerized autopilots that can follow a very tightly defined path, now allows airplanes to fly exact slalom-style 3-D courses through the sky in a way that has never been conceivable before. With older VOR-based navigation, which prevailed around the world until the early 2000s, the "airways" that ran from one point to the next were eight to ten *miles* wide. That was the margin of error allowed planes on cross-country flights. Now the paths that airliners can fly—on departure, to avoid noise-sensitive areas of a big city, or on descent, to avoid hills and towers on the way to a remote or difficult landing site—have a margin of error of a wingspan or two, or a few hundred feet rather than tens of thousands.

Why does this matter? Noise abatement for one, since the planes can more precisely follow paths that minimize neighborhood disruption. But the fuel savings are also significant. When the new path has been calculated to let the plane glide continuously down toward the runway, the final-approach stage of the flight requires only one-third as much fuel as the conventional method, which involves leveling off several times in a stair-step descent.

These benefits apply anywhere, and airports in Western Europe and Australia have taken the lead in installing them. Typically for America's general standing in the infrastructure races, American airports lag behind. But the revolution in aircraft guidance has one more implication that matters far more in China than in most other countries: It promises to bring China's most remote (and politically sensitive) areas within feasible air reach of the rest of the country.

The western half of China, from Xinjiang in the north to Tibet and Yunnan in the south, is very forbidding country for aviation. It includes some of the world's remotest and most mountainous territory. This is dangerous to fly in for obvious reasons: peaks, violent storms, gusty winds. But there is also a less obvious reason. The navigational tools that have let aircraft find their way through bad weather and threatening terrain, and that have let controllers monitor their progress, have long depended on installations on the ground. Radar dishes to track airplanes themselves, radar-and-weather installations, "NavAids" like VOR stations—these all had to be built and maintained, and in a fairly dense network, to be of any use. It is no problem to have radar stations and navigational beacons dotted at intervals of a few dozen miles all across the East Coast of the United States—or of China as well. It is a major challenge amid the mountains and high plateaus of Tibet—and better transportation to Tibet and other western regions where ethnic Tibetans live has been a strategic priority for the central government, so as to bind those areas more tightly with the rest of China. And since both the radar beams and the ground-based navigation signals travel in straight lines, they can't reach into the valleys between mountain ranges. Air-traffic controllers looking for airplanes, and pilots looking for navigation signals, are both effectively blind when a mountain sits between a radar site and the airplane.

Much of western China has until recently been effectively beyond the range of reliable air travel. Navigation was so difficult that planes would often fly only in clear, calm weather—and the weather was very rarely clear and calm. The coming of GPS offered the first prospect of guidance to remote areas without building a network of radar stations and beacons along the way. The more recent advent of the high-precision systems collectively known as required navigation performance (RNP) is almost as important, in allowing safe (and fuel-efficient) approaches, in any weather, to the most isolated and forbidding airports in the world.

Direct flight to Tibet

A small company named Naverus, based outside Seattle, is playing a major role in the opening of these western Chinese airports. This is another illustration of the underpublicized integration of safety and environmental efforts in the U.S. and Chinese aviation systems.

In the 1990s, an Alaska Airlines captain named Steve Fulton

worked with the FAA and with Alaska officials to design the
first RNP approach in the world. It was for the Juneau airport, which is so closely hemmed by mountain ranges that it
had been inaccessible in its frequent bad weather. Traditional
navigational systems were not precise enough to keep airplanes
clear of the mountains as they dropped down toward the runway. Since no roads connect Juneau with the rest of Alaska or
North America, the frequent airport closures were a big problem. Fulton's new RNP approach for Juneau, which plotted out
a very precise set of waypoints for the airplane's autopilot to
follow as it wound its way through treacherous terrain, allowed
safe descent through clouds and served as a proof-of-concept
for making other "impossible" airports more accessible. Soon
he and his team had applied thirty more RNP approaches for
Alaskan airports.

In 2003, with another Alaska Airlines captain, named Hal
Andersen, and a high-tech entrepreneur named Dan Ger-
rity, Fulton founded Naverus to develop RNP approaches for
other airports in difficult terrain. They won contracts in Brazil,
Canada, Australia, New Zealand, and the United States. But
they were determined to make inroads in China, where aviation was growing faster than anyplace else, and where much of
the planned airport expansion was in the harshest mountain
settings.

When I first met the Naverus people, in Beijing, in 2007,
they had just completed one historic project and were preparing
for another. The achievement just behind them was an approach
to what was then one of the highest and most difficult airports
anywhere on earth: Linzhi, in Tibet. Linzhi's runway is at 9,700
feet of elevation, about the same as the highest airport in North
America, the one in Leadville, Colorado. But Leadville is a tiny
ex-mining settlement of perhaps two thousand people, while

Linzhi is one of the major cities of the Tibetan plateau, with a population of perhaps two million. For three hundred days of the year it rains in Linzhi, and on the other sixty-five days the weather is rarely good enough for pilots to fly under Visual Flight Rules and find their way through the 18,000- to 20,000-foot escarpments alongside the narrow valley in which Linzhi sits.

Lhasa is the next airport to the west, two hundred fifty miles away; Bangda, an even more remote Tibetan setting that has the highest-altitude commercial airport in the world, is about one hundred fifty miles to the east. Because the surrounding territory was so impossibly steep, only a few light airplanes had ever landed at Linzhi; no "transport aircraft"—airliners or cargo planes—had ever touched down on its runway. As with so many infrastructure projects in China, the big, new Linzhi airport with its broad runway had been built first, with practical questions about its feasibility coming second. "They just picked a location and built an airport there," Steve Fulton told me in Beijing. "Only after that did the operational people look around to see whether anyone could actually fly there."

After Fulton and his team persuaded Chinese aviation officials to let them try an approach for Linzhi, he got his first in-person look at it. He flew to Lhasa and made the ten-hour drive eastward, through twisty mountain roads, to Linzhi. The airport itself proved to be beautiful and modern, with a long, well-paved runway. But the terminal was practically vacant. "They had their firetrucks, their Jetways—but no action," he said. His next step was to use his own handheld GPS and begin making precise measurements of the location and elevation of significant areas around the airport. Foreigners are in theory forbidden to do this kind of mapping in China, because of holdover national-security concerns. Fulton explained that he had to make the measurements, because the official Chinese maps were so imprecise or wrong. "Through this process, I think the Chinese themselves began to see the importance of accurate terrain information," Fulton said. "If it's wrong, you crash."

By 2006, after eighteen months of work, the approach was drawn up, and the autopilots had done fine—in simulations. But no real airliner had flown the course in real circumstances. On July 12, 2006, Fulton joined a group of Chinese pilots and aviation officials crowded into the cockpit of an Air China 757 as it made a historic first test flight into Linzhi.

The last six minutes of that approach are on video at the Naverus Web site,[7] and they are riveting. The crew is talking in Chinese the whole time, but you can hear Fulton's voice in the international language of aviation, English, calling out altitudes as they head down. Because this was a test flight, and no one had proven that the autopilots could keep them from running into a mountain in the clouds, they were required to conduct the flight under Visual Flight Rules conditions. Fulton had carefully arranged with the Air China crew about the circumstances under which they would break off the flight rather than risk disaster if it turned out that the mapping was wrong or the autopilots didn't work.

"As we turned each corner in the valley and went into each new segment of the approach, we kept being *just* under the clouds," Fulton told me. Indeed, that is what the video shows—the cloud level coming down, and the plane descending just enough below it so that the pilots could still see ahead of them. "It was a kind of ballet down the river valley, with sweeping turns back and forth." Then, at 200 feet above ground level—practically landing, from the layman's point of view—the plane's autopilots made an S-turn around a crag that sat between them and the runway. The plane automatically veered around the final obstacle, aligned itself with the runway, and touched down exactly on the center line. The fifteen people jammed in and around the cockpit—including brass from Air China and the CAAC—gave a round of applause. "Captain Jiang, the senior Air China pilot, turned to me and said, 'I have full confidence in this technology!'" Fulton later told me. "We all knew that people from the minister on down would have been fired if we'd crashed." To say nothing of the effect on those aboard.

Instead, the CAAC vice minister proclaimed that "the future looks good for RNP technology in China."[8] Six weeks later, the first regular commercial airline flight ever to reach Linzhi touched down, guided through clouds and difficult weather along the RNP path. Naverus won contracts to develop several more approaches in China, starting with Bangda, which at 14,219 feet is the very highest airport in the world. Then for another Tibetan airport, Nagqu, which when it opens will be even higher. The business boomed so much that in late 2009 the Naverus company was acquired by GE and is now known as GE Aviation PBN Services. Boeing and Airbus now have their own subsidiaries working on RNP approaches. There is a race to cover China with these new navigation systems that will make travel to remote areas safer, more reliable, and also more fuel efficient.

"The point is that they can navigate to any airport in the world with absolutely nothing on the ground," Sergio von Borries, a pilot from Brazil who had become another Naverus official, told me at a conference in China. "These truly are the highways in the sky, and we are the highway engineers."

China as the world's biofuels lab

The other potential solution to the pollution problem was hard for me to take at face value, but eventually I became semi-convinced. It is shifting to algae as a major future source of jet fuel.

China's great advantage in many fields is that it is the place where so much of the world's *doing* now occurs. In the effort to develop lower-carbon sources of aviation fuel, China has become the locus for efforts by Boeing and others to extract fuel more efficiently from biological sources. The concept here is not a mystery. Algae, like some more complex plants, produce hydrocarbons that can be converted to a form of oil. (Many algae produce a kind of waxy paraffin with a high oil content. Normal fossil-fuel deposits are only rarely the remains of dinosaurs; much more frequently, they come from ancient fossilized algae beds.) The trick is growing algae and harvesting its oil at a large enough scale and a low enough cost to be a plausible substitute for regular petroleum. Projects toward that end are under way around the world. Most within the United States have been sponsored and subsidized by the Pentagon, which has viewed its reliance on imported petroleum as a serious security risk. Within China, the major effort is, yet again, jointly led by Boeing and the Chinese government.

Al Bryant, a career Boeing engineer and manager, moved to Beijing shortly after the Olympics to oversee Boeing's research-and-development efforts within China. He became famous within aviation circles for his role as a traveling proselytizer for the importance of biofuels in general and algae in particular. His presentation centers on a graph that projects likely emissions from airline travel through the year 2050. This chart has been the premise for Boeing's argument that it is time for an all-out effort for practical biofuels, especially from algae. The presentation's main feature was a chart showing that the hoped-for carbon improvements from biofuels would not simply keep the aviation industry from grossly increasing CO_2 emissions as traffic goes up but actually reduce them below their 2009 levels.

When a jet engine burns fuel that comes from algae, it emits carbon dioxide just as if it were burning fuel pumped straight from the Persian Gulf. But the algae would have removed at least as much CO_2 from the atmosphere while it was growing. So in principle, and with allowances for inefficiencies and fuel costs in the production process, algae-based fuel could allow airplanes to run on something much closer to a "carbon-neutral" basis, also sometimes called operating on "current carbon cycles" versus the "fossil carbon cycle" of burning coal or oil.

The aerospace argument for new biofuels takes full account of America's ethanol disaster in the 2000s. In one of the worst policy mistakes of modern times, the U.S. government subsidized farmers to grow crops, mainly corn, that could be converted into ethanol and blended into gasoline supplies. This made no sense in energy-efficiency terms. (It took more energy to plant, fertilize, harvest, and process the corn than the ethanol yielded.) It made no sense in economic terms, except as a subsidy to the farmers and agribusiness. It made no sense in moral terms, since it diverted crops that could be used for human or animal feed into transportation fuel. So the aerospace standard is to find biofuels that don't directly or indirectly compete with the human food supply; that represent true carbon savings, as corn-based ethanol never could; and that can be sustainably grown and harvested without depleting water supplies or doing other long-term damage.

Whatever biofuel the aviation industry creates must have the same "energy content" as current fuels, so that aircraft as big and heavy as today's fleet can fly at comparable speeds. It must be compatible with the design and technology of current jet engines. It must be compatible with the existing worldwide infrastructure of fuel storage and distribution. And—trickiest of all—it must be *interchangeable* with today's jet fuel, which is stockpiled at airports around the world. "You need to be able to leave Beijing with a tank full of biofuel, go to Lima, Peru, refuel there with normal fuel, and fly back," Al Bryant told me in Beijing. "You can't have an airplane stuck in Lima because it can't use regular fuel."

By process of elimination, all these criteria have led mainly to algae. In principle it can produce hundreds of times more fuel, per acre of surface area, as oil palms (which are largely grown on land where tropical forests have been clear-cut), soybeans, corn, or other crops that can be used for biofuels. It grows and produces the oil many times faster than more complex plants—an algae crop cycle is a matter of days rather than weeks or months. It can be grown on land that is otherwise too barren or unusable, and in water that is too polluted or brackish for any other human or agricultural purpose. "The world's entire aviation-fuel needs could be taken care of by algae facilities the size of Belgium," Bryant said. He waited for me to make the requisite joke about the highest and best use of Belgium's landmass, which I did. Other American and Chinese scientists I interviewed were skeptical that algae farming could become practical that quickly, or affordably, or at the needed scale. Nonetheless, Boeing's calculations assume that a sustained world oil price of

$90 per barrel or above would make algae-based fuel economi-
cally practical, once production techniques are improved. World
oil prices peaked at above $140 per barrel just before the world
financial collapse of late 2008. During the crash they fell to as
low as the mid-$30s, then climbed above $80 by early 2010 and
remained there through 2011.

Boeing is now working with a variety of state-owned research
facilities across China on sustainable-fuel projects, especially
involving algae. Chinese universities and technical institutes are
among the world's leaders in algae research, especially one in
Qingdao. That is the descriptively named Chinese Academy of
Sciences Qingdao Institute of Bioenergy and Bioprocess Technology, and it is where the world's hopes for making aviation
more environmentally sustainable may lie.

9 ⋆ The Tensions Inside China

Will China change the world, or be changed?

The theme throughout this book has not just been aerospace and aviation. It has also been balance and tension. The balance and tension between, on the one hand, the innovation, flexibility, chaos, unpredictability, patience, humor, and improvisation that characterize Chinese society in its individual elements and that in combined force have since the 1970s helped reduce poverty and create wealth faster than any other organizational scheme in history. And, on the other hand, the fearful, short-sighted, crude and clumsy, highly personalized and subjective, often self-defeatingly harsh control measures taken by security forces always worried about where Chinese spontaneity might lead.

Crude and clumsy? In January, 2011, U.S. Secretary of Defense Robert Gates made an official visit to China. The purpose of the trip, which included a meeting with President Hu Jintao, was to begin calming U.S.-Chinese relations after an unusually tense year. In the preceding twelve months, the two countries had differed over maritime rights in the South China Sea, American arms sales to Taiwan, the value of the Chinese currency, and of course the selection of an imprisoned Chinese civil liberties activist as the 2010 winner of the Nobel Peace Prize. Gates's trip, which immediately preceded Hu Jintao's own state visit to Washington, was supposed to convey the message that the two countries would try to contain their differences rather than letting the disputes escalate.

The news of the trip, however, was the opposite of what Gates intended. The People's Liberation Army chose that week for a debut flight of its supposedly super-advanced J-20 "stealth" fighter, which was publicized first by Chinese bloggers and then by the mainstream media around the world. By the time the world's aviation analysts had a chance to pore over the photos and performance data of the J-20, they generally pooh-poohed its significance. It was based on decades-old designs, and its rumored stealth capacities to avoid radar were primitive. If anything it suggested the backwardness of the Chinese aerospace establishment rather than its advances. But those analyses took a while to complete, and in the meantime the military's decision to stage the test flight badly undercut Hu Jintao's position during Gates's trip. Either Hu had known all along about the planned flight, in which case he was deliberately saber rattling during what was intended as a peacemaking visit; or he had not known, and the implications of that were worse, in reinforcing long-standing concerns that the PLA was making strategic decisions on its own, without Party control. (Most Western democracies operate on the principle of civilian control of the military; in China, the military is officially under Communist Party control.)

And Chinese measures that are self-defeatingly harsh? Among many possible illustrations is the government's furious response to the selection of Liu Xiaobo for the Nobel Peace Prize in 2010. The foreign ministry all but ruptured relations with Norway, whose parliament oversees selection of the Peace Prize winner. In so doing, the Chinese government naturally frightened and antagonized a range of other nations, who had new reason to wonder what a steady increase in Chinese power might mean. Chinese officials threatened small states with trade sanctions and other difficulties if they attended the award ceremony—and then preposterously claimed that most of the world's governments joined in denouncing the choice.

With a more coldly cynical understanding of how to influence world opinion, or with a greater interest in this component of its "soft power," the government could have registered its disagreement and then underplayed the Nobel Prize episode. It could have conveyed through unflappability the message that it was serenely confident enough to absorb such petty blows. Such calculated calm generally seemed outside the government's capability. Beyond its fury about Liu Xiaobo, China's "diplomatic" efforts as a whole through 2010 were marked by similar oversteps and outbursts, plus threats and insults both intended or unwitting to surrounding nations. All of this eroded its "soft power" even as its economic strength continued to grow. The clearest indication of this backfiring effect was the expansion of Chinese claims to control over the South China Sea, which drew the governments of South Korea, Japan, Vietnam, and several other Southeast Asian nations into closer military cooperation with the United States.

Aviation as test of the Chinese system

China's aviation and aerospace ambitions offer one of many arenas in which these tensions will express themselves. The factors that will shape China's evolution as an aerospace power—trust and honesty in commercial dealings, efficient and honest regulation, transparent dealings with international bodies, stable relations between civil authorities and the military, a culture of free research and innovation—are bellwethers for its development more broadly. The interaction among the forces changing China, and the forces China is exerting on the world, will determine what kind of power China will represent and the speed, nature, and possible limits of its rise.

In the Western media and in most outside discussions of China's future, the contrasts and tensions I am describing are often presented in stark either-or fashion. Either they are sure to continue—or, alternatively, they are sure to be resolved. One way or another we won't have the ambiguity of the controlled chaos, the precarious success, of the China we have seen through the first few decades of its modernization.

The idea that the contradictions will continue, so that China will in the long run be both economically successful and politically controlled, lies behind the widespread projections that the world must soon confront the ripple effects of a powerful new Chinese model of authoritarian capitalism, and a "Beijing consensus" about how the world's economies should interact. In this view, economic vitality ultimately determines the success or failure of the associated political system. The Soviet system was contained for half a century after World War II by Western military power, but—by this logic—it finally failed because it could not keep up economically with market capitalism. By extension, each new high-speed rail line that is opened in China—each supermodern airport, each advanced semiconductor factory, each addition to national output or export surplus or head count of engineers—confirms the viability of the Chinese approach of state-fostered market development coinciding with tight political controls.

Unlike India, with the friction of its multiparty democracy, China has a system that makes sure the country's big jobs get done. The people living in the path of a "necessary" new road in Sichuan or Guangdong might not be happy about being forced to move, but the country as a whole benefits from an improved infrastructure. China is able to build so many new airports, and the United States and Western Europe so few, in part because Chinese officials can commandeer the land. They are not bogged down by lawsuits over noise or pollution concerns. Unlike the old Soviet Union, China has so far found a way to keep businesses vibrant while maintaining political control. Unlike modern Russia, it has so far kept corruption at a level at which it distorts rather than cripples the economy as a whole. Unlike the United States, where political and media attention bounce from one spectacle to the next, China has usually kept the focus of its governmental efforts directed on the main threats to the country's development and well-being. Rulers who don't have to face election campaigns or an unmuzzled press enjoy that luxury.

The upshot of these Chinese achievements, of course, is an implied but potent political message. China's infrastructure is astounding in its sweep and modernity; India's and America's are, in their different ways, depressing for decaying faster than they are rebuilt. The more abundantly the Chinese system delivers, freed from the bothers of democracy, the more it calls into question the ability of liberal democratic systems to keep up.

Many Westerners fear that the more successful China's economy is, the more threatening its model and ideal will inevitably become. And of course it's not just Westerners who think that a shift in economic fundamentals will have a profound political effect. A frequent theme in Chinese discourse is that the growing power of the country's system will finally allow its representatives to talk back to the West, including about the supposedly "universal" values Westerners preach.

This view of the political implications of China's economic

growth coexists with its opposite—the idea that China's material progress would be the best possible guarantor of its eventual political and social liberalization. This is the faith that politicians and, especially, business leaders have used to justify continued Western interactions with China even when oppression is increasing there. Its premise is that as China grows richer it will naturally become freer too. When people can choose what car to buy and what job to accept, sooner or later they'll want choice in other matters too. When some of them grow rich enough to own aircraft, they will want the freedom to travel without waiting weeks for an official okay. How long will citizens who are increasingly prosperous, urbanized, and "empowered" in many walks of life put up with a media system that does not treat them as fully adult, insisting that they be sheltered from certain "unauthorized" facts and viewpoints, and a political system that denies them a direct say in public affairs?

Over the past generation, and the past decade especially, China-watchers have framed this choice for the country: Either the growing power of the Chinese economy will change the rest of the international system, effectively making it more Chinese, or the growing prosperity of the Chinese people will change their own country's system, making it more international.

The contradictory signals from China—the magnificence of the country's hosting of the 2008 Olympics; the crackdown on all dissidence during the Olympics—make us eager for the choice to emerge, clearly and definitively, to end the suspense that has been building for forty years, since Richard Nixon's 1972 visit, so we can know whether to regard China as friend or foe. But because of China's vast resources and because its authoritarian system allows it to marshal them so effectively, the country is able to stave off the choice and, while it is doing so, to continue to transform in astonishingly fast yet contradictory ways. Sometimes they make it appear to be on a path to changing the international system, sometimes to being changed by it.

China's aerospace future is a test case for its economic and technological development as a whole. The more tightly the government maintains internal controls, the likelier that its aerospace industries will evolve toward a more efficient version of the Soviet model. That is, they would have some brute-force technical strengths, but they would lag the Western competitors in innovation, and their products would appeal only to captive customers. But the more that the military is willing to relinquish control over airspace, and that civilian authorities trust their people to travel unsupervised and collaborate with partners anywhere around the world as they choose, the greater the chance of real innovation arising within China.

Other industries have a similar telltale function. Can China move to the frontier of info-tech development, rather than just making low-cost products to someone else's specifications? In the life sciences? In exploration of space? In fostering universities that are such undeniable centers of excellence that scholars will leave Oxford, Berlin, Berkeley or Palo Alto, Cambridge or New York to spend their careers in Beijing or Xi'an? (Much as European, Latin American, Asian, or African scholars have often felt in the past half century that they had to come to North America to be part of the first team.)

The development of institutions and organizations like these will shape China, and the choices China's political leaders are about to make will largely determine whether China can excel in new ways.

Can the Chinese system "catch up," and grow up?

With aerospace as a proxy for Chinese development in the broadest sense, what are the forces that will determine in which direction China goes? A threshold indicator is whether the leaders of a maturing Chinese system will be confident enough in the country's achievements to become thick-skinned. In practice this means not allowing themselves to be baited by small slights in international dealings—and, much more important for the country's development, allowing their own people latitude in pursuing their interests and shaping their society. The deliberately provocative way of raising this point is to ask whether the Chinese system is ready to grow up.

Each national culture has a point about which it is most defensive, because on that point it has its own most serious doubts. You can't provoke most Americans by pointing out that the country has had a very warlike record for a very long time. Many Americans view this heritage as an achievement rather than a failing, and even those who don't aren't likely to feel insulted or personally threatened by this critique.

Yet let a foreigner tell an American that the country is "declining," and there will be a reaction. Denial, assent, an argument that there's still hope—something. The intensity of the reaction obviously underscores the point that this is one of Americans' longstanding sources of self-doubt. Other countries—Japan, Germany, England, Russia—have similar points that provoke defensiveness. What is most deeply concerning to a culture (as for most individuals or families) is often the most difficult or infuriating for outsiders to bring up.

In modern China, one of these always sensitive subjects is the idea of China's full "equality" or "maturity" in modern international society, especially relative to the white Western nations that for centuries have been in economic and political control. (Competition with Japan is a separate and equally tangled question.) This is the significance of the phrase "Hundred Years of Humiliation" to describe China's period of subjugation to foreigners and the repeated insistence by Chinese spokesmen on full dignity, equality, and respect in international dealings. In the late spring of 2011, I had the opportunity to watch the leaders of the world's two largest military forces, China's and America's, sit down for discussion over a meal. Admiral Mike Mullen, then the Chairman of the Joint Chiefs of Staff and as such the senior military adviser to President Obama, as he had been previously for President George W. Bush, had invited General Chen Bingde, the commanding general of the People's Liberation Army and the senior military official in China, to a dinner at Mullen's official residence in Washington.

I was one of a small number of outsiders at the dinner, at which the two senior commanders did most of the talking. The entire discussion was off the record, but I can say that in the following days I listened with a sense of familiarity to coverage of the public events of General Chen's visit to the United States—the first by a senior PLA official in seven years. In nearly every formal statement, response to a question, or impromptu comment in the presence of reporters, he returned to the same note, an insistence on *respect*. Improved relations must start on the basis of mutual respect, he would say. Or: Our nations must seek ways to work together, but on the platform of respect. Or: Only from a vantage point of mutual respect and equality can we make progress. The tone was affable, and the words might have sounded like pointless officialese. But that reflected something far closer to the heart of Chinese concerns than is often appreciated by outsiders, especially by the historically confident Western world.

In Chinese governmental culture, respect is not the only issue with the power to raise hackles or close down debate. Another is the fear of disorder that might call the recent decades of material progress into question. A similar important fear involves the specter of "splittism" that could divide the country and challenge the central government's control. There is simply no point in discussing the merits of autonomy for Taiwan, Tibet, or Xinjiang—the areas of principal "splittist" threat and concern—in any sort of public setting. It's not just that government policy is resolute on splittist questions; the great majority of the mainland Han Chinese public seems to feel the same way (no doubt because that is the only view offered in schools and from state-controlled media), even though they might dissent from government controls or policies in other realms. Chinese people who are familiar with American history point out the many similarities between the current Han attitude and the drive toward Manifest Destiny thinking in the United States from the nineteenth century onward.

But the sensitivity about respect comes up even more often than these other concerns. Paradoxically and predictably, the heavy-handed steps that the government takes to demonstrate its control in domestic affairs often undermine the respect it so craves internationally—as with the absurdity of the Catch-22 "authorized" Olympic protest zones in which no real protest was allowed—and impede its progress toward fostering the high-end, high-tech creative and industrial culture that would magnify China's power all the more.

May 35

During our time in China, my wife and I had two encounters with the nervousness of the security state. Both illustrated the government's nervousness about the kind of openness a fully modern economy would imply. The first was in 2009, on "May 35."

In the spring of the previous year, as the Olympic torch made its highly publicized (at least in China) way across Europe to begin a months-long journey to the opening ceremonies, French protesters clogged the route to demonstrate against China's policy in Tibet. On Chinese TV this received saturation coverage as a shocking and unprovoked affront to national dignity. It also moved police to extra-alert status inside China, lest pro-Tibetan demonstrators managed to stage an "embarrassing" event back home.

Just before the torch relay, China Southern Airlines reported that it had foiled a terrorist plot to blow up one of its Boeing 757 airplanes, on a route from Urumqi, in the Uighur region of Xinjiang, to Beijing. The airline said that a young Uighur Muslim woman had brought soft-drink cans full of gasoline into the plane and was trying to set the gas alight in the bathroom when a flight attendant stopped her. (The airline gave the attendant a bonus worth $17,000.)[1] Until then, airline passengers in China had been able to take drinks or other liquids through security checkpoints without the 3.5-ounce maximum that had become familiar in the United States and Europe. Soon after the incident, Chinese authorities imposed similar limits on liquids or gels. But at most Chinese airports they didn't require passengers to take off their shoes until another bombing scare in Xinjiang in 2011.

In those same spring months before the Olympics, subway stations across Beijing were equipped all at once with X-ray screening machines for bags and parcels. In theory, anyone bringing a purse, briefcase, or backpack into the subway was supposed to put it on a conveyor belt for inspection. In practice, people who looked rushed enough, or were intent enough on dodging eye contact with the half-attentive guards, or whose bulky parcels of goods for sale at open-air markets (or bedroll containing clothes and belongings, if they were migrant workers) were too big to fit inside the X-ray machine could often breeze right past the screeners and toward the ticket gate. As a foreigner, I was reluctant to try the same thing myself until I saw that nothing happened to the Chinese commuters who obliviously barged through. Aha! So this was one of the countless "rules" in Chinese life ignored by most people most of the time, but always available for enforcement if the need arose. By the time we left Beijing, a year after the Olympics' close, I'd perfected the art of hiding a briefcase under my coat or sweater when it was cold, or on warmer days holding it open for a cursory glance by the guards as I quickly strode past the machine.

The Olympics came and went, but the machines in Beijing stayed on—and soon they had spread to the Shanghai subways, in anticipation of its 2010 World Expo. By 2011 they appeared to be a permanent fixture in both cities, and at many subway stops attendants grew more dutiful about making sure all incoming bags went on the belts. I learned later that the screening machines were made by a company owned by Hu Jintao's son-in-law; that business, plus what always looked like make-work for the young women who staffed most of the checkpoints, gave this form of security theater an economic logic in China.

The sixtieth anniversary of the founding of the People's Republic of China, on October 1, 2009, required extra security for the mass rallies and parade of military equipment that day. Shortly thereafter so did the *liang hui* (两会), or annual "Dual Meetings" of political leaders from around the country, and the visit of President Barack Obama a few weeks after that.

But of all the moments of lockdown in Beijing itself that year, the most palpably tense came on May 35. This was the twentieth anniversary of the Tiananmen Square protests and crackdown, which had occurred on the fourth day of June of 1989—or the thirty-fifth of May, as Chinese students put it in blog posts and text messages to avoid screening by automated censors. Day by day in late spring security officials were more and more obviously on guard for anything that could constitute a "surprise" or "incident" on the anniversary.

By the evening of May 34, or June 3, when my wife and I went from our apartment near the Guomao intersection two miles west toward Tiananmen Square, along with our Chinese-speaking Belgian friend Peter Claeys—the same friend with whom I'd flown the Cirrus to Zhuhai—the layers of security were already more elaborate than we had seen in our previous three years in the country. We took the Beijing Metro Line 1 to the Tiananmen Square East Station, and as we trudged up the stairs toward the street, we discovered that we would need to pick our way around large numbers of People's Liberation Army troops, in their familiar light green shirts and dark green trousers. Once outside, on the main Chang'An Road that runs between Tiananmen Square and the Forbidden City, we also saw regular police and security forces, in light blue shirts with dark blue pants. Then scores of blatantly plainclothes policemen—fit young men, looking as if they'd just come in from the parade yard and switched out of uniform into identical-looking "casual" pants and shirts. Then a contingent the likes of which we had not ever seen before, or at least not ever noticed. These were plainclothesmen trying a little harder to be plain-clothed. They looked like the counterparts of the undercover narco detail in a *Mod Squad*–type American police movie: young men with hip-looking fauxhawks or extra-long hairstyles, some dressed in cargo shorts with Hawaiian shirts, or black T-shirts, or white "wife-beater" sleeveless T-shirts, all looking as if they had nothing particular to do—but all scanning the crowd every second, in the fashion of Secret Service agents on an American presidential trip.

As we looked across a broad boulevard to Tiananmen Square itself, we saw that its paved expanses, capable of holding tens of thousands of tourists on a normal day, were empty except for the army and police troops. Waist-high aluminum crowd barriers were on all sides, to keep anyone out—and police were confining all visitors to sidewalks on the far sides of the square. Knowing that dozens of officials' eyes were on us, we looked as innocently as we could toward the monuments, and like the few Chinese tourists there took pictures toward the setting sun.

I heard a commotion behind us, and saw a young Chinese-looking man being hustled away by some of the "informal" plainclothesmen. He was calling out—in Chinese, English, and a language I didn't immediately recognize—asking people for help. We turned to look, and immediately found a short and very toughly built Chinese man, with a shag-cut hairdo and shorts and a wife-beater T-shirt, standing right in front of us. "This does not concern you," he said to us in English. "This is the police's business. It is not your concern. Go on your way."

We walked away from the altercation for thirty or forty seconds, enough to indicate that we were not making trouble and would do as we were told. At that point, when we convinced ourselves that we were a safe distance away, I turned around, to look back to the scene of the police action we'd just watched. And, inconspicuously, I thought, took a picture of the man we'd seen earlier, still struggling with plainclothes police. As soon as I'd snapped the picture, I turned back around, and we quickened our pace toward the south end of the vast plaza. Within a few more strides we were surrounded on all sides by a group of police in mufti.

They waited until a young supervisor who spoke some English appeared. Peter Claeys, who had lived in China for years and was always complimented by Chinese people on his mastery of Mandarin, played dumb about understanding what the rest of the policemen were saying to one another.

"Did you take a picture?" the supervisor asked me. I could see no payoff in dissembling. "Yes." "Why did you do that?" "I don't know." The young questioner stepped away and spoke into a police walkie-talkie. Fifty yards away, we saw the man who'd originally warned us talking on a walkie-talkie too. He seemed to be in charge and to be running the investigation from afar. We could hear both ends of their conversation, which was of course in Chinese. Our Belgian friend listened and gave us quiet updates in French—his first language, and one my wife and I could handle but the Chinese cops could not.

"Are you here on a journalist visa?" the young man said when he had finished his walkie-talkie consultation. I was relieved to be able to say forcefully and honestly, "No." I'd been denied a journalist visa when I first applied at the Washington, D.C., embassy back in 2005—and through the years since then I'd made do with a variety of business, academic, and tourist visas to remain in China. I introduced myself freely to officials as a reporter when requesting interviews; I gave them copies of books and articles after they appeared. No one in Chinese officialdom (except, conveniently, this policeman) had any doubt about my role. And as long as no one I interviewed had to take official responsibility for approving a visa that could conceivably lead to trouble, no one cared whether I was following the letter of the law.

"We're here on tourist visas," I added, helpfully, telling him the literal truth but inviting him to draw the wrong conclusion. "Where are your passports?" he asked. We said we didn't have them—for fear of losing them or having them stolen, we didn't carry them around on the street.

Now we had a problem, since in principle foreigners are supposed to carry passports at all times. And this was the opening for the police: We were in direct and admitted violation of yet another law that was generally ignored but could be applied when useful. After consultation with the boss in cargo shorts, the local sublieutenant began to give us a stern lecture about the importance of showing respect for Chinese law while enjoying the privilege of traveling in Chinese territory, about Chinese laws deserving the same respect any other country's did, about China's refusal to tolerate signs of disrespect, and so on.

At times over the next near-hour, I was worried—within limits. The blunt truth is that in most cases, the worst punishment a foreigner in China will face is to be made to leave the country. That is of course not the worst thing that can happen to local Chinese citizens who cooperate with journalists and other outsiders, a reality that both the Chinese and the foreigners need constantly to weigh. Peter Claeys, who had recently moved from Shanghai to Taiwan, was near the end of his planned visit to China anyway—but my wife and I had trips booked through rural China for the next few weeks. What would we do if we were forced to leave? Would we be able to come back?

After much fretting and consultation over the walkie-talkie, a solution was found. I would write a confession, and an apology—requests redolent of the "self-criticism" that the communist leadership had asked of dissenters through its history. Then we could be sent on our way. I pulled a notebook out of my back pocket and ripped out a sheet of paper, trying to close it before the policeman had a chance to think about the words REPORTER'S NOTEBOOK in big print across its cover. And what should I write?

Sentence by sentence, the young policeman got instructions over the walkie-talkie from his boss and relayed them to me. "You write, 'I am sorry for interfering with the police during their work,'" he told me. "Okay," I said, and started writing some words. I said them aloud to him as I wrote: "I understand that the police feel I interfered with them in their work." He took the paper from me and read it back to his captain, who noticed the difference. "No," the young policeman said. "You will say 'I am sorry.'" "Okay." I crossed out the original words and started again. "I am sorry that the police feel I interfered with them at their work."

That one got through. Then on to the next item of confession. "You should write, 'I broke Chinese law that I must carry my passport.'" "Okay. 'I broke Chinese law that I should carry my passport, because I was afraid of having it stolen after my wallet was taken by pickpockets last week on the Beijing Metro.'"

That was the truth, even though it was the only instance of

even petty crime that had affected us through the previous three years in China. Gangs of Dickensian urchins got on the most crowded cars at the most jammed stations at the peak of Beijing's rush hour—and "accidentally" stood blocking the doors, so that passengers trying to get off essentially had to swim through a sea of bodies from the car's interior onto the platform. By the time they escaped the car and reached the platform and could recognize that their purse or wallet had disappeared, the train was already rolling away. A few days earlier I had performed just such a mid-car freestyle routine, losing contact with the car's floor for several seconds and being suspended by other bodies, as I escaped the train at the super-packed Guomao Station near our apartment. As soon as I got to my feet on the platform and watched the train depart, I could feel the emptiness in my back pocket where my wallet had been. By the time I got back to my apartment and began calling credit-card companies ten minutes later, my Visa card had already been used at a Starbucks two stops down the line—a test transaction, to see if the card worked—and my MasterCard had been used for a small purchase at an art store and then tried (and rejected) for a major buy at a camera store. All this was a nuisance at the time, but it gave me a story to tell the policeman at Tiananmen Square. This departure from his prescribed script, to give my excuse for leaving my passport at home, he also allowed.

A few more sentences, about the importance of respecting China, respecting its laws, respecting its police, and respecting the duties of a foreigner when visiting another country. I told myself that none of the prose I was writing at a Chinese policeman's direction could ever be used against me outside China, because no native speaker of English would think I had "confessed." It would be like a hostage photo in which I was giving hand signals of resistance. The police took all the contact info they could think of—our apartment number, the telephone number of the management, our address in the United States.

At the very end, the boss in the cargo shorts and modish haircut came over, and he watched me erase every photo in my camera that showed police or soldiers. The process was surprisingly delicate. He and his police colleagues didn't seize or smash my camera. They didn't confiscate the digital memory card. They didn't ask that everything on the card be zapped, through a "bulk erase." One by one, the cop in charge looked at my camera's view screen to see each of the thirty or forty shots I had taken, and one by one he asked me to push the "erase" button. When we got to an innocuous tourist vista of the square taken just before the troubles began, he said I could stop.

Then, "You should go home." This time we complied, and fast.

A recent sign of nervousness: the "Jasmine" movement

My wife and I were living again in Beijing through the early months of 2011, as the "Arab Spring" movements spread a mixture of promise and turmoil across the Middle East, the prospect of a parallel "Jasmine Revolution" brought increased security and clampdown in much of China. The government's response again raised doubts about its ability to embrace the openness and experimentation that world leadership in fields like aerospace would demand.

Objectively, there seemed to be very little reason for Hu Jintao and his colleagues to think of themselves in a position anything like that of the quickly deposed Mubarak in Egypt, Ben Ali in Tunisia, or Qaddafi in Libya. Unlike any of those countries, China's overall economy had not been stagnating. Demographically the main Chinese fear was that it had the exact opposite problem of many Arab countries: too few young people entering the workforce relative to the jobs that had to be done and the retirees who had to be supported. While the Communist Party of China had a permanent hold on power, its individual leaders were rotated out as they reached retirement age, rather than hanging on as life-tenure autocrats. Despite a range of sources of serious discontent—inflation, corruption, pollution, the gap between collective national wealth and the uncertain position of each specific family—in the living memory of most Chinese people things had overall gotten better rather than worse.

The leaders of the Chinese Communist Party, unlike the Arab autocrats, faced problems but not crises. Speculating about how "the Chinese electorate" would vote, if it could vote, is difficult, but all evidence I've seen suggests that, if faced with an up-or-down choice on the current regime, more people would vote to stick with it than to throw it out. The economy keeps growing; material circumstances improve for most people in most of the country. And it's meaningless to ask whether a rival party or slate of candidates would be more popular, since none is allowed to emerge. Even the tens of thousands of protests that erupt across the country each year—yes, that means an average of one hundred to two hundred marches or demonstrations somewhere in the country every day—are more often directed against local abuses than against the legitimacy of the Chinese system as a whole. In all the cases I have seen, people were complaining about the local landlord or factory owner and in fact appealing to the central government to come in and straighten things out.

Yet in these circumstances, so different from the powder keg of economically stagnant societies in North Africa and the Middle East, China's security system reacted in early 2011 as if it faced a threat so dire that it dared take no risks at all. Lawyers who had defended those accused of political crimes were themselves arrested, or just disappeared from view.[2] Nongovernmental organizations were closed down. The Nobel Committee expressed concern that it could no longer even make contact with Liu Xiaobo to be sure that he was alive and physically well.

After text and Internet messages spread and recommended that Chinese people gather for "Jasmine Protests" in Beijing, Shanghai, and other big cities, the mobile-phone data networks that are urban China's main communication tools were blocked or interfered with. As each of the appointed days dawned, the public areas were flooded with plainclothes and uniformed police. On the first "Jasmine Sunday" in Beijing, we saw a handful of Chinese demonstrators joined by an equal number of foreign reporters—and five or six times as many Chinese security officials. On the next Sunday, there were virtually no demonstrators, and many of the foreign reporters were roughed up, detained, and warned that under new rules they needed official permission to interview anyone in downtown Beijing. By the following Sunday, the movement had more or less run its course, for now.

Through those same Arab Spring weeks in 2011, the government signaled in countless other ways that between the risks of cracking down too hard, and those of not cracking down hard enough, it would always err on the side of being tough. Leading Chinese papers published editorials saying that, as China continued through a difficult economic transition, people had to understand that political disagreements needed to be contained.[3] Peking University announced that it would screen incoming students for "radical thoughts," to prevent trouble before it happened.[4] On a Friday in early April, Beijing municipal authorities ordered the cancellation of a prestigious annual debate tournament among teams from sixteen leading Chinese universities that was scheduled to begin the next day. The tournament had run every year since 2002, with no previous interference or problems. But the topic for the 2011 tournament, a retroactive assessment of the 1911 revolution led by Sun Yat-sen, was deemed "too sensitive" for public discussion a century later.

Through the previous five years in which my wife and I had been living in or traveling to China, it had been moving toward a condition of "permanent emergency." By analogy: For most of the decade after the 9/11 attacks, the U.S. Department of Homeland Security had persisted with its meaningless color-coded "threat level" system, which for years on end was set constantly at "orange."[5] Society was in a state of permanent threat; it was as if the National Weather Service, on learning that a tornado might strike Kansas, put the entire country on an open-ended alert.

A similar security ratchet has been in effect in China. Month by month, the specific reason that conditions were "unusually sensitive" varied. But, as enumerated earlier, there was always some reason, and special security measures were always called for. There was a year's buildup of special security for the Olympics, and then a year for the Expo in Shanghai. In the early springtime of each year the Dual Meetings of political leaders, or *liang hui*, required special controls, especially in Beijing. One indication that the Dual Meetings were under way: Many of the pirated-video shops near Tiananmen Square and the central government headquarters closed for the week. It was a sign of propriety, or something. In the fall, National Day and its associated meetings and parades has a similar effect.

There was upset in Tibet. There was upset in Xinjiang. Then upset in Inner Mongolia. And the Arab Spring. There had been a year or two of "unusual" sensitivity before Hu Jintao and Wen Jiabao leave the top two party leadership positions in 2012. There will be a year or two of special sensitivity after that.

In the first three decades after China's great opening in 1979, the government's level of nervousness and consequent hyper-control might vary month by month. But year by year, and certainly decade by decade, the trend had been toward opening. When the 1980s are compared with the 1970s, and then the 1990s with the 1980s, and then the early 2000s with the 1990s, it is clear that over each of these periods life within China was becoming freer, more predictable, more connected to the outside world, more bound by the rule of law. The China of the Beijing Olympic era was unrecognizably more open and internationalized than the one I had first visited in 1986. But as I write at the end of 2011, things have been moving the other way. For how long?

The Internet as indicator

The clearest modern indication of a society's confidence or insecurity, and by extension its readiness for modern creative industries like aviation, is its policy toward the Internet. The Chinese government's steady attempt to throttle its people's connection with the outside world is a dramatic sign of its nervousness, and a profound threat to the future of any advanced industry, including aerospace.

What matters to expats, especially in still-developing countries, is an unreliable guide to what matters to local citizens. While living in China, I hated the beer, which like most beer in Asia is "light," weak, and watery. But my taste was clearly at odds with that of Chinese customers, who bought the beer so avidly that China has become by far the world's leading beer-drinking nation. Craft breweries, tailored to expats' taste, keep opening up in big Chinese cities, and most often keep closing down.

A similar-sounding foreign complaint in China—that Internet access is so slow, unreliable, and often interfered with—might seem to be similarly detached from locally important reality. Many Internet problems in China arise from attempts to reach sites located somewhere else. If, like most Chinese users, you are mainly looking for information that is written in Chinese and is on sites and servers within China, you have fewer complaints. Over the past decade, the Chinese media have consistently presented the message that the "uncontrolled" Internet is a wild and dangerous place, full of criminals, perverts, and other threats to the well-being of "netizens," notably youths. Surveys of mass Chinese opinion, as opposed to outspoken "netizen" minorities, have consistently shown large majorities saying that they are grateful for government monitoring of this potential menace.

But even from a purely Chinese perspective, the increasing state controls on electronic communication represent something important. They symbolize an increasing divergence in the post-Olympic years between China's path and that of most other "first rate" nations, and they matter in practical terms.

At the time of the Olympic Games, the genius of China's "Great Firewall" system might have been described as its flexible repression.[6] The guiding principle seemed to be that Chinese censorship would make it just difficult enough to find unauthorized material that the great majority of Chinese citizens wouldn't bother—but would allow enough loopholes and pressure valves that people who really cared about finding something could manage to do so. The loophole mainly took the form of the government's turning a blind eye toward VPNs—virtual private networks, which were in effect ways that anyone willing to spend one or two dollars per week could buy safe passage through, under, over, or around the Great Firewall. You signed up for a VPN service, you made your connection, and from that point on you prowled through the Internet just as if your computer were logged on from London or New York. (Indeed, the VPN worked by making the computer's connection appear to be in one of those cities outside China.)

Why did the government allow the loophole? For a long while, the confident assumption by most foreigners was that the government didn't really care what the foreigners or even the English-fluent Chinese elite might read. In fact, the creator of the Great Firewall, a computer scientist—and university president—named Fang Binxing, made waves in February, 2011 by telling a leading Chinese newspaper that he had six VPNs running on his computers at home. (Within a few hours, that report was removed from the paper's Web site. Foreseeing this possibility, like a number of other foreigners I saved a copy of the page as soon as I saw it.)

Moreover, truly interfering with VPN operations would make it simply impossible for banks and big industrial firms to do their work in China. The survival of their business depends on the integrity of their data. Financial firms rely on accurate and secure transmission trades, transfers, and account information among their offices worldwide. Manufacturing firms are constantly exchanging shipping and production data. The threat that data will be intercepted, monitored, or altered is worrisome enough in the best of circumstances, which is why companies use VPNs for their private data even in Europe or North America. To entrust their information to the "public" Internet in China, for screening by the Great Firewall, would be inconceivable.

Google was evicted from China in early 2010, and within a

year doing business over the Internet anywhere in the country became significantly harder. VPNs suddenly stopped working. The leading ones sent out messages to users in China suggesting new IP addresses to use, with new settings; almost immediately many of those were blocked as well. If you have used the Internet while in South Korea, Japan, or Singapore and then tried it from America, you know that the load time for Web pages in the United States seems shockingly slow. In countries with ubiquitous high-speed broadband, pages load practically as soon as they are selected. By comparison, the half second or so it might take for a complex page to load over a slow U.S. connection can seem an obstacle. In China, during the crackdown, you could wait five, ten, thirty seconds for a page to appear—if it appeared at all.

Google, with its range of services, was a special target, for obvious reasons. One study found that it took forty-four times longer for a Gmail screen to come up than the domestic Chinese system QQ, and eight times longer than Yahoo.[7] The government's Google-specific filtering and interference techniques became sophisticated enough that sometimes users would see a list of messages in their inbox or documents they had stored as "Google Apps," but if they clicked to open a document or send a message they had been composing, the screen would freeze. Eventually it would display the message that in the rest of the world meant an actual connection failure but that in China usually meant that the firewall was at work: "The connection has been reset." When I was grumbling during this period to a foreign tech expert who was on long-term assignment in China, he said that he had been wrestling with the same problem. "If I hadn't spent years in this field, I'd never be able to reconfigure my home network in Beijing simply to connect to Gmail," he told me.

And Google was in a better situation than Facebook, Twitter, LinkedIn, and many other services, which much of the time were blocked altogether. "I have to say, Twitter, Facebook, Google Earth, and the rest didn't do themselves any favors by telling the world they were responsible for Egypt and Tunisia," a Western businessperson who had worked in China for decades told me during the Arab Spring. "What do you expect China's response to be? You have given a gun to the hard-liners—not that there is any 'soft-liner' in the government, but you're playing to the deepest fear of everyone in the government by saying there is a force outside China that they can't control, and that will fundamentally change politics here. That, they will stop."

Just after the disastrous 2011 earthquake and tsunami in Japan, I corresponded with a Western journalist who had returned to his home in Shanghai from the devastated areas of northern Japan, where he was reporting on the villages that had been obliterated and the families whose loved ones were still lost. The Japanese government was being criticized for not saying more, faster, about its problems, he pointed out—but then he drew the contrast with China. "One of the more helpful sites to those of us trying to get a sense of what might be happening at the stricken Daiichi Fukushima plant has been the Union of Concerned Scientists' [site]," he wrote in a note. "The folks there have been almost unerringly—and depressingly—accurate in their postings. Yet upon returning home to Shanghai last night for a few days, I find that the site appears to be blocked here in China (though accessible through my usual proxy)." Then the real reflection on China: "Anyone care to speculate as to why THIS site would be blocked? What are they"—the Chinese government—"afraid of? Or is the answer simply that these days, they're afraid of EVERYTHING . . ."

For many puzzling events in China, like the variation in what laws are enforced in different parts of the country, or the varying messages about foreign policy coming from different branches of the government, I assume an "accident rather than conspiracy" explanation. Coordination is so difficult, divergences are so great; internal friction among rival or disconnected entities is often more significant than any concerted effort to deal with the outside world. But in this case, I came to believe the hypothesis that the Internet controls were a purposeful trial run, an experiment to learn exactly what it would take to close down the VPNs altogether if it came to an emergency. Indeed, I interviewed enough tech officials, from enough companies from enough different parts of the world, to be confident in a conclusion I generally resisted about China: that there was a deliberate plan to cut off all access, that it was being tested, and that it would certainly be used if conditions became tense enough.

"There is a widespread sense of anger and malaise among the foreign community here—myself included," one long-time resident wrote me in an e-mail message. "I suspect it's because this is a reminder that whatever rights we thought we enjoyed here were merely privileges, granted and rescinded by the government." A prominent blogger in China sent out this tweet (using a VPN to escape firewall controls) in the summer of 2011: "Anyone bullish about China should come and try to use the Internet here." Or to put it as the head of an American Internet company did in an e-mail to me during the crackdown, "Ultimately, if they want to take the country's Internet connections 'Third Word,' none of us can prevent that."

"Did the Brits ban steam?"

One of China's main nationalist papers, *Global Times,* has argued that China needed special consideration and understanding in circumstances like these. It was still too early to unleash the full power of free communications on the society. "The Internet has broken China's previous social calm, and forced society to proceed hurriedly in respect of issues like democracy," the official English version of the editorial said. A few weeks later, the same paper argued that since the Pentagon was shifting the international battlefield onto the Internet, the Chinese government had no sane alternative but to exercise its own controls to defend China's national security.[8] The *People's Daily* chimed in around the same time, "Chinese people fear turbulence and worry about being led into troubles and so they ardently hope for stability, harmony and peace."[9]

This was putting a proudly nationalistic gloss on the idea that there was a time and place for each stage of development, and that the proper time had not yet come for Chinese people to choose and filter information on their own. Opinion polls in China, for what they are worth, suggest that many people were indeed comforted by the government's role in shielding them from dangerous views. But I know there are people who feel infantilized and diminished by this reminder that they're not quite part of the modern world. I know because I've met many of them. Students at universities seemed dutiful rather than sincere in explaining that they didn't really miss much by using the Baidu search engine instead of Google. "They are kind of embarrassed," one tech expert said at a program in Bejing in

2011. "It suggests a kind of second-rateism for the country, even now."

In an interview with a Chinese Web site in 2011,[10] Richard Parris, an Australian Internet-technologist living in Beijing, pointed out that the number of Chinese people directly affected by Internet censorship was relatively small. But he argued that the restrictions had a disproportionately large effect on the country and its potential. The small group directly inconvenienced constituted a large share of those Chinese with ambitions to operate at the highest level of scholarship, scientific research, technical innovation, and other elements of truly first-rate international activity. Among others, they would likely include those with the greatest ambitions to learn from and compete with the world's best in aerospace or other advanced high-tech fields. "This is a younger, more Internet-literate group, more likely to have a friend overseas with a Facebook account," Parris said. "Or a new colleague who can't *believe* that they can't get on their Facebook account in China."

Hip and worldly young Chinese might be embarrassed in front of their foreign friends by these remnants of backwardness, Parris said. But the real damage to the country was that in any line of work that depended on international communication, "there was a sense that this could make China second-rate. If you're an Internet professional, *this is not the place you'll want to work* if you want to be competing with the best. This will still be a place where people can make money. But they will go to Silicon Valley—or India" (or other countries he could have mentioned) "to be part of real innovation" in modern fields like infotech, biotech, and aerospace.

"I feel so sorry for China's scientists, engineers, and artists in all of this," a foreign friend of mine who has worked for years as a musician in Beijing told me during the Jasmine crackdowns.

"Just at the moment that should be their 'coming out,' which happens by sheer luck to coincide with the blossoming of the Internet as the very fabric and medium of the scientific and artistic worlds at large, they have these additional handcuffs slapped on them by their own government. They have plenty enough access to the Internet to know how important it is, but just enough obstacles to prevent them from joining and taking advantage of it all."

Or, as another correspondent suggested in an e-mail exchange, "What country ever rode to preeminence by fighting the reigning technology of the time? Did the Brits ban steam?"

China's universities as bellwether

China's universities are at the heart of this transformation. If they can flourish and mature, almost anything will be possible, including eventual world leadership in aerospace. If they cannot, it will be a sign of larger obstacles to the country's emergence. The outsized share of the world's top research universities is one of the three American advantages hardest for any other country to match. (The others: openness to large-scale flow of immigrant talent, and an even more outsized share of world military power. Of course, the first two build greater strength in the long run; the third threatens to sap it.)

The news that the outside world receives about China's output of cars, computers, buildings, and high-speed trains applies to China's approach to higher education as well. Huge amounts of money are being spent; classrooms and laboratories are being equipped at record speeds; larger and larger cohorts of graduates are being tested, trained, and prepared for their own success and their nation's. "In twenty-five years, only a generation's time, these universities could rival the Ivy League," Richard Levin, the president of Yale, said in a speech at the Royal Society in London in 2010, referring to India's ambitions as well as China's. "This is an audacious agenda, but China, in particular, has the will and resources that make it feasible."[11] Soon thereafter, the Royal Society issued its own report on national trends in scientific research, which had a similarly cautionary and awestruck tone. A BBC summary of the report said that "China is on course to overtake the US in scientific output possibly as soon as 2013—far earlier than expected."[12] Also that fall, a report in *The Telegraph* in England was headlined, "China: The Ultimate Brain Drain?"[13] During his time as leader of one of the world's great universities, Levin has placed special emphasis on developing ties with students and institutions within China and has visited the country often. When I asked him in Beijing just before the 2008 Olympics whether it would be possible to create a first-rate academic system within a political and media environment as closed as China's, his response was immediate and positive. "Sure," he said. "The Soviet Union did it." He went on to argue that a surprisingly large share of the curriculum of a leading international university could fit and flourish even within the confines of modern Chinese controls. Certainly in math and sciences, engineering, music, and some other liberal-arts fields, the universities of the Soviet era were strong; and today's China is far less sweepingly totalitarian than the Soviet system was even in its reform era.

Yet by the time the Berlin Wall fell, the Soviet Union and its Eastern bloc nations were as short on the broader cultural and intellectual achievements that great universities both promote and symbolize as they were on high-tech consumer goods. Universities become great by attracting the best scholars and the best students from around the world. Few of the world's most sought-after candidates were competing for places at universities in Leningrad or Warsaw. Few ambitious graduate students or aspiring inventors who had a choice of where to live chose to live in or move to the Soviet bloc to realize their dreams.

China's situation is obviously more promising than the Soviet Union's, and it is already more attractive to students and teachers who want to be part of the excitement that is modern Chinese life. But the culture of China's educational and research establishment symbolizes some of the country's problems now, and a change in that culture would be significant.

When the Royal Society emphasized the output of research papers from scientists at Chinese universities, it counted only the volume of the work, not its quality. This same Royal Society paper showed that while China had nearly matched the United States in total output of papers, it barely registered in international standings of *cited* work—papers significant enough to be referred to by scientists in other laboratories and other countries.[14]

An increasing number of domestic Chinese and international reports have underscored what anyone teaching classes in Chinese universities has noticed: that Western complaints about "publish or perish" pressures are nothing compared with the imperative for industrial-scale output among many Chinese scholars. In 2010, a British scientific journal revoked seventy papers it had received from two scientists at the same university in China; the journal said that the laboratory "findings" had simply been faked. "Academic fraud, misconduct and ethical violations are very common in China," Rao Yi, a professor and dean of the life sciences school at Peking University, told the Associated Press after that episode.[15] Another Chinese professor, Zhang Ming of Renmin University in Beijing, told *The New York Times,* "If we don't change our ways, we will be excluded from the global academic community."[16]

A culture of copying shows up in many ways in China, as it has in other societies during periods of catch-up. As my Chinese friends who have studied American history frequently point out, through much of the nineteenth century American "inventors" and industrialists relied heavily on copying and stealing British and European designs. The most emotional note in Charles Dickens's dispatches from America in the 1840s is his irritation about pirated U.S. copies of his works.

The United States outgrew this phase; the question for China is whether it will do so too, and, if so, when. Thirty years after China's opening to world commerce, more than a decade after its entry into the World Trade Organization, nearly all software and videos used in China are pirated. In 2011, Microsoft's CEO, Steve Ballmer, pointed out that almost as many personal computers were sold in China as in the United States, but Chinese customers bought only one twentieth as many licensed copies of Windows as Americans did.[17] Nearly every day the foreign and local Chinese press in China carries accounts of patients who suffer after taking faked medicines, or pilots who have flown for airlines with faked flight-training certificates.

In my experience, many Chinese students believe that sharing homework (or copying essays or "research" papers from the Internet) is not any sort of cheating but is perfectly standard behavior. Before its climactic showdown with the Chinese government disrupted its mainland operations, Google had made arrangements with Chinese publishers to avoid copyright complaints about the books it indexed in its Google Books program. As it has done in other countries, Google scanned the books' contents and allowed users to search for selected passages, but it did not make the entire contents available for bulk download. Meanwhile its Chinese counterpart, Baidu, had uploaded complete versions of millions of Chinese books, and many non-Chinese works as well, and made them available in their entirety for free download, as if no copyright laws applied. They stopped only after the unusual intervention of a group of Chinese authors, who complained to Baidu's founder and CEO, the billionaire Li Yanhong—known as Robin Li in his days as a computer-science grad student at SUNY Buffalo and as an online developer for *The Wall Street Journal* in New York. In 2011, Li agreed to close the pirated book depository down.

"The reason Li and Baidu are in this public relations mess now is because, for years, they behaved like many Chinese businesses, consumers and government officials," the Beijing correspondent for *Forbes,* Gady Epstein, wrote during the controversy.[18] "They exhibited a casual disregard for piracy, in a culture and economy that did not value intellectual property. . . . Robin Li's problem, in other words, is China's problem." Epstein also quoted the widespread Chinese crack that Baidu should take as its motto the reverse of Google's, or, simply, "Be evil."

The Chinese system strains mightily toward ultimate recognition of its achievements through Nobel Prizes, which was one reason the selection of Liu Xiaobo was so galling. Clearly Chinese scientists are capable of world-leading work, and many Chinese-born or ethnically Chinese scientists have been recognized with Nobel Prizes for their research. But as of 2011, all such awards have been for work conducted in American, British, French, or other foreign laboratories. No one of any ethnicity has won an award for scientific work within a Chinese institution.

A system this vast has many areas of excellence, which will expand; it will certainly win prizes and continue to improve; .

and if funding and other inequalities drive Western systems into a tailspin, it is possible that the Chinese system will catch up. If so, that will say as much about what the West is doing wrong, as what China is doing right.

Accountability and rule of law

The Chinese system is a resounding thirty-year demonstration that ever-growing economic output can coexist with tight political control. But the commercial and technological achievements that would represent China's next great step, including leadership in aviation, create new complications. Everywhere else those achievements have occurred, they have required a "soft infrastructure" of customs, laws, procedural protections, and bureaucratic order. They don't necessarily require fully functioning democracy. Japan's decades of post–World War II development occurred in a system that was democratic yet in which the same party always won; Singapore's system is still a paternalistic-guided democracy; South Korea developed under a military dictatorship; and the established political systems of Europe and North America have struggled to stay on a democratic keel. But through the centuries of industrialization, they have moved continually to build this soft infrastructure—through protection of contracts, rule of law, efforts to provide some equality of treatment and opportunity.

Without these protections, China will ultimately fail to flourish. It won't have leading Internet industries, or biotech companies, or aerospace innovation centers, or whatever field the most ambitious young dreamers are drawn to twenty years from now. It will fail because the world's most talented people will choose to work somewhere other than China—a freedom more and more available to the world's talented elite with each passing year. Thus the nature of China's civil society—not whether its people can count on protections from business competitors, and from the police—will play an enormous part in whether dreamers, like those portrayed in this book, can make their dreams come true.

The foreigners who say that today's China is totalitarian are not paying attention. There are too many people, doing too many inventive things, across too great a stretch of territory to be under direct governmental supervision and control. The system is instead authoritarian and decentralized, with the government cracking down where it feels it must, and observing points of discontent and pressure among the population to address them if it can.

The modern Chinese system of "informal accountability" relies on governmental monitoring of the Internet and other channels of communication, to learn about sources of discontent before they become extreme. It comes from rewarding mayors and provincial governors for calm and prosperity in their areas, rather than just for cracking down. If peasants or migrant workers are about to revolt, the government's Plan B is to send in troops to repress them. Plan A is to placate them, if possible, with jobs, schools, or other benefits.

For instance: After the financial crash late in 2008, many millions of Chinese workers suddenly lost their jobs in export factories that depended on customers in North America or Europe. They went home, in droves, to their villages in the countryside. (From our apartment in Beijing, which directly overlooked a long-distance-bus station, we saw crowds of migrants, all their possessions in big sacks over their shoulders, line up to take the buses home each day.) Rather than let them fester there, the government launched large-scale public-works programs to give them jobs and income, as well as inaugurating health-care programs in rural villages. When traveling through Yunnan and Sichuan provinces in early 2009, we passed along rural road-ways teeming with hoe- and shovel-wielding laborers, dozens per mile employed on repaving projects.

But even the most sensitive network of informal accountabil-ity is different from a predictable, transparent set of rules, just as the informal system of training and checking pilots was different from the formal check airman system that Joe T helped intro-duce. Full modernization depends on the predictability that is another term for the rule of law. It is the sense that personal or company assets, once developed, won't be arbitrarily seized; that a society's basic operating principles won't be changed capri-ciously so that what was taken for granted yesterday is a serious crime today; that the various interests affected by policies and plans won't be entirely ignored as policies change. Capitalist development—for that matter, communist too—depends on some sense that efforts today will have a predictable outcome tomorrow.

Month by month, connection by connection, liberalization by liberalization, since 1979 the Chinese system has moved in this direction. How much further will it move? And how fast?

China has moved generally but not consistently ahead. The biggest jolt backward was of course in 1989, at Tiananmen Square. Minor disruptions have happened repeatedly since then, including the Jasmine upheavals of 2011. An influential essay in *The Wall Street Journal* argued that the increasing crackdowns of the Jasmine era were ominous precisely because authorities barely bothered to pretend that they were following preexist-ing rules.[19] "Signs of tightening control have been visible for several years," the author, a human-rights activist named Joshua Rosenzweig, wrote. "But the authorities are now employing a range of new, illegal methods to silence their critics." During the few weeks after the Jasmine threat, some fifty prominent civic figures—writers, lawyers, bloggers, professors—were either arrested or simply vanished.[20]

In reflecting on these and other crackdowns, a law professor named Carl Minzner wrote that China was "turning against the law."[21] The argument was that regularized legal procedures had been convenient during China's decades of expanded trade. But now they were proving inconvenient and so would be ignored. The treatment of Google was as significant on this score as for what it signified about free speech. Google's big showdown over censorship occurred early in 2010, when it chose to move its search systems out of mainland China rather than continue to comply with orders to "filter" the results. Not long afterward, the Chinese government began "discovering" that Google had been breaking various tax laws all along—and that its mapping software also violated various Chinese security rules.[22] The shifting landscape of "rules" is mainly discussed in China as it affects political activists and foreign groups. Those consequences are important, but the more challenging question for the people and leaders of the country is what the Chinese system is giving up because of the unaccountable nature of its political power.

Inequality as threat to China's development

One other question about China's soft infrastructure will be answered in the next stage of its development. That is whether life in this communist country has begun to seem intolerably unequal and unfair. The Gini coefficient is a statistical measure, usually taught in courses in economics or sociology, that gauges the degree of economic inequality within a society. The lower the Gini coefficient, the more equal the income distribution; the higher, the less equal. The scale runs from zero to one. In a society whose Gini coefficient was zero, every person would have exactly the same assets as every other person. In a society at the other extreme, with a Gini coefficient of one, one person would own everything, and no one else would have anything.

The Gini coefficient of American society has risen steadily over the past half century, as both income (annual money coming in) and wealth (accumulated earnings through the years) have become more unequal. China's has risen higher, faster. China has dozens of billionaires, and hundreds of millions of peasants. Every day in China brings sights like one I glimpsed in 2011 in Beijing: a chauffeur-driven Bentley, its plutocrat passenger behind darkened windows in the backseat, brushing past a man pulling a cart by the wooden yoke across his shoulders. After a while you stop noticing, or at least marveling. But such extremes have a cumulative effect inside China, especially combined with a growing sense that the rules for achieving success have been rigged.

"It is hard to get anyone in Beijing under the age of thirty to indicate anything but contempt for the government," a professor at one of the city's most famous universities wrote to me during the crackdowns of 2011. "There really is a sense among young people and college students that everyone is grabbing everything they can." The professor mentioned a survey prepared by the consulting firm Bain & Company, as part of its annual "China Wealth Report" for a major Chinese bank, whose results were being hotly discussed in China at about that time. It covered the richest people in China, those with investable assets worth more than $1.5 million, and found that almost half of them had considered leaving the country.

China's most precious assets, the aspiring next generation of the best-positioned families, were more and more being sent overseas. Nearly every member of the ruling State Council has a son or daughter with an Ivy League—or Oxford/Cambridge or Berkeley/MIT—degree. Through the final years of the Hu Jintao–Wen Jiabo era, the mayor of Chongqing, a flamboyant speaker named Bo Xilai, had drawn the nation's attention with his "red" campaigns, designed to recall the patriotism and sacrifice of the Mao era. He sent his son to Harrow, then Oxford, then to Harvard for a graduate degree. In 2011, the Chinese personality magazines had features on the young Bo's romance with Chen Xiaodan, daughter of the head of the China Development Bank. This "golden couple" met in Cambridge, Massachusetts, where she was at the Harvard Business School.

Such extensive knitting-together of China's leaders with outside institutions makes it easier for China and the rest of the world to coexist in the long run. But it creates a deep strain inside the country. China's leaders don't believe enough in the country's own school system to place their children in it.

Each nation has its guiding myth about the structure of opportunity that allows people to rationalize inequality of results. For America it's the idea of a fresh chance. In Japan, opportunity is heavily weighted to success and effort in school. Through the ages in China, people have necessarily absorbed tremendous inequalities of result and have found philosophical and practical ways to cope. It's not just a national-image cliché to say that the idea of endurance, stoicism, "eating bitterness" (*chi ku*, 吃苦) means more in today's China than any corresponding concept would in most rich countries of the world.

The tension in China seems less based on absolute extremes of circumstance than with the *ways* people are getting ahead and becoming rich. A foreign professor at a Beijing university posted the following account online soon after the arduous

Spring Festival migrations at the beginning of the year (he felt
he had to use a pseudonym in order to retain his job):

> Over the Chinese New Year holiday, a crowd of passengers
> at the Tianjin Railway Station were held waiting by police,
> left holding their luggage on the platform in the piercing cold
> wind while a small group of Communist Party cadres strut-
> ted onto a first class carriage. Enraged by the unfairness of
> it all, a young law student from Beijing University snapped
> a photo of the scene with her cell phone. Several uniformed
> and plain-clothes police rushed her, yelling at her to surrender
> her camera and come with them. When they grabbed her, she
> screamed "like a fishwife" (in her own words), creating a scene
> until they let her go. The moment she did board the train, she
> posted her story on her school's micro-blog, where it spread
> like wildfire across the Chinese Internet.
>
> Ever since President Hu Jintao took office in 2003, he has
> made fairness a central theme of his agenda . . . The incident at
> the station, however, reveals the disconnect between the gov-
> ernment's fixation with income inequality and what's really
> been rubbing the masses the wrong way. *What people resent
> isn't wealth, it's privilege.* By and large, your average Chinese
> worker admires people who have gotten rich through clever-
> ness or hard work, because that's what they aspire to do them-
> selves. What bothers them, though, is the growing sense that
> there's a special class of people who get to live by a different set
> of rules than everyone else.[23]

During those same Chinese New Year holidays in 2011, a
writer named Yang Jisheng published an essay about the "different set of rules" applying at the top and the bottom of China's
emerging political and social structure.[24] "Fair dealing is impossible," he wrote, according to the translation by David Bandurski. "Under this system, power is on top, power is worshipped.

Everyone lives in a different power class. The power center is like a black hole that sucks in the wealth of society."

One recent video that attracted millions of views on the Chinese Internet showed a young student at Dezhou University, a provincial school in Shandong province, being picked up by her boyfriend—in his family's helicopter, which landed on the school grounds.[25] Even at the snootiest Swiss or New England boarding school this would draw a second glance; at a second-tier university in a Chinese coal-mining province, with a beau known to be from a politically connected family, it opened a vein. The video of the girl being picked up received 3,300 comments in the first twelve hours it was posted, many to the effect of "this is what China has become."

Part of the appeal and flexibility of Chinese society involves precisely the malleability of rules that, when abused, create the impression of a system that is rigged. People get around rules; they find ways to live with them; no one wants them to be applied too rigidly. But as the momentum has shifted back to the big state enterprises; as the penalty for violating the rules has increased; as the progress toward a more rules-based system has slowed and perhaps reversed; the larger question of whether China can become the best version of itself has returned.

These are the signals we will watch in all of China's most ambitious pursuits, including in the skies.

10 ∗ The Chinese Model, Airborne

A nonuniversal nation

When I first arrived in China, I wrote the one and only "I've just arrived, and here is what I'm wondering" article that journalistic convention permits each writer on first immersion in a country. Among the questions I said I wanted to answer was, What is the Chinese dream?

Nearly six years later, I realize that it's a silly or meaningless question, since for the foreseeable future the country's ambitions will be fully satisfied by allowing hundreds of millions of people to realize their individual and family dreams. Grandparents who can live in reasonable health and security to an old age? Great. Students whose education makes the most of their abilities and who have the chance to do their best around the world? Better still. After China's centuries of seeming to move backward as a society and its more recent decades of tragedy and turmoil, the simple bourgeois comforts are much of what the modern Chinese miracle could and should provide.

But there is a way in which the question does make sense, as an expression of concern about what the rise of a "nonuniversal" nation will mean for the rest of the world.

Through the centuries of Western military, technological, and economic dominance, "universalism" of some sort has been so basic a part of international relations that it barely needed to be discussed. The leaders of the French Revolution issued their Declaration of the Rights of Man—not the rights of Frenchmen. The Declaration of Independence began, "When, in the course of human events," not "events in the colonies of North America." With varying degrees of sincerity, Western colonialists tried to create replica British, French, or American citizens in their colonies. Long before the colonial era, Christian missionaries wanted to bring people worldwide to their view of the one true universal faith. The idea that anyone could—and should—"aspire" to Western standards is simultaneously the most and least admirable part of the Western tradition. Most admirable in advancing the principle that people of different origins, races, and religions should be judged and valued by the same standards. Least admirable in the gap between that principle and a discriminatory reality, and in the condescension it implied for the unfortunate non-Westerners of the world.

The best and worst parts of the American model are intensified versions of this Western universalism. In theory, anyone can become an American. Most Americans innocently, or pridefully, assume that in fact most people around the world want to become Americans, and would if they only had the chance. (And many do want exactly that.) The self-satisfaction of this view can make non-Americans roll their eyes, but it is connected to the factor that is the enduring secret of American national strength.

Modern America's power is often calculated in material terms, from the size and strength of its military to the scale of its corporate assets. But everything I have learned convinces me that these are finally reflections of the country's success in attracting and enabling human talent. That success, in turn, has depended on the fortunate interaction of many different circumstances, rules, and decisions. For the United States these have included immigration policies that made it attractive for ambitious people to migrate and realize their ambitions within American institutions and companies. Persecuted Jews, Hungarians, Cubans, Vietnamese, Iranians, Ethiopians, Chinese, in periods of turmoil in their respective countries; highly motivated Indians, Mexicans, Dominicans, Russians, Nigerians, Irish, Poles, Pakistanis, and many others through the decades. At their best, the levels of America's public-education system, from grade school through Ph.D. programs, created opportunities for the ambitious. A research establishment leveraged their work for public and private benefit; an American pop culture kept renewing itself with outside stimulus until it became for better and worse the pop culture of the world.

In its pluses and its minuses, everything about this approach— the approach that has created the world's reigning power of the moment—is fundamentally different from the principles behind the rise of the aspirant great power, China.

America's challenge is strangely conservative: Somehow it has to avoid destroying the cultural conditions that have been so important to its growth. China's challenge is more complicated—which, of course, doesn't mean that it is insurmountable. The country's successes over the past three decades arise mainly from allowing more and more of its people to apply ideas, ambitions, and energies in ways that benefit themselves and their families, and that build the national economy at the same time. To take the next step in its development, it will have to alter that equation in subtle but significant ways, by granting broader scope to individual ambition than has been possible through the Communist Party's decades in control. The institutions at the heart of such "soft" success have until now been areas of signal weakness for China.

At an individual level, and as an accumulation of daily interactions over the years, my experience is of the great permeability of Chinese culture. People are easy to meet, to get to know, to laugh or argue with. And in its vastness, today's China contains people who belong to a variety of universalist faiths, including Islam, Christianity, Baha'i, and Buddhism.

But in its international dealings as well as in most of its domestic operations, today's China gives more weight to duties and ethics based on personal relations than on abstract principles of how people in general should be treated. It is too pat to put the ethical system the way one Chinese friend did: "Everything for my family and friends; nothing for anyone else." But a variant of these sentiments goes through many aspects of Chinese life. Early in my stay in Shanghai I was amused to see that the first occupant of an elevator would instantly push the "close door" button. Then, for a while, I was annoyed; ultimately I acclimated. When my wife and I had been away from China for several months and returned for a stay, my wife saw a charming young boy walking with his mother on a street in a little enclosed neighborhood. He was eating a bag of potato chips. This was itself a sign of a different trend: the obesity epidemic now affecting China. The country is already dealing with one actuarial consequence of its one-child policy of the past generation—that its population will soon become on average so old. It is just beginning to cope with another, the long-term public-health problems, especially diabetes, coming from the rising rate of obesity in people under twenty, especially the often-favored "little emperor" boys.

As the boy finished the last chip, he simply let the bag drop from his hand, onto the sidewalk in his neighborhood. His mother briefly glanced over to see the bag's fall and kept on walking and talking with her son about something else. The instant seemed not to register, since the sidewalk where their bag sat was in no sense "theirs." Of course, moments like this happen all around the world. At that moment in China it struck me as an illustration of the reality that the consciousness of a "general" public interest is underdeveloped, compared with interest that affects individual families in the here and now—and the country relative to other parts of the world.

The still-limited awareness of interests outside China's immediate ambitions will, I think, affect China's ability to project soft power and improve its standing in the world. One illustration of the tension appears in debates even inside China about the significance of a "China Model" for national development.

Starting around the time of the Beijing Olympics, as China's economy seemed capable only of growth, and as people around the world began talking about a "Beijing Consensus" or a "China Model" in tones that assumed away all the uncertainties facing the country, some people inside China also took up the theme. One of the most highly evolved illustrations came in 2011, when a scholar at the Geneva School of Diplomacy and International Relations named Zhang Weiwei gave a lecture in Holland about the distinctive elements that would mark China's new contribution to international affairs.

The central distinction, according to a careful translation and analysis[1] by David Bandurski, of the China Media Project of the University of Hong Kong, was the entirely inward-looking and self-guided nature of the Chinese model. America might consider itself exceptional or unique as the first purely invented nation, but China was unique because . . . it was unique: "China is not a magnified East Germany, nor is it an amplified Eastern Europe," Zhang wrote. "Nor is it any ordinary country." He enumerated all the reasons that what was true of China was not necessarily true of any other society on earth. It was a "civilization-type nation," where the boundaries of a culture (supposedly) overlapped with the boundaries of a state. Japanese, Germans, Turks, and others might challenge the claim, but that was only one item on the list. It has a five-thousand-year history, and a language whose written form had lasted more or less through that time. "It is as though ancient Rome was never dissolved, and continued to the present day . . . with a central government and a modern economy . . . [and] a massive population in which everyone speaks Latin." And on through other traits, until the clinching argument that China was the civilization of the "four ultras": ultra-populated, ultra-vast in geographical scope, ultra-ancient in historical traditions, and ultra-deep in its culture.

Apart from "ultra-populated," the other distinctions clearly reflected a narcissistic view. Russia is almost twice as big as "ultra-vast" China; Egypt, Turkey, and other countries have "ultra-ancient" histories; Indians, Javanese, Koreans, and members of other societies feel their cultures are "ultra-deep." The significant point about the statement is not whether it is true, but that so many people in China might believe it. As individuals they might deal easily with people from other countries and cultures. (I cannot think of a town I have been, anywhere from Western Africa to Eastern Europe, without at least some Chinese residents.) But the standards they would apply to their society would be rules for China, not rules for mankind.

A Chinese intellectual named Yang Hengjun made just that point in response to Zhang's essay. Yang made a trenchant criticism of the crony-capitalism that he said was creating inequality, corruption, and ultimately stagnation in China. (And soon after this essay was published, Yang was among the writers who disappeared from public view, during the Jasmine crackdown.) He also quoted, approvingly, a pre-communist-era philosopher on China's weakness for nationally minded as opposed to universal thinking. "All reactionary thought in contemporary China is of the same tradition," that philospher, Ai Siqi, wrote in 1940. "It emphasizes China's 'national characteristics,' harps on China's 'special nature,' and wipes aside the general principles of humanity, arguing that China's social development can only follow China's own path."

The British in their centuries of strength meant to bring parliaments and courts to their colonies. The Romans had sought to export their systems long before. The Americans preached their universal ideal; the Soviets and the true-believing communist Chinese had a message for all the downtrodden of the world. But, Yang Hengjun said in the conclusion of his essay, the more China emphasized its own uniqueness, as a "civilizational economy" that combined history, scale, and technology in a way that by definition no other society could approach, the more it excluded itself from discussions about alternatives for the world.

Soft power and success

China is steadily gaining the hard power that comes from factories and finance. Its military hard power is increasing, though from an extremely low base. But lasting influence in the world has come more from soft than hard power: ideas for living, models of individual, commercial, and social life that people emulate because they are attracted rather than because they are compelled.

Soft power becomes powerful when people imagine themselves transformed, improved, by adopting a new style. Koreans and Armenians imagine they will be freer or more successful if they become Americans—or Australians or Canadians. Young men and women from the provinces imagine they will be more glamorous if they look and act like people in Paris, London, or New York. If a society thinks it is unique because of its system, or its style, or its standards, it can easily exert soft power, because outsiders can imagine themselves taking part in that same system and adopting those same styles. But if it thinks it is unique because of its identity—"China is successful because we are Chinese"—the appeal to anyone else is self-limiting.

From the Chinese government's point of view, soft power[2] has so far boiled down to using money to win other people's goodwill or acquiescence. Chinese-built roads in Africa and Latin America; Chinese investment and interaction in Europe and the United States. The public-opinion elements of the soft-power campaign have often backfired, since they have been crudely propagandistic in the fashion of the government's internal news management.

Even before the bad publicity China suffered with the jailing of Liu Xiaobo and the Jasmine crackdowns, a scholar from the Swedish Institute of International Affairs, Johan Lagerkvist, argued that China would likely lose more and more international support unless the government fundamentally reconceived its connections with the rest of the world.[3] "China's internal stability/security and survival of the Communist Party will always be more important to China's leaders than the image it projects for outside consumption," he contended. A choice between maintaining domestic order and pleasing outside critics was no choice at all. "Pouring money into Chinese equivalents to CNN and Al-Jazeera won't help [without] reform initiatives," he said.

In every country, internal interests come first. With more time on the world stage, China's leaders may learn to do what their American, British, French, and other counterparts also had to learn: at least feigning awareness of the interest of mankind. China's predicament is more difficult because its emergence is so rapid, and so much is unclear about other ways in which it will change.

I am sitting in Washington, D.C., as I write these words, and I realize how different the world feels to me than when I was sitting in Beijing, or Yinchuan, or Chengdu, or Linyi, with the chaos and achievement of Chinese efforts just outside my window. From a distance, it can seem strange to think that there are limits or challenges to China's progress. The *action,* the sense of can-do, is so different from the political and economic paralysis of America's age of constraint.

But I know how much is in flux, and how much is at stake. It is not an evasion of analysis but a recognition of China's complexity, and the world's, to say that a wide range of outcomes is possible, and that it is worth watching very carefully signals like those I have mentioned to recalibrate our estimates. Nearly every day of these past five years—when watching the earth being scraped away for airports or highways, when seeing apartments put up within a week and the families who used to live in the knocked-down tenements sent scrambling to other parts of town, when seeing the beggars next to the Bentleys and the security agents watching students in the Internet cafés— I have thought to myself, How long can this go on? And nearly every day, when seeing those same sights, I have asked myself, What is this system *not* capable of? Anyone who says China is destined to succeed or fail, to open up or close down, either knows much more than I do, or much less. Anyone so sure is not willing to acknowledge the great unknowability of life in general and life in this quarter of mankind.

Notes

Introduction

1. In flying school, you learn when the instructor asks you to close your eyes and try to control the plane by seat-of-the-pants "feel" alone. When he tells you to open your eyes a minute later, you are inevitably in a spiral toward the ground. Minus the instructor, this is the story of the John F. Kennedy, Jr., accident; he had not yet been trained in these "instrument rules" flying skills and got into an irrecoverable spiral when he lost sight of the horizon in the evening mist over the ocean.

1: This Is Going to Be Big

1. If curious, you can test this yourself: look for any big Chinese city on an online map from Google, Bing, or other major providers, then click back and forth between "map" and "satellite" views. In most other parts of the world, the two views align. For Chinese cities, they're slightly mismatched, by margins of perhaps ten or twenty meters. What's marked as a road in the map view might be the middle of an apartment block in the satellite view.
2. As the passage in a speech by Wen Jiabao said, "We will organize the implementation of industrial innovation and development projects, including those on National Broadband Internet Agenda, cloud computing, the Internet of Things, integrated circuits, flat-panel displays, space infrastructure, regional aircraft and industrialization of general aviation aircraft, as well as major application and demonstration, projects on the health of the people and on using information technology to benefit the people." From the official English version of the plan as carried by China Real Time Report, "China NPC 2011: The Reports," *Wall Street Journal,* March 5, 2011, http://blogs .wsj.com/chinarealtime/2011/03/05/china-npc-2011-reports-full-text/.
3. Of many theories about Buick's present popularity in China, the one I like best involves spillover glamour from its days as a Rolls-Royce-style imported luxury marque in the precommunist era, especially in Westernized Shanghai.

4. Xin Dingding, "Aviation Sector Has High Hopes for Next 5 Years," *China Daily*, February 25, 2011. http://europe.chinadaily.com.cn/china/2011-02/ 25/content_12077726.htm.

5. Lu Haoting, "China May Lead Global Aviation Recovery," *China Daily*, September 17, 2009. http://www.chinadaily.com.cn/bizchina/2009-09/17/ content_8701529.htm.

6. Centre for Asia Pacific Aviation, "Air China Value Greater than United-Continental, American, JetBlue, AirTran & US Air Combined," March 9, 2011. http://www.centreforaviation.com/analysis/air-china-value-greater -than-united-continental-american-jetblue-airtran—us-air-combined-pt-1 -47146.

7. Centre for Asia Pacific Aviation, "World Airport Rankings 2010," March 16, 2011. http://www.centreforaviation.com/analysis/world-airport-rankings -2010-big-changes-to-global-top-30-beijing-up-to-2-heathrow-falls-to-4-47882, and http://www.centreforaviation.com/analysis/world-airport -rankings-2010-hong-kong-eclipses-memphis-as-the-worlds-busiest-cargo -hub-47887.

8. He meant small aircraft, which are roughly ten times more numerous than the large passenger craft in all commercial airlines' fleets.

9. "Details Emerge About the Hurun Report's New Magazine for Chinese Billionaires, 'Wings & Water,'" *Jing Daily*, March 16, 2011. http://www .jingdaily.com/en/luxury/details-emerge-about-the-hurun-reports-new -magazine-for-chinese-billionaires-wings-water. The Chinese name for the new magazine was simply *Qing*, essentially "Lift Up."

10. "The Chinese Private Jet Industry—Set to Soar," *PrivateFly*, January 11, 2011. http://blog.privatefly.com/?p=331.

11. Mo Lingjiao, "China's First Private and Business Jet Expo Sparks Controversy," *Global Times*, August 16, 2010. http://en.huanqiu.com/china/ society/2010-08/564149.html.

12. Thomas A. Horne, "China on the March," *AOPA Online*. http://www.aopa .org/aircraft/articles/2011/111009-china-on-the-march.html.

2: Getting off the Ground

1. By military convention, whatever aircraft is carrying the incumbent President is known during that flight as *Air Force One*—or *Marine One* in the case of presidential helicopters, *Executive One* if it is a civilian aircraft, or *Navy One* if it is a naval aircraft like the one in which George W. Bush flew to a carrier deck during the "Mission Accomplished" ceremonies of 2003. Because the newly sworn-in President, Lyndon Johnson, was on the same flight that carried Kennedy and his widow back to Washington, that plane was still *Air Force One*.

2. Mark Dougan, *A Political Economy Analysis of China's Civil Aviation Industry* (New York: Routledge, 2002), p. 22. As Dougan, an Australian academic, put it, "Because China is so large and so geographically diverse, a coordinated transportation infrastructure was traditionally viewed as both essential to and a reflection of a ruling regime's power and authority." One of the many Americans who have worked in China's aviation development put it this way: "I think Chinese officials wonder whether there has ever been a really strong country that didn't have a strong aerospace sector."

3. Da Hsuan Feng, "The Legacy of Tsu Wong: From Boeing's Genesis to NCKU," *iTainan*, January 1, 2008. http://www.itainan.org/forum/legacy-tsu -wong-%28%E7%8E%8B%E5%8A%A9%29%3A-boeing%E2%80%99s -genesis-ncku.

4. For more on Wong Tsu, see "Wong Tsu in 1916," China National Aviation Corporation, undated. http://www.cnac.org/wongtsu01.pdf; Global Security, "Kuomintang Aviation," undated. http://www.globalsecurity.org/ military/world/china/aviation-history-12.htm; Eve Dumovich, "The 1st and the Best," *Boeing Frontiers,* December 2006, http://www.boeing.com/news/ frontiers/archive/2006/december/ts_sf12.pdf.

5. "Feng Ru," ChinaCulture.org, undated. http://www.chinaculture.org/gb/en _aboutchina/2003-09/24/content_26559.htm.

6. This account of Feng Ru's aviation history draws from Rebecca Maksel, "The Father of Chinese Aviation," *Smithsonian Air & Space* magazine, August 2008. http://www.airspacemag.com/history-of-flight/The_Father_of _Chinese_Aviation.html; also Patti Gully, *Sisters of Heaven* (San Francisco: Long River Press, 2007).

7. Tai Ming Cheung, "Remaking Cinderella: The Nature and Development of China's Aviation Industry," testimony before the U.S.-China Economic and Security Review Commission hearing on "China's Emergent Military Aerospace and Commercial Aviation Capabilities. Panel IV: China's Aviation Industrial Complex," May 20, 2010, p. 3.

   As part of this testimony he also said, "The aviation industry has more than 130 large and medium-sized factories and research institutes employing 250,000 workers scattered across the country, especially in the deep interior, and often possessing the same manufacturing and research attributes. But intense rivalry, local protectionism, and huge geographical distances mean that there is little cooperation or coordination among these facilities, preventing the ability to reap economies of scale, engage in innovation clustering, and also hampering efforts at consolidation."

8. On the general evolution of aircraft companies in the early decades, see U.S. Centennial of Flight Commission, *History of Flight,* "The First U.S. Aircraft Manufacturing Companies," 2003. http://www.centennialofflight.gov/essay/ Aerospace/earlyU.S/Aero1.htm.

9. *History of Flight*, "Commercial Aviation: the 1920s." http://www.centennial offlight.gov/essay/Commercial_Aviation/1920s/Tran1.htm.
10. Dougan, *A Political Economy*, pp. 38ff.
11. Ibid., p. 39.
12. The best known of these, Embry-Riddle, itself exemplifies the diverse and chaotic business conditions of aviation's early days. A wealthy aviation enthusiast, T. Higbee Embry, joined with a former military pilot and air-show performer, John Paul Riddle, to form the Embry-Riddle company in Cincinnati in 1925. They sold airplanes, carried airmail, and offered flight instruction. By 1930, their flying services were absorbed into the newly formed American Airlines. A few years later, Riddle led the development of what became the Embry-Riddle Aeronautical University, in Florida.
13. Dougan, *A Political Economy*, p. 56. "The quality of the aircraft which would have had to be used were so inferior to what other industrialized countries were using, that it would have been an embarrassment to the government and detrimental to its image abroad."

3: The Men from Boeing

1. E. E. Bauer, *China Takes Off: Technology Transfer and Modernization* (Seattle: University of Washington Press, 1986), p. 5. "Small clouds of vapor rose from each silent figure as we waited in the dimly lighted interior. In an all-saving society, there was no logic in heating the massive terminal building during the night."
2. Bauer, *China Takes Off*, p. 101.
3. At the time, Boeing's main competitors were other American companies, Lockheed and McDonnell Douglas. By the early 2000s, after Boeing acquired McDonnell Douglas and Lockheed merged with Martin Marietta and stopped making commercial aircraft, the main competition for large passenger airliners was, of course, the national-champion battle between Boeing and Europe's Airbus. This is the battle that China aspired to join with its national champion, C919.
4. Bauer, *China Takes Off*, p. 31.
5. Ibid., p. 32.
6. Ibid., p. 177. Bauer gave this example: "The deputy director of maintenance stood attentively on the ramp, watching. He took no notes and reported nothing; it was not his job. Also watching were at least twenty maintenance and ground personnel. Of course, none of them would report it, either. To report would put them in double jeopardy. First, they were supposed to be minding their own business, and, second, criticism of the planning unit would be taken unkindly. Our interpreter, watching with us, would never dare to utter a word. Most frustrating of all, the controllers would be reluc-

tant to criticize the planning orders. They could only laugh among themselves, passing the event off as a joke."

7. Randy Baseler, "China Rocks!" *Randy's Journal,* April 20, 2006. http://www
.boeing.com/randy/archives/2006/04china_rocks.html. Also, Embassy of
the People's Republic of China in the United States, "President Hu Jintao
Arrives in Seattle for US Visit," April 25, 2006. http://www.china-embassy
.org/eng/zmgx/zmsbzyjw/c1/111/t248787.htm; and Associated Press, "In
Visit to Boeing, Hu Emphasizes Trade," *Boston Globe,* April 20, 2006. http://
articles.boston.com/2006-04-20/news/29246222_1_president-hu-jintao
-china-trade-deficit.

8. With the quaint earnestness that would be recognizable to anyone who had
listened to official Chinese rhetoric, he closed his remarks by expressing
confidence that "beneficial cooperation and win-win outcome" between the
United States and China would "fly further and higher, just like a Boeing
plane."

9. For more information on this crash, see the online Air Disaster searchable data-
base, http://www.airdisaster.com/cgi-bin/view_details.cgi?date=05081997&
reg=B-2925&airline=China+Southern+Airlines.

10. For background on Yang's career, see the ChinaVitae Web site, http://www
.chinavitae.com/biography/Yang_Yuanyuan%7c313. The site is the most
easily available English-language source on Chinese government officials.

4: The Chinese Master Plan

1. Tom Orlik, "China's Ties That Bind," *Wall Street Journal,* August 26, 2011.
http://online.wsj.com/article/SB10001424053111904875404576530361
948603924.html. "Diminishing returns from more roads and railways and
continued efforts to constrain a real-estate bubble mean the scope for investment to step into the breach a second time if foreign demand disappoints is
limited. . . . China's real weakness is that the gap in GDP left by retreating
exports has been filled not by a sustainable increase in domestic consumption
but by more investment."

2. The energy business illustrates the phenomenal reliance on infrastructure
construction. After the Japanese tsunami and nuclear disaster in 2011, the
world's survey of nuclear plants showed that more new plants (nearly thirty)
were under construction in China than in the rest of the world combined. A
similar pattern prevails in coal-fired plants, solar- and wind-powered installations, and almost any other kind of heavy investment.

3. Without getting too much into the details: China's national savings rate has
in recent years been about half of its GDP. That is different from saying that
each Chinese family saves half of its earnings, although some of them may.
Rather it reflects the share of "consumption" in the whole national economy,

which accounts for only half of what the Chinese economy produces. The rest is either exported for foreigners to buy, with the proceeds often turned into T-Note holdings in the United States, or devoted to capital projects inside China.

4. Damien Ma, "Is Chinese Growth Sustainable?" *The Atlantic,* August 18, 2011. http://www.theatlantic.com/international/archive/2011/08/is-chinese-growth-sustainable/243795/.

5. The transition from one Chinese leader to another takes a couple of years, because of the staggered schedule on which various power bases in the Communist Party, the Military Commission, and the government are transferred.

6. Casey was the subject of a cover story I did in *The Atlantic:* James Fallows, "China Makes, the World Takes," *The Atlantic,* July/August 2007.

7. Andrew Batson, "Not Really Made in China," *Wall Street Journal,* December 15, 2010. http://online.wsj.com/article/SB10001424052748704828104576021142902413796.html.

8. It is known in Chinese as 鸿海 Hon Hai, or 富士康 Fushi Kang.

9. Helen H. Wang, "Myth of China's Manufacturing Prowess," March 10, 2010. http://helenhwang.net/2010/03/myth-of-manufacturing/. Emphasis added.

10. These accounts are from a foreign blogger who goes by the name Tom: "Four Jobs That Highlight China's Ineffeciency," *Seeing Red in China,* May 17, 2011. http://seeingredinchina.com/2011/05/17/four-jobs-that-highlight-china%E2%80%99s-inefficiency/. "Perhaps the most perplexing example of this I've seen was in Chengdu at the Sichuan Museum," he wrote. "The museum was free to enter but it employed 3 people to hand out tickets, and two more to check them."

11. Here is one illustration, from an assessment early in 2011 of the Twelfth Five-Year Plan: "Goal #6. Create an innovation driven society by encouraging education and training of the workforce.

"The plan seeks to shift China from its role as the factory of the world to a new role as a technological innovator for the world. There are two components to this approach:
- China will need to become a domestic innovator in all areas of current modern technology, with an emphasis on practical industrial applications.
- Where China is not capable of domestic innovation, China will continue to import technology from advanced economies. However, China will seek to actively domesticate that technology through a program of 'assimilate and re-invent.' The recent program for production in engines for high speed rail is offered as an example of the 'assimilate and re-invent' approach.

Dan Harris, "China's 12th Five Year Plan: A Preliminary Look," *China Law Blog*, March 3, 2011. http://www.chinalawblog.com/2011/03/chinas_12th_five_year_plan_a_preliminary_look.html.

12. State Council of the People's Republic of China, "China National Environmental Protection Plan in the Eleventh Five-Years (2006–2010)." http://english.mep.gov.cn/down_load/Documents/200803/P020080306440313293094.pdf. The paper went on, "The quality of coastal marine environment is at risk. . . . The number of days with haze in some big and medium sized cities has some increase, and acid rain pollution is not alleviated. . . . The phenomena of no strict observation of laws, little punishment to lawbreakers, poor law enforcement and supervision are still very common." And on through a very long list, with this stark conclusion: "China is facing [a] grim situation in addressing climate change."

13. The Chinese government's major air-pollution measure is PM 10—that is, relatively large particulate matter, with a diameter of 10 microns or more. Particles this size can be visible, and they make the air look hazy. But PM 2.5, or particulate matter of 2.5 microns or more, is medically more dangerous, because the pollutants are fine enough to penetrate deep into the alveoli of the lungs. As of late 2011, the Chinese government was still "considering" including PM 2.5 measures. In a cable revealed by WikiLeaks in 2011, the U.S. embassy in Beijing sent back alarmed reports in 2006 about the dangerously high PM 2.5 measures its own sensors were detecting. By 2008 the embassy had put a PM 2.5 sensor on its roof, which sent hourly PM 2.5 readings out via Twitter. These were typically high enough that they would have caused school closings and public-health emergencies in most European or North American countries.

14. Harris, "China's 12th Five-Year Plan." "Currently, for every 1% increase in GDP, China's energy use increases by 1% or more," Harris writes. "If this rate continues, China will need to increase its energy consumption by 2.5 times to achieve its 2020 economic goal. To put this into perspective, this would mean increasing the current consumption of coal from the current 3.6 billion tons per year to an astronomical 7.9 billion tons a year. No one in China thinks this can be done. . . . The new plan advocates an all out program in this area."

15. McKinsey Global Institute, *Preparing for China's Urban Billion* (San Francisco: McKinsey Global Institute, 2009), p 18. "There will be unprecedented investment opportunities for business among a booming middle class and a stratum of affluent consumers," the McKinsey study says. "The scale of urbanization will be large and migration will be its main driver."

16. On the problem of the phantom towns, see April Rabkin, "China's Potemkin Cities," *Mother Jones*, August 18, 2010. http://motherjones.com/politics/2010/04/china-ghost-mall: "Economists have raved about China's double-

digit growth—which dropped to a still-impressive 9 percent in 2008 and 2009, even as much of the world slouched through the recession. But this turbocharged expansion is less about the invisible hand than the iron fist: the enormous engine of the state geared to drive GDP at the expense of everything else. . . . The country has entombed its new wealth in concrete and steel. You can see it in Dongguan, in Guangdong province, where the world's largest mall stands empty, save for a few hamburger chains. And in Beijing's tallest building, a year old and still unopened. It is evident in six-lane boulevards where most of the traffic is bicycle carts. And in cities like Erenhot, where the relentless construction continues, oblivious to a dearth of demand."

17. Sky Canaves, "Shanghai Building Collapses, Nearly Intact," *Wall Street Journal,* June 29, 2009. http://blogs.wsj.com/chinarealtime/2009/06/29/shanghai -building-collapses-nearly-intact/.

18. Two veteran analysts explained the connection between passenger and freight traffic on China's rail lines: "China's businesses—ranging from manufacturers to coal mines—have complained for years about the difficulty of securing space on freight trains, which forces them to move a lot of their cargo on more expensive and less efficient trucks. An increase in rail capacity will enable them to put their freight back on trains, generating huge savings. Ton for ton, freight carried by rail costs nearly 70% less than carriage by truck, uses 77% less energy and produces 91% less carbon dioxide emissions." Will Freeman and Arthur Kroeber, "China's Fast Track to Development," *Wall Street Journal Asia,* June 4, 2010.

5: An Airport in the Wilderness

1. I spoke by phone with a pilot originally from New Zealand who had decided to leave the Linyi school, even though it still owed him several months' back pay. "I had to ask myself every time I strapped on the seat belt whether this is the flight I wouldn't come back from, and my little boy in New Zealand would grow up without a dad," he said.

2. Christopher Jackson, "An Introduction to China Aviation," *China Law Blog,* December 6, 2011. http://www.chinalawblog.com/2011/12/christopher _jackson_has_written_this.html.

3. As the ACP's mission statement says, its Chinese counterparts "find it's easier to coordinate with the US if our government and industry come together in one partnership for Sino-US cooperation developing Chinese aviation safety, capacity, and efficiency." American Chamber of Commerce in China, Beijing, "Aviation Cooperation Project Mission Statement," undated. http:// www.uschinaacp.com/news/163.

6: An American Dream, Turned Chinese

1. The body screening the sale is the Committee on Foreign Investment in the United States, generally referred to by its acronym CFIUS, pronounced *siff-ee-us.*
2. "China's Aviation Industry Soars onto the Global Stage," *The Link,* March-April 2010, China Europe International Business School. http://www.ceibs .edu/link/latest/51104.shtml.
3. "China Completes Cirrus Merger," by Dan Namowitz, *AOPA Online,* June 28, 2011. http://www.aopa.org/aircraft/articles/2011/110628cirrus_completes _china_merger.html.

7: China's Own Boeing

1. Cheung, "Remaking Cinderella," p. 2. He also wrote: "Reform-minded technocrats took charge of the defense and aviation sectors and vigorously implemented far-reaching reforms, including slashing costs and laying off tens of thousands of workers. Funding for R&D activities was also revamped with more money going into viable high priority projects and the culling of lower priority and failing projects."
2. For valuable background on the Chinese efforts, see Roger Cliff, Chad J. Ohlandt, and David Yang, *Ready for Takeoff: China's Advancing Aerospace Industry* (Arlington, VA: Rand Corporation, 2011).
3. L. J. Hart-Smith, "Out-Sourced Profits: The Cornerstone of Successful Subcontracting," paper presented at Boeing Third Annual Technical Excellence Symposium, February 14–15, 2001, p. 4. Paper is available at https:// www.documentcloud.org/documents/69746-hart-smith-on-outsourcing .html. "Suppliers are under just as great pressure as prime manufacturers to maximize their profits, maximize their return on minimized investment, and the like," he wrote; "indeed their interest rates on borrowings are usually higher than for prime manufacturers. So they have no incentive to design assembly tools that permit minimized rework for derivative products, for example, particularly when they have no guarantee that derivatives may ever be made or that they would be awarded the work. Indeed, they may not even have the expertise to foresee such opportunities."
4. Michael Hiltzik, "787 Dreamliner Teaches Boeing Costly Lesson on Outsourcing," *Los Angeles Times,* February 15, 2011. http://articles.latimes.com/ 2011/feb/15/business/la-fi-hiltzik-20110215.
5. "With adequate resources provided by an aggressive industrial policy, China's aviation scientific and engineering talent has the potential to be among the

best in the world (just like in the Soviet Union)," he wrote in his November, 2009 "Monthly Newsletter" for the Teal Group. "China also has a superb home market (just like the Soviet Union had). China has adequate capital (just like the Soviet Union's aviation industry had). China wants to construct a broad array of jet families (just like the Soviet Union did). But without economic freedom, particularly the freedom to move away from an autarkic and vertical industrial policy, it means nothing. If China continues down this path, its aviation industry will be heading down the same Soviet dead end street."

6. Aubrey Cohen, "Analyst: Don't Fear Embraer, or Bombardier, Comac and Sukhoi," *Seattle PI,* October 9, 2009. http://blog.seattlepi.com/aerospace/ 2009/10/09/analyst-dont-fear-embraer-or-bombardier-comac-and-sukhoi/.

7. As Aboulafia said in a report for his clients, the ARJ21 "is disastrously heavier than its closest competitor, Embraer's ERJ-170. . . . Given the razor-thin margins associated with regional airline operations, it is quite inconceivable that any airline would voluntarily operate this aircraft." Richard Aboulafia, "China's Commercial Aircraft Industry: The Limits of an Autarkic Industrial Policy," Teal Group, private newsletter, 2010.

8. Cheung, "Remaking Cinderella," p. 3.

9. Clyde Prestowitz, "It Won't Be on Immelt," *Foreign Policy,* October 3, 2011. http://prestowitz.foreignpolicy.com/posts/2011/10/03/it_wont_be_on _immelt.

10. Gabe Collins and Andrew Erickson, "Jet Engine Development in China: Indigenous High-Performance Turbofans Are a Final Step Toward Fully Independent Fighter Production," *China SignPost,* June 26, 2011. From the same post: "Enough is left out so that the exporting companies can comply with the letter of the export control laws, but in reality, a rising military power is potentially being given relatively low-cost recipes for building the jet engines needed to power [both military and civilian aircraft]."

8: The Environmental Consequences of Aviation

1. Ma Xiangshan, "China's Actions and Positions on Greenhouse Gas from International Civil Aviation," address to the International Civil Aviation Organization colloquium on Aviation and Climate Change, May 11–14, 2010. http://legacy.icao.int/CLQ10/Docs/0_Ma_en.pdf. From his presentation: "Developed countries should assume their responsibility and take the lead in reducing emissions due to their own background of historic emissions growth. Full consideration should be given to the fact that developing countries are in their own growth stage and are facing a considerable shortage in terms of finance, technology and capability."

2. "China Fires First Salvo in War Over EU Aviation Emissions Cap," *Clean-BizAsia,* June 29, 2011. http://www.cleanbiz.asia/story/china-fires-first-salvo-war-over-eu-aviation-emissions-cap.

3. As carbon-dioxide levels continue to rise, the main uncertainties about future warming center on what will happen when "positive-feedback loops"—i.e., the hotter things get, the faster they will get even hotter—kick in. The main way this would happen would be through melting of the polar ice sheets, which would mean less white ice surface to reflect the sun's heat, and more blue water surface to absorb it. Similarly, the vast Arctic permafrost areas could have a positive-feedback effect as they thaw. They are essentially frozen peat bogs, which contain huge amounts of methane. As they began to melt, they would release their methane, which in turn could trigger even faster melting and more methane release.

4. Shipping may have a smaller greenhouse effect than aviation because its emissions come at sea level—but it has a greater overall polluting effect, because the fuel is "dirtier" (with heavier sulfur concentrations) and maritime engines have been less subject to cleanup rules than those used on land or air.

5. From 2 percent of a world total of 37 billion tons—or, three quarters of a billion tons from airplane engines—the aviation share is expected to rise sharply by 2030, to 3 percent of a 50-billion-ton total. That would mean a billion and a half tons of CO_2 just from airplanes, or twice as much as in 2010.

6. The 1950s-vintage VOR system is a network of beacons that send out a different signal for each of the 360 degrees of the compass, so that planes with the right equipment could fly the 90 degree "radial"—due east—from one of the stations, or the 270 radial—due west—from another. Most of the en route instrument charts in developed countries are still defined by these VOR beacons.

7. Another video of the approach and landing is available online at http://www.youtube.com/watch?v=PdSMk01l2wQ&feature=related.

8. David Hughes, "Air China's First RNP Approach into Linzhi Airport, Tibet," *Aviation Week,* September 26, 2006.

9: The Tensions Inside China

1. Associated Press, "Woman confessed to 'terrorist' hijack attempt, China says," *Taipei Times,* March 28, 2008. http://www.taipeitimes.com/news/world/archives/208/03/28/2003407384. Also B. Raman, "Foiled Attempt to Blow Up Plane from Urumqi," *International Terrorism Monitor,* March 29, 2008. http://www.southasiaanalysis.org/%5Cpapers27%5cpaper2654.html.

2. For more on these episodes, see Joshua Rosenzweig, "China Abandons the Law," *Wall Street Journal Asia,* March 24, 2011.

3. One example from a large possible sample of such declarations: In late May, the official organ the *People's Daily* published a lead editorial arguing that in a time of world ferment, the last thing the Party could do was tolerate dissent of any sort. It began (according to the paper's official English translation), "The Party's political discipline, as the most important discipline of the Party, is essential for safeguarding the Party's political principles, political orientation and political lines as well as regulating political speech, political actions and the political stance of Party organizations and members. It is also the basis of all the Party's disciplines." Editorial, "Firmly Safeguard Party Political Discipline," *People's Daily,* May 27, 2011. http://english.people.com.cn/90001/90780/91342/7393262.html.

4. Zhang Jiawei, "Peking University Clamps Down on Radical Thought," *China Daily,* March 25, 2011. http://www.chinadaily.com.cn/china/2011-03/25/content_12228217.htm. After the plan was announced and attracted international ridicule, the university said that it really meant only to find students who were performing poorly in class. See He Dan, "Peking University's Plan Stirs Questions," *China Daily,* March 26, 2011. http://www.chinadaily.com.cn/china/2011-03/26/content_12230681.htm.

5. Finally, in 2011, this manifestation of American permanent-emergency thinking was eliminated when Janet Napolitano, the secretary of homeland security—a term that itself betokens permanent emergency—had the gumption to dismantle the system and replace it with a more fine-grained and localized warning system.

6. For more, see James Fallows, "The Connection Has Been Reset," *The Atlantic,* March, 2008. http://www.theatlantic.com/magazine/archive/2008/03/-ldquo-the-connection-has-been-reset-rdquo/6650/.

7. Jessica Colwell, "Gmail now 45 times slower than QQ in China," *Shanghaiist,* March 22, 2011. http://shanghaiist.com/2011/03/24/gmail_now_44_times_slower_than_qq_i.php. My own experience confirmed those results.

8. Editorial, "The Internet Belongs to All of Us, Not Just the US," *Global Times,* March 31, 2011. http://www.globaltimes.cn/opinion/editorial/2011-02/623812.html.

9. Editorial, "China Is Definitely Not the Middle East," *People's Daily,* March 10, 2011. http://english.peopledaily.com.cn/90001/90780/91342/7314966.html.

10. Josh Gartner, host, "What Is Up with the Chinese GFW?" *China Policy Pod,* March, 2011.

11. Levin fleshed out this analysis in a magazine essay: Richard Levin, "Top of the Class," *Foreign Affairs,* May–June 2010.

12. David Shukman, "China 'to Overtake US on Science' in Two Years," BBC News, March 28, 2011. http://www.bbc.co.uk/news/science-environment-12885271. For the Royal Society finding, see "Knowledge, Networks,

and Nations: Final Report," the Royal Society, March 28, 2011. http://
royalsociety.org/policy/reports/knowledge-networks-nations/.

13. It continued, "China's Peking University is determined to become a seat of
world-class learning to rival Oxford and Cambridge, Harvard and Yale."
Peter Foster, "China: The Ultimate Brain Drain?," *The Telegraph,* October 23, 2010. http://www.telegraph.co.uk/news/worldnews/8080644/China
-The-Ultimate-Brain-Drain.html.

14. The United States accounted for 30 percent of all citations between 2004 and
2008, followed by the U.K. at 8 percent, Germany at 7 percent, and Japan,
France, and Canada with 5 percent apiece. China came after that, with 4 percent of world citations with the rest of the world making up the difference.
China's total output of papers was nearly three times larger than the U.K.'s,
but was cited only half as often.

15. Gillian Wong, "Rampant Cheating Hurts China's Research Ambitions,"
Associated Press, April 11, 2010.

16. Andrew Jacobs, "Rampant Fraud Threat to China's Brisk Ascent," *New York
Times,* October 7, 2010.

17. This was not a question of a U.S. company's failure to adapt its products to
local tastes. Microsoft employs thousands of engineers and salespeople inside
China and produces fully Chinese versions of all its products.

18. Gady Epstein, "Profiting from Piracy: Robin Li's Problem Is China's Problem," *Forbes,* March 29, 2011. http://blogs.forbes.com/gadyepstein/2011/
03/29/profiting-from-piracy-robin-lis-problem-is-chinas-problem/.

19. Rosenzweig, "China Abandons the Law."

20. A list of those detained was compiled by C. Custer, "Perspective . . ." *Chi-
naGeeks,* March 29, 2011. http://chinageeks.org/2011/03/perspective/. On
March 15, 2011, the New York City Bar Association sent a formal letter to
China's minister of justice, Wu Aiying, and other judicial officials to express,
as the letter put it, "our grave concern with respect to reports over the past
several weeks that lawyers in various parts of China have been harassed,
beaten, and detained at the hands of agents of the government." It included
about a dozen examples, including this one: "Tang Jitian, a prominent rights
defense lawyer in Beijing, was picked up by police on February 16. Tang's
home was also searched and some of his belongings were seized. Tang has
faced much retaliation for his rights defense work and had his license to practice law permanently revoked in April 2010. Tang has not been heard from
since his February 16 disappearance, but reports now indicate that a notice
imposing 'residential surveillance' on his home indicates that he is suspected
of inciting subversion of state power." A few days later, in a much more
remarkable man-bites-dog story, the Working Group on Arbitrary Deten-
tion, part of the United Nations Human Rights Council, formally demanded
that the Chinese government release a well-known human rights lawyer, Gao

Zhisheng, who had been held without trial for more than a year and said he had been tortured. And about the same time, one of the country's most prominent writers, Ran Yunfei, was arrested and charged with incitement to commit subversion, the same charge on which the Nobel Peace Prize winner Liu Xiaobo had been sentenced to eleven years in prison.

21. Carl Minzner, "China's Turn Against the Law," *China Law and Politics Blog*, March 26, 2011. http://sinolaw.typepad.com/chinese_law_and_politics _/2011/03/chinas-turn-against-law.html. He added, "Central authorities worry that decades of official rule-of-law rhetoric are fueling surging numbers of petitions and protests by citizens seeking to protect their rights, and even leading some officials to perceive law as superior to Party policy. They also fear that China's cadre of public interest lawyers might emerge as a core of Mideast-style protest movements."

22. "New Campaign Targets Illegal Online Maps," *Global Times*, March 8, 2011. Also, "Google Maps Fails to Apply for License, Faces Shutdown," *People's Daily Online*, April 1, 2011. http://english.peopledaily.com.cn/90001/ 90778/90860/7337874.html. Xiao Qiang, of the journalism school at U.C. Berkeley, who had left China after the Tiananmen Square repression, found messages from the state propaganda office ordering that the news of Google's tax problems be highlighted by all Chinese news sites for a certain period of time. For instance, the English version of the instruction read, "All websites are requested, on their front pages and headline news pages, to repost the story 'Unlawful Tax Activity by Google's China Business Discovered Again.' Leave the story up until April 1, 8:00 am."

23. William de Toqueville (pseud.), "China's George Orwell?," *The Diplomat*, June 2, 2011. http://the-diplomat.com/whats-next-china/george-orwell% E2%80%99s-china/.

24. David Bandurski, "Zhang vs. Yang on the China Model," *China Media Project*, March 29, 2011. http://cmp.hku.hk/2011/03/29/11205/#_jmp0_.

25. Fauna (pseud.), "Female Student Picked Up by Helicopter at Dezhou University," *ChinaSmack*, March 23, 2011. http://www.chinasmack.com/2011/ videos/female-student-picked-up-by-helicopter-at-dezhou-university.html.

10: The Chinese Model, Airborne

1. Bandurski, "Zhang vs. Yang."

2. The term "soft power" was coined by Joseph Nye, of Harvard, and he has argued that China's charm-offensive efforts were bound to defeat themselves, because they brought all the more attention to the lack of rules in its domestic practices. In 2010, he wrote, "The Shanghai Expo was a great success but was followed by the jailing of Nobel Peace laureate Liu Xiaobo. And for all the efforts to turn Xinhua and China Central Television into

competitors of CNN and the BBC, there is little international audience for brittle propaganda"—and little possibility, for now, of other than propaganda coming across those channels. Joseph Nye, "China's Repression Undoes Its Charm Offensive," *Washington Post,* March 25, 2011.

3. Johan Lagerkvist, "The Coming Collapse of China's Soft Power," *China-roader,* March 23, 2011. http://johanlagerkvist.org/2011/03/23/the-coming-collapse-of-chinas-soft-power/.

Index

local, 112–13
Nobel Prize and, 186–7
production shifts and, 149–50
Sichuan earthquake and, 127
soft power and, 187, 235
Weinan and, 112–13
"Chinese 'Heart' for Large Civilian
   and Military Aircraft, A"
   (Collins and Erickson), 166
Chinese master plan, 81–106
   addiction to growth in, 84–6
   aerospace in, 81–4
   and China as new America, 86–90
   way ahead in, 90–106
Chinese National Aviation
   Corporation, 51
Chongqing (formerly Chungking),
   52, 53, 225
Cirrus Aviation, 34, 35, 154
Cirrus Design Corporation, 129–44
   employment declines at, 138–9, 140
   Israviation and, 130–1
   reform from within and, 134–7
   sale of controlling interest in,
      132–3
   sales collapse of, 137–8
   sold to China, 140–4
   start of, 130
Cirrus SR20, 131, 132
Cirrus SR22, 3–5, 12, 34, 35, 38,
   100, 123, 131, 134
Cirrus ST50, 130–1
Cirrus VK-30, 130
cities, 99–104, 117
Civil Aeronautics Board, 61
Civil Aviation Administration of
   China (CAAC), 32, 62–3, 65–7,
   109, 123, 160, 180
   Fiduccia and, 135, 136
   flight liberalization and, 127–8
   "Relevant Measures" document
      and, 136–7
   safety issues and, 72–3, 76–9, 135
Claeys, Peter, 21, 38, 133–4, 135

in flight to Zhuhai, 4, 5, 11–19, 34
in Tiananmen Square, 197, 199,
   201
Clissold, Tim, 110
clouds, flying in vs. out of, 16
coal, 27, 28, 104, 108, 122, 133,
   182, 243n
coal-fired plants, 241n
"cockpit integration," 162–3
Cold War, 54–5
Colgan Air crash, 75
Collins, Gabe, 166–7
COMAC (Commercial Aircraft
   Group of China), 47, 147–8,
   150, 162, 167
   obstacles faced by, 153–8
Commerce Department, U.S., 123
Communist Party, communists, 51,
   53, 62, 102, 186, 201, 204,
   222, 226, 230, 235, 248n
   regional boss of, 115–16
computers, 43, 57, 93, 209, 218
construction, 82–3, 85, 86, 91–2, 99,
   173, 241n, 244n
   accidents and, 102–3
   of "ghost cities," 102
consumption, 85–6
   energy, 98, 101, 243n
control towers, 73
copying, 218
copyright, 218–19
corn, 182, 183
corruption, 40, 189, 204
crashes, 57, 66, 72, 75, 132
credit cards, 202
Crescent Capital, 132–3, 139–40
crime, 201–2
Cultural Revolution, 111
cultures, defensiveness of, 192
currency, 134, 185
Curtiss, 58
customers, 96, 130, 132, 133, 134,
   138, 139
customs inspectors, 134

About the Author

James Fallows is a national correspondent at *The Atlantic,* for which he has reported from around the world for more than thirty years. He also holds the professional Chair in U.S. Media at the United States Studies Centre at the University of Sydney, in Australia. He has been a frequent contributor to NPR since the 1980s, most recently as a regular analyst for *Weekend All Things Considered,* and has written for *The New York Review of Books, The New Yorker,* and other publications. He has won the National Magazine Award, the American Book Award, and a New York Emmy Award for his role as host of a documentary about China. His website is www .jamesfallows.com. He has a long-standing interest in technology, aviation, and China, which he first visited in the 1980s and where he and his wife lived from 2006 through 2009.

A Note on the Type

This book was set in Adobe Garamond. Designed for the Adobe Corporation by Robert Slimbach, the fonts are based on types first cut by Claude Garamond (c. 1480–1561). Garamond was a pupil of Geoffroy Tory and is believed to have followed the Venetian models, although he introduced a number of important differences, and it is to him that we owe the letter we now know as "old style."

Typeset by Scribe, Philadelphia, Pennsylvania

Printed and bound by Berryville Graphics, Berryville, Virginia

Designed by M. Kristen Bearse